中国哲学关键词50讲

（汉英对照）

吴 怡 著

花山文艺出版社

河北·石家庄

图书在版编目（CIP）数据

中国哲学关键词50讲：汉英对照 / 吴怡著. —石家庄：
花山文艺出版社，2020.9
ISBN 978-7-5511-2582-6

Ⅰ.①中… Ⅱ.①吴… Ⅲ.①哲学－研究－中国－汉、英
Ⅳ.①B2

中国版本图书馆CIP数据核字(2020)第145071号

书　　名：**中国哲学关键词50讲**（汉英对照）
著　　者：吴　怡
策　　划：张采鑫　崔正山
责任编辑：张采鑫　李　鸥
特约编辑：柯琳娟
责任校对：李　鸥
装帧设计：好天气工作室
美术编辑：胡彤亮
出版发行：花山文艺出版社（邮政编码：050061）
　　　　　（河北省石家庄市友谊北大街330号）
销售热线：0311-88643221/29/31/32/26
传　　真：0311-88643225
印　　刷：北京天宇万达印刷有限公司
经　　销：新华书店
开　　本：880×1230　　1/32
印　　张：13.5
字　　数：278千字
版　　次：2020年9月第1版
　　　　　2020年9月第1次印刷
书　　号：ISBN 978-7-5511-2582-6
定　　价：68.00元

自　序

这本书的原文是英文，是我于 1986 年所写。因为在教学上，发现西方的学生对于中国文化和中国哲学的了解没有其他来源，只有靠书本，甚至靠课堂中教授所规定的课本，这些书本和课本，都是把中国思想翻译过来，再加上作者的理解不同，西方式的写法又喜欢逻辑推理，很少能把握中文的原意，使读者有会于心。譬如李雅各（James Legge）的著名翻译《四书》，对于这个儒家最重要的"仁"字，在每处的翻译都各不相同。读者又如何能"一以贯之"？至于当时在西方的出版界，也没有中国哲学字典之类的书籍可资查考。所以当时为了教学起见，我准备写一本简易的中国哲学词典，给自己的学生用。

当时我选了三百个字和词。但在着手写第一个"一"字时，我就发现有问题了。本来我准备每个字或词写几条简单的定义，因此每个字和词最多不超过一百字的解释，但我在写"一"时，参考一本西洋哲学字典的"一"，其中一个定义是中国学者所写，说"一是道"。我想不对，老子书中虽然"一"很重要，但"道生一"，如果一是道的话，岂非道生道了吗？所以"一"显然和道不同，我必须详细说清楚，这一说下去，"一"的字头就写了二千多字。如果以这种方法，去写三百个字和词，显然不是我当时的英文能力所可及。于是，我改选了五十个重要的单字，这就是本书的内容。

这本书自出版以来，已有几十年了，广受西方学生的喜爱，他们曾要求我教"中国哲学术语"一课，我也教了近二十多次，有一位韩国的禅师金君曾两次参加这门课。目前我已退休，也把这本书束之高阁。半年前，内人方俶看到这本书，好奇地翻了一下，突然兴起，觉得这本书介绍中国哲学字义，很有意思，因而想到对一般中国学生或许有益，所以自愿帮我翻译成中文。为此，她查找引证，遍查经书甚至用手机查出处，好像玩游戏似的，兴趣盎然；她也读了很多原文，自谓虽辛苦，也值得。如今她已译毕。为了配合她的辛劳，我也把教授这门课程时的一些看法，写成"按语"，排在各字的末尾，作为自己对这些字义的心得，一并献给读者。

目 录

·Contents·

V

1. 一

"一"在中国哲学中用来描述道的本质、功能和实践。在道家那里，道是无形的、超然的，无法描述或操作的；因此中国哲学家总是把"一"作为道的象征。"昔之得一者，天得一以清，地得一以宁，神得一以灵，谷得一以盈，万物得一以生，侯王得一以为天下贞，其致之。""故贵以贱为本，高以下为基。是以侯王自谓孤寡不谷，此非以贱为本邪？非乎？故致数舆无舆，不欲琭琭如玉，珞珞如石。"（《老子》第三十九章）

在这一章第一句中，老子用"一"相当于道。我们可以把"一"换成道，为什么我们却没有直接用"一"代替道呢？这是因为老子在后半章要强调谦和无欲。"道"这个字象征最高的原理，但是谦虚和无欲的含义却不能用道直接表现出来。而老子在此用"一"却不一样。这个"一"一方面，是象征道的内涵，是开始、融合和整体性；另一方面，却含有少和最低的意思，也就是说它可以象征谦虚和无欲。

"一"在中国哲学里扮演很多角色，最特别的是创造力、融通性和基本原则的概念。而"一"在中国哲学家的运用，也可以分六种情况来讲。

1）"一"的概念

一是生生（创造力）。

"道生一，一生二，二生三，三生万物。"（《老子》第四十二章）"道生之。"（《老子》第五十一章）"天下万物生于有，有生于无。"（《老子》第四十章）但是如何能道生万物？如何能有生于无？老子以"一"去解决这个难题，因为"一"是有和无中间的桥梁。因此，道的生生，第一步是生"一"，通过"一"，而有了二，"二"就是相对原则或阴和阳之气。

二是融通性。

"厉与西施，恢恑憰怪，道通为一。其分也，成也；其成也，毁也。凡物无成与毁，复通为一。"（《庄子·齐物论》）这是说，所有不同的事物都是"一"。

"参万岁而一成纯"（《庄子·齐物论》），这就是说，所有时间是"一"。"安排而去化，乃入于寥天一"（《庄子·大宗师》），这就是说，天和人是合一的。

三是基本原则。

"天下之动。贞夫一者也。"（《易经·系辞下传》第一章）这里，"一"是原理，是最高和最基本的规则。这个"一"，在《易经·系辞》中被称为"太极"。例如，"是故易有太极生两仪，两仪生四象，四象生八卦。"（《易经·系辞上传》第十一章）宋明儒家总是以"太极"为"一"。例如，"太极，一也，不动；生二，二则神也。"（邵雍《皇极经世·观物外篇》）

2）"一"的运用

道的实践，"一"在中国哲学家的运用上，至少有六种情况。

一是抱"一"。

"载营魄抱一，能无离乎？"（《老子》第十章）这里"一"是指道。老子用的词是"抱一"，意思是使自己和道合一。换言之，无论你做什么事，都必须遵循道。

二是合"一"。

"天地与我并生，而万物与我为一。"（《庄子·齐物论》）"自其异者视之，肝胆楚越也；自其同者视之，万物皆一也。"（《庄子·德充符》）庄子的思想是道贯通万物，而万物也存在道中。因此，我们要体认万物与我是一体的，我们也实际生存在道中。

三是"一"以贯之。

孔子曰："参乎，吾道一以贯之。"曾子曰："唯。"孔子出去以后，其他学生问曾参："何谓也？"曾子曰："夫子之道，忠恕而已矣。"（《论语·里仁篇》）孔子不像道家一样强调"一"，也不告诉我们"一"是什么。但是，依照他的思想，"仁"是基本的德性或是中心思想，相当于"一"。他强调那些实际对父母行孝，对君上尽忠，对人民仁爱和对万事尽己之心，都是以仁"一"以贯之的。

四是专于"一"。

"闲邪则固一矣。然主一则不消言闲邪。有以一为难见，不可下功夫，如何？一者无他，只是整齐严肃，则心便一。一则自是无非僻之干。此意但涵养久之，则天理自然明。"（朱熹《近思录》卷四引《二程遗书》卷十五）程颐是宋朝理学家，强调专"一"的方法。大凡心之所想，行之所为，持久地专注于善，或照着天理去做，就不会有偏差。大多数的宋明理学家也把"一"当他们最主要的方法去修养心性。

五是无欲之"一"。

"或问：'圣可学乎？'濂溪先生曰：'可。''有要乎？'曰：'有。''请问焉。'曰：一为要。一者无欲也。"（朱熹《近思录》卷四引周敦颐《通书·圣学》）周敦颐是宋朝理学家，也名周濂溪，受道家的影响，此处"一"的意义就是无欲。

六是归"一"。

"僧问赵州：'万法归一，一归何处？'州云：'我在青州，作一领布衫重七斤。'"（《碧岩录》第四十五则）赵州从谂是唐朝禅师，常以好像不相关的话回答学生的问题。"一"是超越万物，不附属于任何事物的。何为"万法归一"？我们不能得到答案，因为这是一个不能问的问题。一般而言，"一"在佛法中象征真如，也是究竟法，中国禅宗旳意思是真心。在此点上真心是不须要讨论的。在这里，我们强调为何禅师总是给人困惑？其实他们提出"万法归一，一归何处"，就是用这话刺激学生去达到证悟。

怡按

就修养功夫来说，如何能"一"？尝试言之，可以有以下各端：

（1）无欲：无欲则心不外逐，内心自能归于纯一。

（2）主静：静则不躁动，内心自然宁静而清明，清明则一。

（3）存诚：闲邪存诚，无邪则心念归一。

（4）致虚：虚其心，则心无挂碍，旷然而明澈，明澈则一。

（5）安命：顺从天命，心无旁骛而一。

（6）素位：素其位而行，别无所求，心念即能专一。

（7）顺道：一切所为，顺道而行，自能"道通为一"（《庄子·齐物论》）。

2. 人

"人"是指人类。是象形人的形体。在中国哲学上的意义很多，各学派都有论说。

1）"人"在儒家

人类总被视为宇宙的中心。"故人者，其天地之德，阴阳之交，鬼神之会，五行之秀气也。"（《礼记·礼运》）"天地之德"表示人是有责任生产或生生万物。"阴阳之交"，在阴阳和谐中，是宇宙万物的开始发展。"鬼神之会"，意思是人有灵魂，可以和鬼神相通。"五行之秀气"意思是人在五行的生化中是最有智慧的。

从这里，我们发现在孔子的思想中，人和动物是不同的，人能修养自己以至于天人合一。孔子知道人有欲望是不好的，但他们会面对这些欲望而试着解决它，或和谐地转换它成为建设性的目标。

因此，孔子的思想中，人是至关重要的；只有通过人性，宇宙才能生生不已地发展。

2）"人"在道家

人在宇宙的变化中，是一个最主要的组成部分。庄子特别强调天和人之不同，"牛马四足，是谓天；落马首，穿牛鼻，是谓人。"（《庄子·秋水》）由此可知，庄子的意思是指自然的变化是天，人为的设计是人。因此，在庄子的思想中，如果人是随着自然发展的话，将是完美的和真正的人，不然他将苦于为肉体所限，为欲望所束缚。

3）"人"在中国佛学

特别是在中国禅宗，人的一般定义有如道家思想。如"一切修多罗及诸文字，大小二乘，十二部经，皆因人置。……不悟即佛是众生。一念悟时，众生是佛。"（《六祖坛经·般若品》，以下简称《坛经》）因此，人和佛之间没有不同，人能成佛只在一念顿悟。

从以上的引文中，我们发现，在中国哲学体系中，人是一个最基本的概念。虽然学派不同，但他们都同意人性有善的和德性的因素。如果发展出来，能使人成为圣人、真人或佛。由于此理，中国人说"做人"。虽然我们现在的人不完美，但只要修养我们的心智和去实践德性，我们就能成为完美的人。

怡按

就这个人的相关词语来说，人的分类层次，儒家有圣人、仁人、贤人、君子之分；道家有神人、天人、至人、真人、圣人之别。道教讲神仙。佛教也有佛、菩萨、罗汉等的差别。一般学者都以最高的境界为追求的理想，要成圣、成仙、成佛。其实我们研究这个"人"字，最重要、最基本的，也是最下层、最普通的"人"，即"做人"。孔子真正的教化是"成人"，老庄的真意也是做个"不争"的人、"无待"的人，中国的人间佛学也主张"人成即佛成"。所以总而言之，一句话，最重要的，甚至最高的理念就是"做人"，这两字已概括了所有的中国哲学。

3. 天

"天，颠也。至高无上，从一大。"（许慎《说文解字》）在宇宙中，天是最高、最大的。而且天在形式和意义上是从人性中展现出来的，所以天与人类是有关联的，这一点可于很多特别用法之中得知。除了一般的意思天空外，"天"在中国哲学思想中至少有六种含义。

1）终极权威（权威性）

"予惟小子，不敢替上帝命。天休于宁王，兴我小邦周。"（《尚书·大诰》）此处，"天"是被解读为上帝，它具有绝对的权威性，能掌控人民的命运。天的概念和规范兴于周朝。在此以后，很多哲学家认为天是最高和最终的有德性的神，把权威性的天变成最流行的信仰。在这里，我们可以看出，这个一般形体的"天"，是如何逐渐被转换为上帝、权威性的神、创造主或最高的精神的。

2）最高的德性

"天地之大德曰生。"（《易经·系辞下传》第一章）生生本是天的功能，这里，由天的权威，转化成天的德性，这种德性能使万物生生不已。

3）物质性的自然

"天行有常，不为尧存，不为桀亡。应之以治则吉，应之以乱则凶。"（《荀子·天论》）荀子，生于战国末年（约公元前313—公元前238），在秦朝之前，他是极少数强调物质自然重要的儒者，而且主张人必须参与到自然之天的造化之中。

4）生命性的自然

"知天之所为，知人之所为者，至矣。知天之所为者，天而生也。"（《庄子·大宗师》）虽然在庄子的思想中，"天"有时是指物质性的自然，但更多的时候是指超越性的天道，"天"的存在是超过我们的认知能力的，但我们却可以通过心性和他相通。

5）是最高标准

"天垂象见吉凶。圣人象之。"（《易经·系辞上传》第十一章）这是说，"天"是我们最好的楷模，我们应该遵循它。

6）超然的天命

孔子的学生子夏说："死生有命，富贵在天。"（《论语·颜渊》）这是说，"天"好似决定我们的命运，而且安排我们的生命；我们无力改变它赋予的一切。

怡按

以上我们只就"天"这一个字来分析，这个"天"常和其他的字连结成许多复合词，如天道、天理、天命、天行、天良等，因而有各种不同的作用。如天道，指生生不已的动态；天理，是指内在于人物的理路；天命，是指天赋予人的性能和责任；天行，是庄子的用语，是指自然的流衍；天良，是儒家用语，是指我们本具的良心。但无论是哪一个"天"字所组成的复合词，我们强调"天"都是为了"人"，也就是说为了使我们"人"能向上提升。

4. 仁

"仁"字很难翻译成英文，因为中国哲学和哲学家用他们自己的方式解说它的内涵。一般而言，它的意思有善心、爱心、好心、慈爱、慈善和慈悲。而且这些只是部分意义，每个人都有其独特的表达方法及他们的观念意识。我们不能接受仅以"慈悲"作为适切的定义，因为"仁"能用来包括社会的理想性，不只是一个道德名词而已。

"仁"的字源，如许慎说："亲者，密至也。从人二。"（许慎《说文解字》）"仁"建立在二人的关系上，没有人与人的关系就没有仁。无论如何，汉儒的解说是相对的，不含"仁"的形而上的意义。

在孔子之前，"仁"只是一个简单的道德行为，主要指爱民的意思。如"仁，所以保民也。"（《国语·周语》）"明慈爱以导之仁。"（《国语·楚语》）

无论如何，孔子选"仁"为主要概念，这是他整个哲学思想的根本。在他的思想中，"仁"有时是指仁爱的德性，但最主要的还是指完美的人格，这一点可分六方面来看。

1）"仁"的意义

孔子对"仁"没有下过一个确切定义，因为他认为仁不是知识之事。在《论语》中，都是学生问到"仁"，然后孔子回答学生如何去行"仁"。我们发现在《中庸》一书中有比较确切的定义，孔子说"仁者，人也。"此处，"人"的意义是"仁"或是"人道"。也就是说，"仁"是完美的人或为人的规范。

2）"仁"的本质

在《论语》中，孔子没有谈到"仁"的本质。然而，如果我们同意《易经》"十冀"是孔子写的或记录他的思想的，我们就会发现"仁"的本质是"天地之大德曰生"（《易经·系辞下传》第一章）和"夫大人者，与天地合其德"（《易经·乾卦·文言》）。由此二引语，我们发现"大人"，同具有天地生生之德。对人来说，生的意思一方面是具有发展天地生化的潜能，另一方面是维系人与人的美好关系，及帮助别人发展他们的事业。例如，"唯天下至诚为能尽其性。能尽其性，则能尽人之性。能尽人之性，则能尽物之性。能尽物之性，则可以赞天地之化育。"（《中庸》）所以帮助别人发展他们的人性和赞助天地的化育功能，都是"仁"的本质。

3）"仁"的功能

"子曰：'参乎！吾道一以贯之。'曾子曰：'唯。'子出，门人问曰：'何谓也？'曾子曰：'夫子之道，忠恕而已矣！'"（《论语·里仁》）这里的忠是尽己之心，恕是推己之心。也就是说，"仁"的功能是成就自己，也成就别人。

4）"仁"的内涵

"仁"是所有德行中最重要的主德。在《论语》中，当学生问到仁，孔子告诉他们要根据自己的个性去实践。因此，有很多种方法去实践仁。例如，当颜渊问仁，孔子回答"克己复礼"（《论语·颜渊篇》），当樊迟问仁，孔子说"爱人"（《论语·颜渊》），当樊迟再问，孔子回答："居处恭，执事敬，与人忠。虽之夷狄，不可弃也。"而当子张问仁，孔子说："能行五者于天下，为仁矣！"请问之，曰："恭、宽、信、敏、惠。"（《论语·阳货》）所有这些德行都是"仁"。我们可以说"仁"是爱人和敬人，但是我们不能说爱人和敬人是仁；"仁"不是任何一种德行，它包括了所有的德行。

5）"仁"的实践

孔子说："仁远乎哉？我欲仁，斯仁至矣。"（《论语·述而》）

虽说"仁"是完美的至德，但它的实践在每天的生活中。如果你有意要行"仁"，你立志要成为"仁人"，你可以随时随地去实践。开始实践之处是家庭。因此，孝道是实践仁道的基础。

6）"仁"的功用

普通道德总是给予我们限制，或者要求我们做一些牺牲。"仁"是不同的。"仁"是自然的，它的表现是愉乐、美好的。例如，"仁者不忧"（《论语·子罕》）和"仁者寿"。实践"仁"是与万物和谐相处而且永远快乐的。

孔子以后，所有的儒家学者依照他的解释，把"仁"当作修养的最高标准，而且成为他们个人哲学体系的重心，继续延伸它的意义，增加它的运用功能。例如，孟子将其发展后说："仁，人心也。义，人路也。"（《孟子·告子》）强调人心是善的，从而建立了性善的理论。这是延伸人心到"仁"的行为和治道上。孟子常把它与"义"连结而说"仁义"，因为他相信"义"是实践"仁"的途径。对于孟子，他把"仁"解作心，而说仁爱和仁义，这是把"仁"落到实践的层面来运用了。

宋明理学家强调形而上的"仁"。"仁者，浑然与物同体。"（程颢《宋元学案·明道学案》）"万物之生意最可观，此元者善之长也，斯所谓仁也。"（程颢、程颐《二程集》）"仁只是个浑然温和的。其气则是天地阳春之气，其理则天地生物之心。"（朱熹《续近思录》）"大人之能以天地万物为一体也，非意之也，其心之仁本若是。"（王阳明《大学问》）。程颢、朱熹和王阳明都将"仁"的概念，从人心扩大到万物的本质了。

怡按

在中国哲学史上，这个"仁"字自孔子以后，被历代的哲学家提得很高。以孔子为例，他周游列国，以"仁"去劝说各国君主，但好像因为其理想太高，不为各君王所接受这一点，已由孔子和子路、子贡、颜回的讨论中提了出来。接着孟子把"仁"解作爱，已浅近了许多，但很多君主仍以爱货爱色为借口，不想谈"仁"。庄子已注意到这点，批评儒家"藏仁以要人"（《庄子·应帝王》）的不当。至于后代儒家，尤其宋明儒家仍然把"仁"推得很高，但仍然都是停在理论上。

今天的社会，我们很少在政治上或生活上用这个"仁"字了，除了中医上还沿用这些名词，如仁医、仁丹等，很少有人再说仁君、仁政或仁人了。好像"仁"字已走出了我们的生活圈。虽然我们已少用"仁"字，但却改用了一些和"仁"相等的字如人道主义、人权思想，以及宗教的大爱，虽然它们和"仁"字仍有差别，但至少也是"仁"的一种实践。我曾在数篇文字中强调，我们可以推行一种容易为人接受的德行，即老子的知足和孔子的恕道，因为这两者不是一味地要求我们付出或牺牲，是人人可以做得到的。而这个恕的"己所不欲，勿施于人"，正是"仁"的实践之德。所以今天我们可以少谈点"仁"的高标理论，多做点人人可行的合乎人性的事情。

5. 心

中国古时，"心"一般是指脑、精神和心情，有时当谈论到疾病时，它的意思也可能是指心脏。在中国哲学里，这个"心"字就是指心思。

对西方人士来说，要了解中国哲学里的"心"有两个问题：第一是需要认清各种不同学派中的不同用法。第二是比较困难的，因为这个"心"包含了智力、精神和感觉的交互作用，在西方它们是绝对分开的。

为了避免一提到中国的"心"，只想到心脏的心或脑子的心，我们把它融合起来，再分成以下八种作用来了解。

1）一般意义的"心"，没有特别强调情感和思想

在《论语》中，"心"字只出现六次，全都是普通的心的意思。例如，孔子说："七十而从心所欲，不逾矩。"（《论语·为政》）这里只是泛指那个心，没有特别的含义。

2)"心"是精神和生命力

"复其见天地之心乎。"(《易经·复卦·彖辞》)在孔子老年时,他研究《易经》而延伸一般心的意思,具有哲学意涵,是强调天地之心,也就是说宇宙的生命和精神。

3)"心"是善之端

"恻隐之心,仁之端也;羞恶之心,义之端也;辞让之心,礼之端也;是非之心,智之端也。"(《孟子·公孙丑》)孟子强调人性是善的;在他的思想中,心就是善的端点。

4)"心"是智慧的

"人何以知道?曰:'心'。……心者,形之君也,而神明之主也。"(《荀子·解蔽篇》)荀子的基本思想是主张人性是恶的,但却认为可通过教育的方法来纠正它。人们可以有德性,乃是因为心有智慧,可以控制欲望。

5)"心"是有欲望的

"不见可欲,使民心不乱。"(《老子》第三章)在《老子》中,谈到"心"的有六章。一般的意思是有情绪的和欲望的。但在老子的思想中，欲望是恶的。因此，老子强调要"虚其心"，也就是说要除掉心中的欲望。

6)"心"是精神的，是真我

"彼为己，以其知得其心，以其心得其常心。"(《庄子·德充符》)"心"在《庄子》中常常出现。由上面的引句，可见第一个"心"是指一般的精神，而第二个"常心"就是真我。

7)"心"是佛、佛法、自性，包括所有的德性

"是心是佛，是心作佛。"(《观无量寿佛经》)道信说："夫百千法门，同归方寸。河沙妙德，总在心源。一切戒门、定门、慧门，神通变化，悉自具足，不离汝心。"(《景德传灯录》第四卷)"菩提自性，本来清净。但用此心，直了成佛。"(《坛经·自序品》)从这些禅师的引文中，说明了"心"的本质，以及如何把这个"心"用在以心传心的教法中。(顺便一提，禅宗所言的"心"，不是儒家和理学家所言的"心")。

8)"心"是理、性、太极，包括万事万物

宋明理学家为禅宗所影响，由"理"的无所不包，而扩大了这个"心"去包含万事万物。"心为太极"(邵雍《观物外篇》上)，"理与心一"(程颢《二程语录》第五章)，"宇宙便是吾心，吾心

即是宇宙"(《陆象山全集》第二十二章)，"心与理一……理便在心之中"（朱熹《朱子语类》卷五），"心外无物，心外无事"（王阳明《传习录》卷一）。从这些征引中，可见宋明理学家都是先把心和理合一，然后由理去说心的无所不包。

怡按

上面谈到修心，但我们究竟要如何修心呢？总括起来，可以有下列各端：

（1）求其放心（孟子主张，收回向外，逐欲之心）。

（2）把心放下（禅宗主张，放下执着之心）。

（3）以仁存心（儒家主张，要有恻隐之心）。

（4）以诚敬存心（宋明儒家虽说用于打坐时，但也用于平日）。

（5）顺忠恕而行（儒家思想，推己之心以及物）。

（6）虚其心（道家思想，要消除心中的欲望）。

（7）化其心（道家思想，扬弃是非之心，而化入于道）。

（8）明其心（禅宗思想，明心见性的明心是认清不善之心，而归于清净之心）。

6. 化

"化"是庄子书中非常重要的字,《庄子·逍遥游》首段:"北冥有鱼,其名为鲲。鲲之大,不知其几千里也。化而为鸟,其名为鹏。"这里我们很容易地把这个"化"当作一般意义的变,如蝌蚪变青蛙或鱼子变大鱼。但是鲲是鱼,而鹏是鸟,如何能从鱼变成鸟?显然,"化"的意义不像最初看到的变一样简单。分析所有庄子书中的例子,我们发现有三个意义。

1)"化"的暂时性

我们观察到宇宙之间的暂时性变化,如生、老、病和死,荣誉、卑贱、灾害和幸运等,这些都是不可避免的,也是顺着时间变化的。如庄子所谓的"是万物之化也"(《庄子·人间世》)。

2)大自然的循环

宇宙在不断的循环,它包罗万象,没有事物能例外。如庄子说:"安排而去化,乃入于寥天一。"(《庄子·大宗师》)"安排"即安于宇宙的排定,即指这个必然的循环。

3）通过功夫的转化之道

功夫是一种心的修养。它努力去成就最高的精神或真我，而与道合一。它超越肉体，而顺乎自然的变化。如庄子所说，"不如两忘而化其道"（《庄子·大宗师》）。

最后，我们再看鲲化为鹏的寓言，它是描写超越肉体的我，而升华为精神的我。这不是变而是转化，它是不断修养我们的心，使我们能超越短暂的生命、知识、经验，而和天地同化，这种修养庄子称为"坐忘"，我们往往把它当成打坐，但其实它是忘掉现实的世界，而与道同化。

怡按

这个"化"有许多复合词，如消化、融化、教化、同化、文化、感化、转化等。其中最重要，可以作为修养功夫的是转化。转化有以下名种特色：

（1）精神化（精神重于物质）。

（2）不执着于外境（不为现象所拘）。

（3）不落于两边（超脱两边的执着，如是非、成败、生死等）。

（4）向上提升（不拘于小知小成）。

（5）忘我而自化（放掉自我）。

（6）忘物而物化（认万物都有真性）。

（7）忘神而神化（要虚掉在上的神性）。

7. 中

"中"是大家最熟悉的字，我们自称中国，提醒我们是在东亚各国的中心，我们也期待中国在物质和精神文明上是中心的位置。在中国哲学里，"中"不是只指中心位置，而含有很多特别的意义。

1）正道

"允执厥中。"（《尚书·大禹谟》）"大哉乾乎！刚健中正，纯粹精也。"（《易经·乾卦·文言》）这个引文表明"中"的原始意义在中国哲学里是指"正道"。"中"有很多用法，特别在《易经》中，意思是正和对的时间或位置。一般来说，在宋朝儒家中，这个用法是很普遍的。

2）性的本体

"喜、怒、哀、乐之未发，谓之中。"（《中庸》）这里"中"的意思是性的本质，是平衡而没有情绪作用的。这种形而上的意义影响到后来的宋明儒学家。

3）是心之虚

"多言数穷，不如守中。"（《老子》第五章）这个"守中"，即保持无欲之心，就好像深谷的空虚，而能生万物。

4）不动摇的心

"且夫乘物以游心，托不得已以养中。"（《庄子·人间世》）这里"中"的意思是心性的和谐而不为外物所动摇。

5）从不偏不倚，极至，到道或太极

宋明理学家提升"中庸"的"中"而为中道。最先，程颐说，"不偏之谓中。"（朱熹《中庸章句》）而后，他说："中是极至处。"（《二程遗书》卷十九）后来，朱熹说："程子曰：中即是道。"（《朱子语类》）陆象山说："中即太极。"（《陆象山全集》）这些都是把"中"扩大到形而上的至高境界。

怡按

我读《中庸》，几十年来都受朱熹的注中那句"不偏之谓中，不易之谓庸"的影响，都强调这个不偏的"中"，都在"中"字上去做文章。最好的例子就是用古代的秤做比喻，我们称物时，随物的轻重，而秤砣在秤的指标上移动，放在最适当的点上这就是不偏之"中"，无过与不及的"中"。可是最近我发现这个例子只能用在称物上，因为物的轻重是固定的，容易测量。可是我们生活上的人事问题，如何去求其不偏？譬如对父母的孝，对人的爱，如何才是不偏，如何才能不过与不及？这一点不能用外在的秤，或道德规范、礼制标准来测量。因此真正的作用乃是求之于心，也就是说"中"在心里。并不是说心里有个"中"的标准，这样有了标准，这个心又不"中"了。

因此我发现要真正把握这个"中"，有两个功夫：一个就是《中庸》后半篇讲的"诚"；一个是老子讲的"虚"。《中庸》为什么在首章讲"天命之谓性"，"喜怒哀乐之未发谓之中，发而皆中节谓之和"？这是指内在的心性与外在的中和，就是为后来的"诚"铺路。我们靠理智无法真正判定处事的不偏，不致过与不及，只有反求自己心中之诚，能诚，处事自然能合乎中道了。如果我们的心中有不诚，那是由于自我太强、私欲太重，所以老子要"虚其心"，先要把心中的欲虚掉。程伊川所谓"闲邪则诚自存"（《二程集》），基于这个道理，我认为这一虚一诚才是致中正、求中和的真正功夫。

8. 反

"反"字，一般意思是反转或反回，在《易经》和《老子》二书中却有甚深的哲学内涵。

1）在《易经》中的"反"

就《易经》的"易"字来说，易是变动。"反"字是变动的正和反。在《易经》的卦义中，是讲宇宙人生变动的相反和返回。我们来看以下三种情况。

一是"反"在每个卦爻辞中。

在《易经》六十四卦中，每个卦由两组三个爻构成，在下面三爻叫"内卦"。"内卦"多半代表思想、家庭和其他主观个人的或内在的事物。在上面三爻叫"外卦"，一般来说，多半象征外在的行为、政治事务等。在每个卦中，都有两爻特别关系到返回，这就是第三爻和第六爻（注意这些爻都是从最下面往上算）。当一个人在第三爻上，即将进入第四爻，代表他必须从理念进入行动，或从安全的家庭内转向有责任的政府。因此，卦爻辞的判断都是停下来检验自己。例如，乾卦的第三爻爻辞是："君子终日乾乾，夕惕若厉，无咎。"（《乾卦》）孔子的小象补充说，"终日乾乾，与时偕行。"即从事于自我反省的道德活动。

另外一条有关返回的是第六爻，它在卦的最上面。任何事情到了极点和达到限制点时，就会返回或变成相反的作用。所以，此爻在卦的极限，常处在变的位置或返回到原始点。例如，《家人卦》第六爻说："有孚威如，终吉。""象曰：威如之吉，反身之谓也。"（《家人卦》）"反身"就是反省自己，返回到内心或返回家内（第三爻），即以德修身而齐家。

第二是"反"在两个卦之间。

所有的六十四卦是相互关联的，其中有十二个卦的意义是相反而又相成的：例如否（十二卦）和泰（十一卦）、复（二十四卦）和剥（二十三卦）、解（四十卦）和蹇（三十九卦）、损（四十一卦）和益（四十二卦）、鼎（五十卦）和革（四十九卦）、既济（六十三卦）和未济（六十四卦）。每对两个卦的爻辞不仅有相反的对比，而意义也为我们提供了从相反中求它们相辅的作用。如果我们能检视并理解它们阴阳的交互作用，就会知道如何解决问题了。

第三是卦的复返。

复卦的"复"字和"反"字相同，而有不同的字形。复卦的第一爻（最底下的）是阳，上面的五爻都是阴，表示阳爻的刚强之气向上发展，而上面的阴柔之气逐渐减弱。在自然界，阳气开始替换阴气，显示春天将至。"反复其道，七日来复，天行也。利有攸往，刚长也。复其见天地之心乎？"（《复卦·彖辞》）这就是说阳气又返回到人间了。

这段话是孔子的评注，它是强调阳爻之气和万物的生生不息之态，这是表现出天地之心。这和老子强调宁静表现的天地之心是相互对照的。虽说生动之气和宁静是不可分割的，但在《易经》中却强调生生之气的重返人间。"反复"是阴阳之气的相交，所以"反"或"复"是《易经》的中心旨趣，在这里"反"变成一个道德的名词，告诉我们每件事情都可以通过变化而变好。

2）在《老子》中的"反"

"反"作为一个特别的词语，在《老子》中出现了很多次。例如，"大曰逝，逝曰远，远曰反。"（第二十五章）"反者，道之动。"（第四十章）"玄德深矣，远矣！与物反矣，然后乃至大顺。"（第六十五章）"正言若反。"（第七十八章）可见整个老子思想充满了"反"的理念，它是道的功能。在老子的思想中，"反"有两种意义："反转"和"返回"。

先看"反转"。

每件事物继续活动，以至于转变成对立的一方，这样就产生了各种不同的相对关系。老子描述这些都是现象界的作用，如万物的变化、政治的消长，以及日常生活的得失、成败等。下面分三种情况来说。

首先，反转是现象界的相对。"故有无相生，难易相成，长短相较，高下相倾，音声相和，前后相随。"（第二章）

其次，反转是理念的对立。"明道若昧，进道若退，夷道若纇，上德若谷，广德若不足，建德若偷，质真若渝，大白若辱，大方无隅，大器晚成，大音希声，大象无形。"（第四十一章）

再次，反转在政治和日常生活中。"绝圣弃智，民利百倍；绝

仁弃义，民复孝慈；绝巧弃利，盗贼无有。"（第十九章）

再看返回。

"反"用在返回上，是借由修养而返回到真我，或借由复命、复明、复朴而返回于道。也有三种情况：

一是复命："夫物芸芸，各复归其根。归根曰静，是谓复命。复命曰常。"（第十六章）

二是复朴："知其荣，守其辱，为天下谷。为天下谷，常德乃足，复归于朴。"（第二十八章）

三是复明："见小曰明，守柔曰强。用其光，复归其明。"（第五十二章）

"反"不仅是老子的中心学说，也影响其他哲学思想和以后的道家学者。这个原理，兵家和法家把它用在战略和管理上，神仙家把它用在炼制丹砂上（见"丹"字），他们只知用相反，而不知返回的修养。他们忽视老子思想的重点在返回上，因而走上极端和终点，与道相反。

怡按

这个"反"字在老子书中已说了很多，但用在修养功夫上却在于一个"返"字。如何知返、用返、能返，有以下各点可以参考：

（1）不要只看表面现象（庄子思想，不执着于是非成败等）。

（2）能知反躬自问（儒家思想，遇到挫折困难时，先要检讨自己）。

（3）先要把自己放在最低处（老子思想，水向低处流能，低才能转身）。

（4）要知退不争（老子思想，进道若退，退一步天地宽）。

（5）要虚掉向上的障碍（禅宗思想，不要以佛为佛；以道为道，才能使自己的人格和自性向上提升）。

9.丹

丹是朱砂，是红色矿石从汞熔炼出来的。后来的道士混合其他的矿物质以炼金术的方法精炼成"丹"，他们希望发明丹药（灵丹妙药）可以使他们长生不死而成神仙。它的理论和源自阿拉伯的欧洲炼金术相似，但它用了老庄思想为指导原则，因此，"丹"成为特别的术语，它综合了魔术、科学、宗教和哲学等因素。由于这些原因，炼金术士变为道教的神仙家。

1）"丹"的定义

神仙家认为"丹"有三个意义：一是真气，这是人的本性；二是心身的修炼，这可以带给人真气；三是金丹或仙丹，这个药物或丹药炼成是混合朱砂，精炼的汞、锡和其他矿物质而成。朱云阳说："不同而同者，先天自然之本体，至真也。即内药。非异而异者，后天颠倒之妙用，乃从妙用而返至真也。即外药也。"（张紫阳《悟真篇》，朱云阳注疏）这里，内药是真气，外药是指金丹的运用。

2）真气

"抱一即成丹。盖一生二，二生三，三生万物。顺去生人生物者，此一也。而三返二，二返一，一返虚无，逆来成圣成仙者，亦此一也。"（朱云阳《参同契阐幽》）这个"一"在老子思想是道，于神仙家来说，就是真气或丹。

3）"内丹"和"外丹"

这部分可从两方面来说。

一是保养三宝。

神仙家所谓"三宝"即精、气和神。朱云阳谓："修道之士有内三宝，有外三宝。元精元气元神，内三宝也。耳目口，外三宝也。欲得内三宝还真，全在外三宝不漏。"（朱云阳《参同契阐幽》）这"外三宝"就是我们的九窍，它们会泄掉我们的精、气、神三宝。保精就是要我们不乱泄精液，而要还精补脑；行炁就训练我们的呼吸，使我们的口不会泄漏真气；保神就是要我们制欲，保持心的安宁。

二是服一大药。

"欲求神仙，唯当得其至要。至要者，在于宝精、行炁，服一大药。"（葛洪《抱朴子·内篇》卷八）"大药"即是金丹，它是由炉火锻炼而成的。炼丹的方法详细记载在葛洪的《抱朴子》和魏伯阳的《参同契》二书。前者详述采药和炼丹的方法，后者用《老子》和《易经》思想介绍炼丹的原理。虽然两书都很详尽，但它们的说法充满奥秘和假设性，这两本书对读者来说，是充满着神秘彩色的。

4）丹道和老子之道的关系

丹道的理来自老子的"反"。朱云阳说："金丹之超出常情也。何谓反？常道用顺，丹道用逆。"（朱云阳《参同契阐幽》）所有丹道的方法是在用一个"反"字。例如还精、不用口呼吸、不食谷米。在表面上，这些做法好像是依照老子的"反"之理，但实际上，却违反了老子的"反"是返于常理和自然。但这却是丹道所违背的。

怡按

道教的神仙之学，丹道有内外之分。外丹指吃由炉鼎所制的金丹，《抱朴子·内篇》就是专讲外丹。魏伯阳的《周易参同契》是以行炁的内丹为主。王阳明少时学金丹之道，也希望能羽化成仙，但"龙场一悟"后才发现金丹之术是错误的，他由此转向内心，不求丹而求道，他写下了几句警语，说："大道即人心，万古未尝改。长生在求仁，金丹非外待。谬矣三十年，于今吾始悔。"

王阳明对金丹的批评是经过他的亲身体验而来的，认为已明金丹不是大道。

10. 玄

扫一扫，
进入课程

本来，这个"玄"字是指颜色深红几乎接近黑色。在《论语》和《孟子》中，"玄"字只是表示颜色；务实的儒家学者没有把哲学意义附于玄字。在《老子》中，我们发现"玄"用在哲学上表现神秘和深度的思想。

1）"玄"是深度的源头

"故常无，欲以观其妙。常有，欲以观其徼。此两者，同出而异名，同谓之玄。玄之又玄，众妙之门。"（《老子》第一章）这里，"玄"用来描述深度的源头，是有和无混而为一的境界。

2）"玄"是慧眼

"涤除玄览，能无疵乎？"（《老子》第十章）这里，"玄览"意思是精神视力，是真心的意思。它被称为"玄"，是因为它的慧眼可以看到事物的本源。

在老子、庄子之后，"玄"被推展到最高境界，如玄天、玄宫、玄黑、玄古、玄圣、玄德和玄珠等。但是在老庄思想中，"玄"

字只是指深度和玄妙而已，并没有太多附加的神奇彩色。

3）"玄"是道

后来的道家以玄为道。"夫玄也者，天道也，地道也，人道也。"（扬雄《太玄·玄图》）扬雄是汉朝儒学家，他的哲学有道家思想的成分，因为他在文章中用"玄"作为关键术语。

扬雄以后，有很多魏晋新道家以"玄"当成他们的中心概念，被称为"玄学"。

怡按

这里的"玄"字来自老子，但后来魏晋玄学家虽然以易、老庄的"三玄"为主，但绝非易与老庄的思想，因为他们是乐于空洞的谈玄，但易与老庄却不谈玄。

另外西方有一门哲学的学问，叫 metaphysics，中国学人常把它译成玄学和形而上学。其实这三者都不同。metaphysics 研究的是西方抽象的观念，它们是被看作宇宙最高的真理，并乐于清谈。至于译成形而上学，虽然是公认的正译，但中国的"形而上"三字来自《易经·系辞传》的"形而上者，谓之道；形而下者，谓之器"（《系辞上传》），所以中国的形而上学是道学，与西方哲学研究抽象观念自然不同。

至于形而上学与玄学也不同。我们可以说儒家的形而上学，如儒家的讲天道、天命、天理以及理、气、心、性的问题，但不能说儒家的玄学，因为儒家绝不谈玄。我近年来对"形而上"一词有新解，认为人在道和器之间，人如果向下堕落，追求物欲就会流于形而下的器世界；如果向上追求道，就是形而上的提升，进入道世界。所以"形而上"不是一个静的境地，而是向上的动的发展，形而上是一种修养的功夫。

11. 名

这个"名"字一般的意思是人名和物名。中国哲学扩展它的意义为官衔、名誉、家庭的名分等。

1）家庭角色

孔子的学生子路说："'卫君待子而为政，子将奚先？'子曰："必也正名乎！'"（《论语·子路》）"名"在此对话中是影射卫君父子的关系，因为当时卫君是儿子，他的父亲曾被放逐在外，回不来。父子相争，所以孔子以"正名"批评他们。后来"正名"便指家庭中父子、夫妇、兄弟的关系，也成为孔子齐家治国的政治理念。

2）官位头衔

"名实当则治，不当则乱。"（《管子·九守篇》）管子是孔子之前早期的法家。这里，"名"是官位头衔，是依据他们的实际工作而定的。从此，后来的法家发展出一套考核名实的制度，查看他们是否符合他们的官衔。

3）名望

用"名"表示名望或名誉，在中国哲学中有两种内涵。在儒家，"名"是好事，它是表现人的荣誉。例如，孔子说："君子疾没世而名不称焉。"（《论语·卫灵公》）而在道家和佛家，"名"是一种欲望或妄想，庄子认为它是产生问题的原因，如他说："德荡乎名，知出乎争。"（《庄子·人间世》）

4）法家、名家和名理派的"名"

"所以谓，名也。所以谓，实也。名实耦，合也。"（墨子《墨经·经说上》）。这里"名"的意思是指物名，或指事实。后来学者研究和分析这方面的"名"，注重名实相符。用之于法律的，称法家，如管子、韩非等人；只讨论"名"的观念，而用于辩论的，称为名家，如惠施、公孙龙等人；只讨论"名"和理，用之于玄谈的，就成为名理派，如刘劭、钟会等人。

怡按

在"名"字中，"正名"是特别重要的，但"正名"有广狭两义。狭义的是指孔子去卫国时，对子路的问题，提出"正名"两字。当时是因卫君父子相争，而要正名，所以是指"父父子子"的伦常关系。以前孔子三十六岁到齐国时，齐景公问政，孔子回答的"君君、臣臣、父父、子子"是指当时齐国大臣掌权，景公失势，这也是正名的意思。可见，"正名"是孔子政治伦理思想的要点。广义的要点有二：一是延续孔子的正名，荀子有《正名篇》，讨论名辞也强调伦理；二是谈名实相符问题，可以包括所有名家、法家等。如果我们再扩大意义来看，《易经》的"位"，《中庸》的素其"位"而行，也都可看作"正名"的运用。十年前，我在北京的一次演讲中，呼吁大家注意自己的名字，都是为父母所取，选择好的、鼓励性的字，因此我们看看自己的名字，想想自己是否做到，这也是一种新的"正名"，即正名字。

12. 志

"志"字是决心成为一个有理想的人，在中国是一个比较流行的术语。特别在儒家哲学中，有特殊的功能，这方面是值得注意和赞赏的。

1）"志"是实践仁的开始

孔子说，"苟志于仁矣，无恶也。"（《论语·里仁》）孔子认为，一个人要实践仁道，第一件事是先立志，要把仁的理念在生活中实践出来。

2）"志"是气、精神和生命的指导

"夫志，气之帅也。气，体之充也。夫志，至焉。气，次焉。"（《孟子·公孙丑》）"志"，是我们精神和身体的主宰，能指导我们所有的行为。

3）"志"是基本的哲学思想训练

陆象山说："学者须先立志，志既立，却要遇明师。"（《陆象山全集·语录》）陆象山是宋朝的儒家，他认为"志"是努力学习的基石。所有理学家都强调"志"，以为"志"不只是重要的理念，而且是哲学的基本训练。

关于"志"，道家和佛家不同于儒家。老子主张"弱其志"（《老子》第三章），也就是减少自我意识或个人的野心。所有禅师强调的是"不执着"或"无心"，也就是无欲或随缘。但实际上，道家和佛家始终努力成为完人或真人。甚至在禅宗，尝试避免执着于佛，如大慧宗杲禅师说："丈夫自有冲天志，不向如来行处行。"一个人应该随着自己的佛性走，不要执着外在的形式。所以，即使禅宗，也有他们自己的"志"。

在中国哲学里，"志"是最重要的，是能支撑学者去实践德行和求道，而且承担责任去寻求方法缓解人们的痛苦。以前文天祥，他选择被杀而不愿投降蒙古敌人，他在他的腰带上写着"孔曰成仁，孟曰取义，唯有义尽，所以仁至。读圣贤书，所学何事？而今而后，庶几无愧。"（《宋史·文天祥传》）这是我们的古代有志之士的典型形象，也是大家常用的例子，这里表现了儒家立志完成人生最高目标的理想。

怡按

在古代，儒家教育的"志"是希贤求圣，学生们也了解谁是圣是贤。可是今天的社会中，年轻的学生们根本没有圣贤的榜样，如何去立这个"志"？有位美国的心理学家到中国小学去做心理调查，对五十个小学生问卷，问他们将来立志做什么？四十九个学生是做企业家和演艺明星，只有一人愿意做教员。这是今天教育的现况，或是今天教育的失败？总之，我们批评这些已是多余。那么我们上面所谈的"志"，是否已经走入历史，而无关紧要呢？甚至毫无意义呢？不然，这点我们可以从两方面来解决。

一是就幼童教育来说。西方心理学家阿尔弗雷德·阿德勒（Alfred Adler）在他的人格的理论中，认为幼童在四五岁时建立了他们的终极目标（final goal），即立志，将会影响他们的一生。这个"志"不是过去的希贤求圣，也不是今天有些父母只一味希望小朋友能上影视表演，我认为这个"志"是德性。为父母的不必像过去一样地教孝，要培养幼童的同情心、责任感和爱物、诚实的德性，这些自然能影响他们的一生。成为一个人格完善的人，这不也是孔子的"成人"，也即"成仁"吗？

二是就成人的修养来说。"志"的字义是士之心，即一个知识人或学者的心念。今天西方的学者只专注于他们的研究，也就是说他们只求理论体系完整，观点独出，并不考虑与天道的相合，以及对人心的影响。所以我认为他们也应一如张载所谓的儒者的抱负，"为天地立心，为生民立命，为往圣继绝学，为万世开太平"。这四句话说的就是对自然界、人民、历史和人类未来的关怀和责任。

13. 忘

"忘"的平常意思是忘记或漠视。仅庄子使它具有哲学意涵，而成为道家思想中超脱相对观念，达到心的最高境界的功夫。

1）庄子的三种"忘"

一是忘自己。

"忘自己"不是指迷失自己和失去记忆，它的意思是不执着于肉体和自我。庄子说，"堕肢体，黜聪明，离形去知，同于大通，此谓坐忘。"（《庄子·大宗师》）"坐忘"就像是在打坐中忘记自己，但却是和道相通的。

二是忘万物。

"忘万物"和"忘我"是相同过程中的两面，两者是互补的。没有"忘己"就不能"忘物"，反之亦然。"忘物"不是说否定万物的存在，它的意思是一个人看透外在事物，而不执着它们的形体。《庄子》中，有一个庖丁的故事，庖丁屠牛的技术很高明，文惠君请他去表演，表演之后，他说："臣之所好者道也，进乎技矣。……臣以神遇，而不以目视，官知止而神欲行。依乎天理，批大郤，导大窾，因其固然。"（《庄子·养生主》）当一个人明白真相，自然能超越所有物质的阻碍，这是"忘物"的真义。

三是忘逍遥。

如果一个人要"忘己"和"忘物"，而执着于舒适的状况，就不能真的"忘"。庄子说："忘足，履之适也；忘要，带之适也；知忘是非，心之适也；不内变，不外从，事会之适也；始乎适而未尝不适者，忘适之适也。"（《庄子·达生》）"忘逍遥"就是要我们连追求逍遥之念也要忘了，也就是不要变成执着于"忘"。如果你要"忘"，反而忘不了。

2）忘于道

"忘"容易被误解为普通的忘记。但庄子的"忘"不是忘记。如果一个人把"忘"当成他的目标，他就不能真忘。"忘"的真意是生活于道中而不知有道。如"鱼相造乎水，人相造乎道。相造乎水者，穿池而养给；相造乎道者，无事而生定。故曰：鱼相忘乎江湖，人相忘乎道术。"（《庄子·大宗师》）"忘于道"是指，当我们觉悟后便能物我双忘，但也是我们的真我和万物的真性各自并存。

怡按

"忘"是庄子思想的用语，它与佛家的"不执"和西方的"超脱"相似，但又不同。"不执"是不执着于外境，即不执着于是非、生死的分别境界。但"不执"往往变成另一种执着。因为念念不忘"不执"，"不执"也成为一念，与外境形成了对立。至于"超脱"，也同样地先确定了外境的存在，然后再企图超脱它们。这已是把超脱的主体与客体先对立了起来。庄子的"忘"却不一样，庄子把是非的观念和物的自体分成为二。庄子要忘的是观念的是非执着，这个执着在自己心中，所以庄子要忘的是忘掉自己的分别心，因而庄子先要"丧我"。至于对外物的自体，庄子不是去忘，而是通过道的"道通为一"，而浑然与万物同体。

14. 孝

"孝"字有两部分；上部分意思是"老"，下部分意思是"子"，表示子必须对父母顺从。在中国文化和哲学中，"孝"是一个重要的德性。特别在儒家思想里，"孝"在与其他德性连接上是有重大意义的。

1）"孝"和其他德性的关系

"有子曰：'其为人也孝弟，而好犯上者，鲜矣；不好犯上，而好作乱者，未之有也。君子务本，本立而道生。孝弟也者，其为仁之本与！'"（《论语·学而》）有子是孔子的学生中比较重要的几位之一，因此他说的也是符合孔子思想的。在这段话中，我们可以发现，"孝"在儒家实践仁道的过程中，是开始，也是基本的德行。孔子的"仁"包括了所有的德行，也就是说"孝"是实践所有德行的开始和基本。

2）"孝"的实践

在所有的德性中，"孝"是依据实际情况去做的。孔子根据实际情况而有以下的各种内容。

一是不违。

孟懿子问孝，孔子说："无违。"即，"生，事之以礼；死，葬之以礼，祭之以礼。"（《论语·为政》）在《礼记》中，顺从是儿子对待父母必须依据的规则。

二是承志。

孔子说："父在，观其志；父没，观其行；三年无改父之道，可谓孝矣。"（《论语·为学篇》）虽然不是所有父亲想做的，都是好的，在儒家看来，父亲代表的理念是智慧的累积，所以老人的经验的传承可以指导他们的孩子。

三是"几"。

孔子说："事父母几谏，见志不从，又敬不违，劳而不怨。"（《论语·里仁》）孔子不要儿子盲目地服从他们的父亲。如果儿子认为父亲是错的，他应该说明，但是要用温柔的方式。如果父亲不接受他的劝告，他还是保持尊重父亲的态度。

四是持敬。

"今之孝者，是谓能养。至于犬马，皆能有养；不敬，何以别乎。"（《论语·为政》）孔子敏锐地意识到孝变成一种习惯，流于空洞形式的危机，所以他强调要以尊敬之心去行孝。

五是色难。

孔子说："色难。有事，弟子服其劳；有酒食，先生馔，曾是以为孝乎？"（《论语·为政》）孝道不在于形式，也不只是一种勉强的责任。孝顺的儿子要以笑脸去服侍自己的父母。照顾父母不能因自己的烦恼而影响他们的快乐。

六是大孝尊亲。

尊亲是要能使父母受到别人的尊敬。如，"身体发肤，受之父母，不敢毁伤，孝之始。立身行道，扬名于后世，以显父母，孝之终也。"（《孝经·开宗明义章第一》）这是指的大孝，儿子为了人民和国家牺牲，也是为了让父母受到他人的尊敬。

3）"孝"在儒家中的重要性

儒家哲学中，"孝"不只是伦理的要素，也是普遍秩序的基础。如，"天地之性，唯人为贵。人之行，莫大于孝。孝莫大于严父，严父莫大于配天。"（《孝经·圣治章第九》）父道和天道等量齐观。天的德是生万物。"孝"继承天的功能，因为孝顺我们的父母是感谢他们生养我们，所以孝就是延续父母给予我们的生命。

4）"孝"在中国文化里的重要性

后来的儒家，把孝当作社会的基础。他们把孝与宗教、政治、伦理和所有社会的成分之间建立了不可分的关系。孔子说："武王、周公，其达孝矣乎！夫孝者：善继人之志，善述人之事者也。春秋，修其祖庙，陈其宗器，设其衣裳，荐其时食。宗庙之礼，所以序昭穆也；序爵，所以辨贵贱也；序事，所以辨贤也；旅酬下为上，所以逮贱也；燕毛，所以序齿也。践其位，行其礼，奏其乐，敬其所尊，爱其所亲；事死如事生，事亡如事存，孝之至也。"（《中庸》）这一段话详述了孝在中国古代社会中，不仅是实践的原则，而且是稳定的基础。

怡按

"孝"是中国文化里，最重要的一种德行。它的重要，是深入人们的实际生活中，即使不读书、不识字的人，也能知、能行，甚至比一个饱读诗书的人，还行得真诚。由于"孝"是在人们的实际生活中，甚至《礼记》《论语》都有明确的规定和论述，但人们的实行都因人而有不同，因此不免有许多错解和误导，而产生负面的影响。时至今日，由于文化的变动，社会的变迁，"孝"也逐渐不受人重视，不仅子女淡忘了孝，做父母的也放弃了以孝来期许子女。在这样的环境中，如果孝是一种美德的话，我们该如何给予"孝"以新的生命？庄子曾说："以敬孝易，以爱孝难。"（《庄子·天运》）庄子说这话的本意是，由爱而行孝比以敬行孝重要。由爱行孝是指真正从心而发的尽孝，以敬行孝是由礼制道德的规范而行孝。今天庄子的话也许能给我们启示，"孝"应该跳脱礼制道德的规范，把它的意义建筑在父母与子女的真爱上。前面我们在"志"的按语中，强调应在孩童四五岁时，就培养他们的同情心、爱心，试想这样的孩子长大后，对他人都有同情心、爱心，难道对父母没有孝心吗？只是这个"孝"，少了几分道德条文，多了几分温暖的爱心。

15. 命

在中国思想里，"命"是一个常用的字。除了"命令"的意思是用作动词外，中国哲学家把它用在以下的六个方面。

1）生命

"不幸短命死矣。"（《论语·雍也》）这里简单的意思就是"生命"或"寿命"，没有哲学的意义。

2）命运

伯牛生病，孔子去探望他，把手从窗口伸进去握住他的手，说："亡之，命矣夫！斯人也而有斯疾也！斯人也而有斯疾也！"（《论语·雍也》）这里"命"是命运，是我们不能改变的。在儒家哲学中，这种"命"是不讨论的。庄子认为，命运如"死生存亡，穷达贫富，贤与不肖毁誉，饥渴、寒暑，是事之变，命之行也"。（《庄子·德充符》）依据庄子所说，如果我们对所有事变，不知原因，不能控制，就是命运。我们不能因它们影响我们心的宁静。

3）天命

到孔子，"命"有一个更深的意义，就是天命。"道之将行也与？命也。道之将废也与？命也。"（《论语·宪问》）"文王既没，文不在兹乎？天之将丧斯文也，后死者不得与于斯文也！天之未丧斯文也，匡人其如予何？"（《论语·子罕》）从这些引言中，我们可以看出，孔子指的是天命。在《论语》中，"命"最常有的意义是至高无上的权力，它可以安排每件事物。这权力不是上帝所有的，或来自神秘的力量，它是合理的原则，是我们可以理解的，但不是可以随意改变的。"不知命，无以为君子也。"（《论语·尧曰》）也就是说作为一个君子，我们的责任是做我们该做的去实践天命。

4）本性

"归根曰静，是谓复命。复命曰常。"（《老子》第十六章）这里，"命"是万物的本性或宇宙的本质。它是真性或真命。

5）理

宋明理学家发展孔子"命"的定义为天理或天道。程颐说："在天为命，在义为理，在人为性，主于身为心，其实一也。"（《二程遗书》卷十八）朱熹说："如天命谓性之命，是言所禀之理也。"

（《续近思录·道体》）可见理学家为了使"命"容易了解和实践起见，把这个"命"解作天的禀赋，而把命运、生命合在一个"理"上。

6）精神

"为生民立命。"（张载《横渠语录》）这里，"命"的意义不只是指人民形体的生命，也是指其精神的生命。而精神的生命比形体的生命更重要。精神生命是指德性和智慧的生命。因此，儒家学者认为应该实践德性来替代执着于生命；我们应该完成我们的职责，因为那来自天命，而不只是物质的存在。

怡按

这个"命"在中国人的生活上，有三句非常重要的成语，即"乐天知命""安身立命""居易俟命"。这三句的"命"都是"天命"。可见"天命"在中国人信念中的重要性。可是"命运"也是一个极普通的词语，我们经常会用到它。那么"天命"和"命运"究竟有些什么不同？我们试分析如下：

（1）"天命"和"命运"共有一个"命"字，这个命是生命。也就是说，从生命的本质来说，它们是相同的，由生至死的历程相同，在生死间的遭遇也相同。

（2）"天命"来自天之所禀，是我们的性；"命运"来自气之运，是我们的物质生活。

（3）对"天命"我们虽无法知，但我们可以尽性，即尽自己的责;对"命运",我们也无法知,但屈于气运的环境,只有任其摆布。

（4）相信"天命",我们的努力是无限发展,没有止境的;相信"命运",我们会放弃努力,自怨自艾。

（5）例如有人出家做和尚,他认为是命运,说"做一天和尚撞一天钟";如果他相信天命,每次撞钟,他知道那暮鼓晨钟,是在撞醒世人的迷梦,是在修行。

16. 和

这个"和"字原始的意思是指两个事物的和合，再转变成为"和平"。哲学家们在不同的情况下用它有不同的意义。

1）天和

"天和"是指乾道的太和。如，"乾道变化，各正性命。保合太和。"（《易经·乾卦·彖辞》）"太和所谓道。"（张载《正蒙》）"太和"与"太极"是同义字。太极生阴阳两仪，所以阴阳之间也是天然的和。如，"万物负阴而抱阳，冲气以为和。"（《老子》第四十二章）

2）心和

"喜怒哀乐之未发，谓之中；发而皆中节，谓之和。"（《中庸》）这是指我们心的作用能够相应和谐。

3）时和

庄子说："一龙一蛇，与时俱化，而无肯专为。一上一下，以和为量。"(《庄子·山木》)这是指在一个不确定的关键时刻，有理智的人总会考虑现实情况，作出适当的决定。这要比我们只问，"如何以道德的观点处理它？"或者"如何以是非的标准解决它？"要重要得多。我们可以根据过去圣人留下来的经验、面前事实和智慧的教言来解它。这里没有固定的标准，只有把握"时"，进而求其"和"。

4）超越相对的"和"

庄子说："是以圣人和之以是非，而休乎天钧。"(《庄子·齐物论》)这里，"和之以是非"是指超越是非之外，也指超越古今、失败和成功、贫穷和富有等现象。假如我们超越这些相对性，我们就能像道家和禅师们，能借修养而达到心之"和"。

5）道德的"和"

"利物足以和义。"(《易经·乾·文言》)这个"义"就是宜的意思。义是道德行为，行义必须以"和"为贵。

怡按

"和"是中国哲学里彻头彻尾的一个非常重要的字，从宇宙的阴阳相和、神人以和，到日常生活的家和万事兴、和气生财。中国人讲"和"代替了西方哲学的追求真埋。譬如说，什么是社会的真理、家庭的真理？我们找不出一个真理来，而就中国人来说，社会中各阶层能和谐，家庭中各分子能和合，这就是社会和家庭的真理。但如何去致和？主要有两个德性：一是虚，就是虚掉自己的私欲。如庄子说，"游心乎德之和"（《庄子·德充符》），这样虚己，不凸显自己，才能与人、与物相和。二是恕，是"己所不欲，勿施于人"。能够多以自己之心去体谅别人，或站在别人的立场上想问题，就不会有人我之间的争斗，而易于和谐相处了。

17. 直

"直"是一个很普通的字，却有着很深的哲学含意。儒家用它于正直，道家用它于真心，佛家用它于无欲。

1）正直的行为

"直"一般的意思是包括正义、正直、正确、诚实和有关的概念。哀公问，"何为则民服？"孔子回答："举直错诸枉，则民服；举枉错诸直，则民不服。"（《论语·为政》）这里的"直"，是特指诚实和正直的官员。

2）真情

叶公对孔子说："吾党有直躬者，其父攘羊，而子证之。"孔子回答："吾党之直者异于是，父为子隐，子为父隐，直在其中矣。"（《论语·子路》）这里，"直"是指父母与子女间天生的真情，没有做作。

3）真我

庄子说："内直者，与天为徒。与天为徒者，知天子之与己皆天之所子，而独以己言蕲乎而人善之，蕲乎而人不善之邪？若然者，人谓之童子。"（《庄子·人间世》）这里，"直"的意思是一个人知道他的真心是天赋的，我的真我和万物是平等的。

4）清静无欲

"一行三昧者，于一切处行住坐卧，常行一直心是也。《净名经》云：'直心是道场，直心是净土。'"（《坛经·定慧品》）这里，"直心"是无杂无邪之心，也就是清净无欲之心。

怡按

孔子的"父为子隐，子为父隐，直在其中矣"，常引起法家和现代人的批评。但孔子只是解释"父为子隐，子为父隐"的父子之间的真情，至于做儿子的，不会以攘羊为是，仍有劝谏父亲的责任，不能因此而陷父母于不义。《论语》所载都为孔子师生谈论之主题，每一标题都会有较长时间的讨论，他们之间不可能只谈这几句话。当然对这段对话，孔门弟子也一定还有讨论，但都没有记录下来，这是读《论语》的后人不能不了解的很重要的一点。

18. 易

　　"易"的原始意思是"改变"。"易，蜥易，蝘蜓，守宫也。"（许慎《说文解字》）蜥蜴，据说一天能改变很多次颜色，因此"易"字是取蜥蜴的形象和改变的意义来作为它的字义的。道教的《秘书》说"日月为易，象阴阳也"，意思是日月交替，也就是改变的意思。

　　《易经》用"易"，有三种哲学含义。

1）改变

　　"易之为书也不可远，为道也屡迁。变动不居，周流六虚，上下无常，刚柔相易，不可为典要，唯变所适。"（《易经·系辞下传》第八章）这里，"易"是指宇宙万物的变化和六十四卦中各爻的变动。

2）不变

　　这个"易"字，用于两方面。一个是关于卦中爻的位置。"天尊地卑，乾坤定矣。卑高以陈，贵贱位矣。动静有常，刚柔断矣。"

（《易经·系辞上传》第一章）这是指爻的位置是固定的。另一个用法是有关于"易"的本质。"天地之道，恒久而不已也。利有攸往，终则有始也。日月得天而能久照，四时变化而能久成，圣人久于其道而天下化成。观其所恒，而天地万物之情可见矣。"（《易经·恒卦·彖辞》）永恒是不变的意思，却是变化的本质。什么是"易"的本质？最好的回答是生生，也就不断给予万物以生命。"在天成象，在地成形。"（《易经·系辞下传》第一章）"成象""成形"就是给予万物以生命。所以"易"的不变，本质是生生，或给万物以生命。

3）容易

"乾以易知，坤以简能。易则易知，简则易从。易知则有亲，易从则有功。有亲则可久，有功则可大。可久则贤人之德，可大则贤人之业。易简而天下之理得矣。天下之理得，而成位乎其中矣。"（《易经·系辞上传》第一章）因此，依照《易经》的道理，如果一个人掌握得好刚和柔（阳和阴的作用），就能掌控宇宙万物的变化，而掌握刚柔阴阳的作用却是易简的。

这三种意义虽然是《易经》之理，但它们对中国哲学的影响却是极深且大的。所有中国哲学家都强调易简的原则。他们表达自己的学说都是非常简单易懂的，他们自己的生活也是非常简朴寡欲的。

怡按

这里只是就《易经》有关"易"字的三义来说。"易"字是讲变化，我们虽每天生活在变化中，但不能盲目地听任变化摆布，我们真正的学易之后，须有一套处变的功夫。譬如"居易以俟命"（《中庸》），便告诉我们如何用"天命"来解决变化的问题。这是说我们在变化中，一定会遭遇到很多挫折和困难，如果我们能了解天命、相信天命，我们便不会被一时的挫折困难所击倒。我也曾写过《处易知化》一文，说明我们在变化中要能知道如何转化。

19. 物

"物"字原本的意思是世上任何的物质。这是极普通的解释，但是它却有很深的哲学意涵。

1）"民胞物与"的情怀

中国哲学家不认为"物"只是简单地被我们控制和利用的物质而已。他们把"物"看作与人相似相关的存在。宋代张载说："乾称父，坤称母；予兹藐焉，乃混然中处。故天地之塞，吾其体；天地之帅，吾其性。民，吾同胞；物，吾与也。"（张载《西铭》）这就是把"物"看作我们人的同类。

2）万物与我一体

庄子说，"天地与我并生，万物与我为一。"（《庄子·齐物论》）庄子认为万物无所不在，万物都在道中。而万物在道中，共有一个道的本质。因此，我与万物都是道的一体，可以互相转化。

3）物欲

"物"在道家和佛家那里，有一个负面的意思，有时也发生在儒家思想中。庄子说："一受其成形，不亡以待尽。与物相刃相靡。其行尽如驰而莫之能止，不亦悲乎。"（《庄子·齐物论》）慧能说："菩提本无树，明镜亦非台。本来无一物，何处惹尘埃。"（《坛经·般若品》）孟子说："耳目之官，不思而蔽于物；物交物，则引之而已矣。"（《孟子·告子》）在这里所有引用的"物"都是指物欲，就是对外在物质的贪执。

怡按

魏晋时期的佛家僧肇，曾在他的《物不迁论》中说过："近而不可知者，其唯物性乎！"就这一点来看，僧肇是受庄子思想影响，承认有物性。在印度佛学中，物无自性是空的。中国哲学与印度佛学的主要不同是，前者主"有"，后者主"空"。所以作为中国哲学的禅宗，尽管一面受般若"空"的影响，不免讲"空"，但骨子里讲自性重物性，仍然强调"有"。所以僧肇的重"物性"，倡"物不迁论"，实是从庄子到禅宗的桥梁。

20. 忠

扫一扫，
进入课程

在中国早期，"忠"是一个德行。原来，它的意思只是官员和人民期望对他们的君主和国家尽忠。而哲学发展赋予了这个词语新的意义。

1）"忠"于君主

孔子说："君使臣以礼，臣事君以忠。"（《论语·八佾》）这里的"忠"是指臣子对君主最基本的责任。

2）"忠"于朋友和其他的人

曾子说："吾日三省吾身：为人谋而不忠乎？"（《论语·学而》）这里"忠"的意思是特别为儒家所强调的，是指对朋友和别人的忠诚的态度。

3）对民和教民以善之"忠"

"贼民之主不忠。"（《左传·宣公二年》）孟子说："教人以善谓之忠。"(《孟子·滕文公》)这两处引证的"忠"不是一般的忠心,而是指君主仁爱人民和教民行善,这是仁君对民的"忠"。有趣的是,国父孙逸仙,回顾古代忠的用法,把"忠"解释为:主要是要善于治理国家和对人民负责任。

4)"忠"是诚和天道

宋明理学家给"忠"新的定义,都来源于《中庸》,它与诚意有关。他们解释"忠"是心的诚意或天道。例如,朱熹说:"尽己之心为忠。"(朱熹《中庸章句》)程颐说:"忠者天道。"(朱熹《论语集注》)在这些注释里,"忠"是被理学家们给予很深的哲学意义,是在心中修养他们的"忠",甚至视同天道。

怡按

"忠"本来是一个外在之德,是指的忠君、忠国,常常忠孝连言,都是指这个忠君忠国的忠。在《论语》中,曾子的"为人谋而不忠乎"(《论语·学而》),已经转向对人、对朋友,也转向自我内心的自省。接着,孔子说"吾道一以贯之",曾子解释说"夫子之道,忠恕而已矣"(《论语·里仁》),这就把"忠"字完全转向内心。所以,朱熹在《四书集注》中说"尽己之谓忠,推己之谓恕",这里把"忠"解作尽己之心,完全内在化了。所以"忠恕"连言,这个"忠"是内在的,是尽己之心。

21. 知

"知"和"智"在中国文字中是通用的。一般说，"知"能用作动词或名词，但是"智"只能用作名词。荀子说："所以知之在人者，谓之知；知有所合，谓之智。"（《荀子·正名篇》）荀子的意思是指，这个能知之心是知，两及于物是智。在一般的用法上，两者无须作这样的区别。但重要的是，这个"知"有"知识"和"智慧"的不同。

1）儒家的"知"

在儒家看来，"知"是一个基本的德行。所谓"知、仁、勇三者，天下之达德也"，又"力行近乎仁，知耻近乎勇"（《中庸》）。当我们感觉自己的无知，而要多多学习以求完美，这是知的作用。在这里，"知"包含知识和智慧两方面，开始学习是知识，继之以求完美而成君子或圣人就是一种智慧了。

2）道家的"知"

在道家看来，知识和智慧是分开的。道家是重视智慧而超越知识的。老子说："知者不言，言者不知。"（《老子》第五十六章）这里，"知"意指智慧。他也说："常使民无知无欲，使夫智者不敢为也。"（《老子》第三章）这个"知"是指的知识，或利用别人的知谋。在《老子》中，大多数的"知"是属于后者。在《庄子》中，两种"知"是不同的。庄子称它们是"大知"或"真知"（智慧）和"小知"（知识）。例如，"且有真人而后有真知"（《庄子·大宗师》）和"知通于神"（《庄子·天地篇》），这是大知或智慧。他也说："知也者，争之器也"（《庄子·人间世》）和"而知为孽"（《庄子·德充符》），这是指小知或知识。在道家看来，这个小知的知识只是一种追求名利的欲望，而大知的智慧乃是看透事物的现象而能知道。

3）佛家的"知"

这个"知"在佛家也有知识和智慧的不同。知识定义为去分别相对关系的事物，像是生和死、对和错等。而智慧则定义为无分别心，是指心的最高境界。中国佛家始终用梵文"般若"去解释智慧，因为在佛家思想中，"般若"是接近佛性的，也有佛家同时用"般若"和"知"两词。例如，僧肇说："然则，智有穷幽之鉴，而无知焉。"（僧肇《肇论》）这里，第一个"智"是智慧，第二个"知"是指知识。全句意思是指智慧是超越了知识的。

怡按

这个"知"有内外二义。外在的，是指对一切事物的知识。

如过去的"六艺"(礼、乐、射、御、书、数),今天的科学及学校所教的知识等,这些知识都是书本的,世代相传的,在本质上是有益的,当然也有某些是错误的。庄子在《养生主》一文中认为这些知识是无止境的,庄子以为用我们有限的生命去追求这些无限的知识是有危险的。内在的知有三种:一是知谋,二是理智,三是智慧。第一"知谋",这是由庄子提出的。他认为我们心中有欲,因此我们心中的知就为欲所操纵,去向外争斗。所以他说:"知者,争之器。"(《庄子·齐物论》)第二理智,为儒家所强调,指哲学、道德所训练的理性之知。第三是智慧,这在中国哲学里,是指神性之知,在佛家是指般若之智,它是由"知"和"德"的结合而提升的。如果只是这样客观地去分析这些"知"的种类,并无特别的价值,重要的是如何把这些"知"向上提升的功夫。在佛学上讲"转识成智",这个识是指意识、知识,即前面说的知谋,也是被私欲操纵的"知"。能转掉这种"知"而成智慧,这也是整个佛学的主旨。至于中国哲学,我用两句话来概括,即"转知成德,转德入道"。这里我插入了一个"德"字,这是中国哲学的特色,这和佛学的由识直接转为"慧"不同。我在这里说"由德入道",而不提"慧",是因为中国哲学的"道"已是包含了慧的。

22. 法

"法"字，原形字是"灋"，由字形可以知道是指公正判决，不能有偏爱或偏见。许慎定义，"灋"的意思是处罚，象征"法"的准则要像水的表面一样平。因此，它的字形左边是水，另外一边是去掉歪曲的一面。（许慎《说文解字》）由这些基本的概念，"法"发展出各种哲学学派的不同注释和看法。

1）法律

大多数儒家即使不在乎"法"的琐碎，但也不强调"法"。对他们来说，德行在治国上比法律更重要。在《论语》中，"法"字只出现两次。在《孟子》中，提到"法"的地方有十次，但只有三次是关联实际法律的，例如"徒法不足以自行"（《孟子·离娄》）。荀子的书中则有许多谈到有关"法"和它的重要性的，例如"法者，治之端也"（《荀子·君道》）。荀子也引起以后的哲学家对法产生更深的关注。荀子的学生韩非，是最有影响力的法家，他有关法的理论成为法家的中心概念。例如《韩非子》在《五蠹》篇中把儒、道、墨、纵横家和工商，当作国家的五种蛀虫，甚至主张不法先王，而以"法"为师。

2）理或自然法

孟子说："君子行法以俟命。"（《孟子·尽心》）虽然这个"法"一般可解作法律，但孟子此处并不是指管理上的法律，而是自然法或天理。这个概念的"法"也是庄子所强调的。如他说："天地有大美而不言，四时有明法而不议。"（《庄子·知北游》）这里的"明法"就是自然之理。

3）典范、规则或方法

虽然"法"一般是用来当作典范、规则或方法，在语意上与哲学无关，但在老子思想中它是一套特别的体系。老子说："人法地，地法天，天法道，道法自然。"（《老子》第二十五章）这里，在前三句中"法"的意思可以解释为"跟随"，而在第四句"道法自然"中却不能这样来解，因为道和自然是同一个层次的。因此，这个"法"意思是"符合"，表示人跟随着地或天的法则，而天跟随的道，却是符合自然的，即以自然为法的。

4）佛法的"法"

当印度佛教传到中国，中国佛家翻译梵文的 dharma 为"法"。"法"的意思是指一切境界，包括最高层次的佛法和最低层次的欲望。慧能说："佛法是不二之法"（《坛经·自序品》），"若见一切法，心不染著，是为无念"（《坛经·般若品》）。在第一条引言中"法"是指真实或真如，在第二条引言中"法"是指所有的事物或观念。

怡按

今天我们看到这个"法"字，有两种看法：一是从中文的原始意义，是指法律的律法，这没有哲学的意义。当哲学家把"法"进一步当作自然法，它就摇身一变，和理结合，成为理法、天地之法，就是天地之理。"理"是道之理，是道在现象界的理路，是"有"。自从佛学进入中土，把 dharma 译成"法"之后，这个"法"即指现象界的一切存在。但依据佛学的看法，一切现象的存在是空，虽然把"法"提升为佛法，但佛法也因"法"的空而空其性，所以佛学始终是以"空"为主的。佛学虽把我们的"法"借了去，却变了它的质性，而成为"空"。一有一空之区别，我们不能不知。

23. 性

"性"是特别重要的哲学术语，因为中国哲学赋予它以特色，就是当学者修养时，特别重视心和性。因此在中国思想史上，不同学派和体系有不同的定义。

1）生命、生活

"天生民而立之君，使司牧之，勿使失性。"（《左传·襄公十四年》）这里，本来性的简单意思就是人民的生命和生活。当哲学家开始研究生命的本质和用性去定义这种本质时，性就变成一个哲学性的重要术语。

2）人性

老子不用"性"这个词。在孔子的《论语》中，它只出现了两次。一是子贡说："夫子之文章，可得而闻也，夫子之言性与天道，不可得而闻也。"（《论语·公冶长》）一是孔子说："性相近也，习相远也。"（《论语·阳货》）在这两段话里，"性"的意思只是普通的人性，孔子并没有使它成为话题而加以讨论。在老子和孔子以后，战国时期的大多数哲学家，包括孟子、荀子和庄子等，对"性"开始感兴趣而大加讨论。"性"被理解为人性。孟子和荀子的看法不同，几乎完全相反。在他们学说中，孟子认为："人性之善也，犹水之就下也。人无有不善，水无有不下。"（《孟子·告子》）荀子则认为："人之性恶，其善者伪也。"（《荀子·性恶篇》）这种争辩在中西方思想史上，已成为人们关注的话题。

3）生命的本质

在《庄子》中，内七篇没有出现"性"，这七篇是庄子自己写的。"性"字却常出现在后面的篇章中，经常用来表现"性者，生之质也"（《庄子·庚桑楚》）。这个"生之质"被以后的道家，尤其道教拿来发展为神仙修炼之学，如所谓"性命双修"之学。

4）本能

"生之所以然者谓之性；性之和所生，精合感应，不事而自然谓之性。"（《荀子·正名篇》）这里，荀子把"性"定义为"精合感应"的本能，也可诠释为欲望。

5）万物之性

"能若婴儿之无所欲乎，则物全而性得矣。"（王弼注《老子》

第十章）这里，"性"意指万物之本性。

6）自性、真性或佛性

"菩提自性，本来清净，但用此心，直了成佛。"（《坛经·自序品》）"性"在中国禅宗里是一个中心的术语，意思是真心、真我，本来面目或佛性。

7）理、气和心

宋明理学家基于"天命之谓性"（《中庸》），发展出一个"性"的学说。程颢和程颐定义"性"是理和气："性即理也，所谓理性是也"（《二程文集》卷二十二），"生即是性。性即是气，气是性，即是命"（《二程文集》卷一）。

怡按

在中国哲学上，对于"性"的问题，大约有两条路向：一是观念理论，一是实际修养。走观念理论的路，如孟子讲性善，荀子讲性恶。其实"性"的本质是超乎二元对立的，讲性善性恶已落在二元对立上，而非那本体的"性"，所以他们所谈的只是理论。理论不能讲真假，只能讲是非。所以性善性恶是真是假，绝无定论。至于他们的各是其所非，而非其所是，却可以为他们的理论，建立各自的体系。孟子基于性善，而提倡仁义，以建立仁心的政治。荀子根据性恶，而主张人为，以建立礼法的政体。至于第二实际修养的路，如庄子、禅宗和宋明理学家们，都把"性"当作目标，在自心上下功夫，他们各自通过心斋坐忘、涵养诚敬和自悟其心，以达到尽性、见性的境地。

24. 勇

一般用法，"勇"是简单描述人类行为的词语。在中国哲学里，它是一个有深度的主要德行。在儒家看来，"知、仁、勇三者，天下之达德也"（《中庸》）。孔子说："勇者不惧。"（《论语·子罕》）从这个定义，很清楚地看出，"勇"远不是字面上的那么简单。

1）有羞耻心

"知耻近乎勇。"（《中庸》）意思是指一个人知道什么是错，而不去做它；或者，假如他已经做错了，他有勇气去做修正。

2）符合正义

孔子说："君子义以为上。君子有勇而无义为乱，小人有勇而无义为盗。"（《论语·阳货》）这是说，我们要有道德的勇气；真正的勇气必须行于正义。

3）本于慈悲之心

"慈故能勇，俭故能广，不敢为天下先，故能成器长。今舍其慈且勇，舍其俭且广，舍后且先，死矣！"（《老子》六十七章）佛教分享"慈悲"的理念，是以勇气为本质的。佛被称为"伟大的慈悲者"和"伟大的勇者"。孔子说："仁者必有勇，勇者不必有仁。"（《论语·宪问》）这里，孔子的意思是指仁者能勇，也能"爱人"；这也即是说，真正的勇者必须是仁爱或慈悲地对待所有人的。

4）知天命

"知穷之有命，知通之有时，临大难而不惧者，为圣人之勇也。"（《庄子·秋水》）真正的勇者，把他遭遇到的一切都当成天命，而不受到任何的影响。

5）克己

"凡人言语正到快意时，便截然能忍默得；意气正到发扬时，便翕然能收敛得；愤怒嗜欲正到腾沸时，便廓然能消化得；此非天下之大勇者，不能也。"（王阳明《与黄宗贤书》）。这里是指在修心养性的关头，要有决断的勇气。

怡按

西方哲学讲"勇"，都着重无惧的勇气，如亚里士多德讲"勇"，便是将勇敢和懦弱相对。也就是说，西方哲学的"勇"是建立在气上的。而中国哲学的"勇"，却是建立在义理上、仁心上。也就是说，中国哲学的"勇"是道德的表现，是修养的自然流露。

25. 真

"真"在《论语》《孟子》或"五经"等书中没有出现。这个字第一次出现在《老子》中,《庄子》中出现了六十六次。儒家学者专注于区别是和非;道家学者热衷讨论真和假。这些哲学的立场并不是互相排斥的。在儒家,"诚"字也有真的意思。但儒家学者主要关注伦理和政治,是以是与非作标准的。道家学者兴趣在形而上学和修心养性的功夫,所以他们并不关心于理论的是和非,而重在修养上的真与假。"真"的意义出现在道家书中,多半指"真实""本质"和"真我""真性"。

1）真实

"其精甚真,其中有信。"(《老子》二十一章)这是指真实和诚信,也指万物的本质是真实存在旳。

2）本质

"如求得其情与不得,无益损乎其真。"(《庄子·齐物论》)这里的"真"是指万物的本质,它们都是真实实的存在。

3）真我和真性

"不离于真，谓之至人。"（《庄子·天下》）这里的"真"是指真我或真性。另外，在《庄子》中有关"真心""真我"或"真性"的很多，如《齐物论》中所提到的"真君"或"真宰"，这些都是"真"。

怡按

"真"，如果是真理，是英文的 truth 的话，那这个真理是西方人追求的，而不是中国人所关注的。西方所讲的哲学是爱智，他们追求的是宇宙的实体 reality。可是二三千年来，西方哲学根本没有看到实体，他们自解哲学就是永远的追求，提出问题，而不一定得到答案。可是中国哲学的"哲"是"知人则哲"（《尚书·皋陶谟》），中国哲学就是为了解决人类的问题，先秦诸子百家的兴起，都是提出救世的方案。在这里也可看出，中国哲学和西方哲学在起步时已截然不同了。

26. 神

"神"原来的意思是"上帝",但是运用上都指"精神",因为中国哲学家教导人在精神上为须与天(天道)合一。

1)上帝或神明

在《论语》中,"神"出现了六次,每次都是指上帝、祖宗或神。例如,"敬鬼神而远之"(《论语·雍也》)。在这些话语中,"鬼"和"神"经常用在一起当成一个复合词,指上帝或神明。

2)祖先

孔子说:"禹,吾无间然矣!菲饮食,而致孝乎鬼神。"(《论语·泰伯》)禹重视祭祀他的祖先,因此,"神"在这里是指祖先。

3)德和性的神妙

在《孟子》中,"神"出现了三次。一次是指精神,另外两次是关联到最高的德和性。"夫君子所过者化，所存者神，上下与天地同流"，"大而化之之为圣；圣而不可知之之谓神。"（《孟子·尽心》）

4）精神

在《老子》中，"神"出现了四次，都是指精神。在《庄子》中，"神"出现很多次，一般来说是指"精神"或最高修养的境界。例如，"其神凝，使物不疵疠而年谷熟。"（《庄子·逍遥游》）

5）神妙或智慧

"神"常常出现在《易经》的"十翼"中，很多时候是指精神、上帝、神明。但还有两种特别的用法：一是指神妙。"神也者，妙万物而为言者也"（《易经·说卦》第六章）和"阴阳不测之谓神"（《易经·系辞上传》第五章）。第二种用法是指智慧。例如，"神以知来，知以藏往。"（《易经·说卦》第十一章）

6）神仙

在道教中，"神"变成"神仙"。"知白守黑，神明自来。"（魏伯阳《周易参同契》第七章）这里的神明即炼丹之学所达成的神仙境界。

怡按

这个"神"字，在中国文化里，无论是精神、神明或神仙，都被看作最高境界。可是这其中有两个问题：一是我们是否能达到这境界，二是达到这个境界又如何。先说第一个问题，这个"神"是阴阳不测的，我们又如何能达得到？如神仙学派都把神仙修炼之术说得头头是道，可是在历史上又有谁真能成仙？第二个问题是，在这个境界上，我们如何自处？由于前一个问题不能解决，所以我们根本看不到任何回答第二个问题的资料。我近年来用"道""理""用"构成的整体等边三角形来描述整体生命哲学，这个三角形似乎可以解答这两个问题。

"用"是指人生实用，通过了"理"的研究，而提升入"道"。入"道"之后，不是停在那里永远不动，这样就死于"道"了。所以达到"道"之后，又须回到人生日用，这时的"用"不是小用，而是大用。这个三角形的圆环作用，我称之为整体生命哲学。我在很多书及文章中都有详细的介绍，此处不赘述。但在这里，我要说的是"神"。我是把这个"神"放在"道"的位置，因为它们有同样的作用。我曾一再强调"道"是虚的，它的作用是虚掉我们的一切执着、自以为是。同样"神"也是虚的，它的作用就是虚掉我们的所有欲念，使心地纯净。但这个"神"之所以能有虚的作用，是因为它本身是虚的（虚不是无，不是空）。也就是说，它的存在不是我们执着的对象或客体，道教的神仙学如果把"神"当作一个实体来追求，必然会成为梦幻空花的悲剧。事实上，我们入"神"，只是由这个"神"的虚的转化，使我们回到人生日用；我们不是在"神"之中，而是"神"在我们心中。也就是说，虚在我们心中，我们处理任何事情，都能"虚其心"，自然是游刃有余，无入而不自得了。

27. 时

"时"是非常普遍的字，但中国哲学家在学说中用它去标示合时宜，这种思想关连到每天生活的实际时间。

1）"时"在《易经》

虽然"时"在《易经》六十四卦中，只出现一次，但在"十冀"中，却出现五十七次。总括它在《易经》的作用，至少有三种意义：

一是四季。

"变通配四时。"（《易经·系辞上传》第六章）根据上下文，"四季"是指实际的季节。

二是机会和机遇。

"君子进德修业，欲及时也。"（《周易·乾文言》）当机会来临时，必须把握。西方有同样的俗语，即"要抢先把握时间"。

三是在六爻中的变动。

"六位时成，时乘六龙以御天。"（《周易·乾卦·彖辞》）这里，"时"是指爻位的改变。

2)"时"在儒家

孔子被尊为"圣之时者",他的思想和行为总是很适当,能把握住时机。孔子的"时"有两层意思:

一是,每件他所提倡或做的事情都表现得合时宜。孔子说,"使民以时"(《论语·学而》)。例如,在季节不适宜去种植、除草和收成时,人们必须从事政府公布的公众事务。又说"夫子时然后言,人不厌其言"(《论语·宪问》)。

二是,他的思想合于时代,但也适当地考虑过去。"行夏之时,乘殷之辂,服周之冕"(《论语·卫灵公》),这是说孔子能够采用不同朝代的制度的好的方面,而不会执着于任何一个。

3)"时"在道家

"时"的意思,在《老子》和《论语》中是相同的。然而,在《庄子》里增加了两个特别的意思:命运和绵延。"安时而处顺,哀乐不能入也。"(《庄子·养生主》)这是接受命运,即顺着时间流转的意思。"知通之有时。"(《庄子·秋水》)这里"时"的意思是指时间的绵延不绝,不是指把时间分段来看。

后来的道家学者,特别是道教,希望用把握时间去控制宇宙的变化。"须知此中作用,俱是攒簇之法。簇年归月,簇月归日,簇日归时。止在一刻中分动静。其中消息,全赖坎离橐籥。所谓覆冒阴阳之道者也。"(魏伯阳《参同契·乾坤门户章》朱云阳注)

他们认为通过阴阳的交会，一个人能够控制一分一刻，就能控制整个宇宙的变化。

怡按

在西方哲学中，宇宙论里最重要的两个概念就是时间和空间。在中国哲学里，"宇宙"两字首次出现在《庄子》中，正巧所谈的也是时间和空间的概念。如，"有实而无乎处者，宇也；有长而无本剽者，宙也。"（《庄子·庚桑楚》）即是指空间中有实物存在，但它们的位置不是固定的，这叫宇；时间有长度却没有始终，这叫作宙。庄子讲的"宇宙"和西洋哲学所论相同，所以今天我们翻译西方的cosmology为"宇宙论"。可是中国哲学家对讨论抽象概念没有兴趣，因此"宇宙"两字在中国哲学里很少提到，我们代之而讲的是天地和现实生活的时空，如四时、古今、四方、位置等。但我们讲的时空是另一套可以凭修养而转化的系统。如《庄子·大宗师》里讲的"三日而后能外天下"，"七日而后能外物"，"九日而后能外生"，这是庄子的忘空间；接着此心能"朝彻""见独"，这是觉悟；然后，"无古今而后能入于不死不生"，即打破被空间分割的古今，而进入永恒的时间，这在道家和中国禅宗就是"性"的境界，可以称"自性""佛性""真心""真我"或"道"。这就是中国哲学的一整套"空""时""性"的转化功夫。

28. 气

"气"是一个复杂的字。它不只在不同的哲学派别中有很多不同的意义，它本身是一个合成的字，是由物质和非物质形成的。有时它是形而上的；有时却是现象界的。"气"是看不见的东西，但是它和看得见的事物有密切的关联。它在道家和后来的儒家中扮演了一个重要的角色。

1）空气、天地的能量

"空气"是原始意义。古代中国人定义"气"为云气，意思是宇宙的能量。在道家和宋明儒家中，这个用法很普遍。"人在气中，气在人中，自天地至于万物，无不须气以生者也"（《抱朴子·至理》），"夫大块噫气，其名为风"（《庄子·齐物论》），"二气感应以相与"（《易经·咸卦·彖辞》）。这里，二"气"是指阴和阳的能量，具有宇宙生成发展的互补互成作用。

2）呼吸

在人的身体中"气"是指呼吸。这个呼吸，包括空气和能量，它是道家的打坐和炼丹成仙的重要功夫。如，"若一志，无听之以耳，而听之以心，无听之以心，而听之以气。"(《庄子·人间世》)"初学行炁，鼻中引炁而闭之，阴以心数至一百二十。乃以口微吐之。及引之，皆不欲令已耳闻其炁出入之声。"(《抱朴子·释滞》)

3）精神

在《论语》中，"气"合并了能量和精神。"君子有三戒：少之时，血气未定，戒之在色。及其壮也，血气方刚，戒之在斗。及其老也，血气既衰，戒之在得。"(《论语·季氏》)这里"气"是肉体的血气，是能量。在孟子的思想中，"气"的意思从情绪和能量转变到了精神。如，"夫志，气之帅也；气，体之充也。"(《孟子·公孙丑》)

4）天地之精华

在庄子的思想中，"气"是宇宙无所不在的本质。"故万物，一也。是其所美者为神奇，其所恶者为臭腐；臭腐复化为神奇，神奇复化为臭腐。故曰通天下一气耳。"(《庄子·知北游》)这里，庄子意指"气"是阴和阳的能量，转动宇宙的因子。后来的道家和儒家，发展这个思想而强调这个"气"是宇宙的本质。如，"天地之气，合而为一，分为阴阳，判为四时，列为五行。"(董仲舒《春秋繁露·五行相生》)

5）事物和物质力量

后来的道家和儒家转变阴和阳的能量成为五行的能量，于是"气"被分成两种：纯粹的成为精神原理，混浊的成为构成事物的形体。如，"气坱然太虚，升降飞扬，未尝止息……太虚为清，清则无碍，无碍故神；反清为浊，浊则碍，碍则形。"（张载《正蒙·太和第一》）

怡按

"气"在今天的科学中指的是空气，由于有氧，是生命之所需，因此也可转为能量，为宇宙不灭的动力。中国古代虽然没有对"气"的科学认识，但哲学上对气的了解，非但不违反科学，甚至有超过科学的运用。在中国哲学中，最先提出"气"，并将之作为整个思想系统基础的是庄子。他强调天地自然之气，是道在现象世界的流衍，认为人如能顺天地自然之气而行，便不会计较人生的成败得失，而能逍遥而游。其后讲"气"较多的，有道教的《参同契》《抱朴子》，儒家的《春秋繁露》等书。而纯以中国哲学的心性修养为主来探讨"气"的，乃是宋初的张载《正蒙》一书。他一面讲宇宙太虚之气的生物，一面讲"变化气质"的修养功夫。他的"气"的思想也影响了此后宋明理学家程朱、陆王的理气之论。

29. 悟

"悟，醒也。"（许慎《说文解字》）醒是悟的原始和一般意思。在《论语》《孟子》《老子》中没有"悟"的例子。虽然在《庄子》中"悟"出现了四次，但没有一个影响以后的中国哲学的。然后，印度佛学开始影响中国思想，"悟"被用为概念的觉醒或觉悟，在中国佛学上扮演了重要的角色。特别是在禅宗，它成为一个关键的思想。因此，在哲学上，觉悟是佛学的词语。值得注意的是，这个"悟"在《庄子》中有一般的觉醒意思。《庄子》用的另外一个字"觉"，这个"觉"却可以通向中国禅宗的"悟"。

悟，在中国禅宗，有以下几个层次。

1）普通的悟

"欲令众生悟佛知见故，出现于世。"（《法华经·方便品》）这里的"悟"是单纯明理的意思，以通过读经和实行佛的教训。有时，它的意思是明白真实的原理或真如。虽然它的意思是明道，但它本身没有特别的意义或内容。

2）小顿悟

"小顿悟者，支道琳师云：七地始见无生。"（慧达《肇论疏》）在佛教，有各种学说谈到"十地"，这是指十个步骤从菩萨变成佛。第七地是指这个菩萨已明白无生之旨，佛法是永恒的，没有生和死。而"七地"是无生，要达到没有生死的佛地，还有三个步骤，所以这个层次叫作小的顿悟。

3）大顿悟

"竺道生法师大顿悟云：夫称顿者，明理不可分，悟语照极。以不二之悟，符不分之理。理智恚释，谓之顿悟。"（慧达《肇论疏》）这个引文是指道生的顿悟。没有阶段或步骤，称为"大顿悟"，这是对照"小顿悟"而说的。可惜道生自己没有留下记录，我们不能确定他的真正意思。

4）在中国禅宗里的顿悟

"顿悟"是禅宗所建立的一个特色。在禅宗的文献中，"悟"出现很多的方式，有些是普通的悟，有些是小悟，有些是大悟。这使得读者去明白其中的不同实属不易。但在禅宗里，最高理想和中心思想的却是"顿悟"，那就更不易了解了。慧能的学生神会曾替"顿悟"下了各种不同的定义说："事须理智兼释，谓之顿悟。并不由阶渐，自然是顿悟义。自心从本已来空寂者是顿悟。即心无所得者为顿悟。即心无所住为顿悟。存法悟心，心无所得，是顿悟。知一切法，为顿悟。闻说空不著空，即不取不空，是顿悟。闻说我，不落（我），即不取无我，是顿悟。不舍生死而入涅槃，是顿悟。"（《神会语录》）虽然神会的叙述是有关了解顿悟的意义，但它被批评过于琐细，对"顿悟"的了解是不必要的。在所有各种定义中，有三种基本原理：

一是超越外在的修养。

"若开悟顿教，不执外修，但于自心常起正见，烦恼尘劳，常不能染，即是见性。"（《坛经·般若品》）外修是指读经、守戒、禅坐等。

二是一念的"悟"。

"若起正真般若观照，一刹那间，妄念俱灭。若识自性，一悟即至佛地。"（《坛经·般若品》）在一念间，没有疑虑和执着，这就是顿悟。

三是"悟"自性。

"不悟即佛是众生，一念悟时，众生是佛。"（《坛经·般若品》）在禅宗，自性虽然可以等于佛性，但比较深的是指个人的个别的性。它是人的原始心念和真我。"顿悟"是看见自性，这是终极目标；没有看到自性的经验，就不是顿悟。

怡按

"觉"和"悟"两字，由于"觉悟"连在一起，因此我们都没有特别注意它们的不同。它们的不同约可分为以下几端：

（1）"觉"是中国人和中国哲学常用的字。不仅庄子用"觉"，在生活各方面也都用"觉"。如，诸葛亮的"大梦谁先觉"及"先知先觉"等。在佛学来华前，我们都是用"觉"。佛学来华后，凡是学佛的人，都用"悟"字。

（2）就印度佛学来说，在一般佛学也是都用"觉"的。如我们注解"佛"字为自觉、觉他、觉行圆满。佛经也是都用"觉"，如《八大人觉经》《圆觉经》。至于"悟"字，在中国禅宗却变得重要而且普遍。

（3）"觉"字来自"梦觉"，主要在觉醒。但"觉"字不仅用于自己，而尤在觉人。如儒家的"先知觉后知，先觉觉后觉"（《孟子·万章》）。佛学上菩萨的"觉"有情。至于"悟"字都属自悟和悟自性、悟禅理。如果这种说法可通，我们可以说"觉"是觉今是而昨非（道家）和万物性空（佛家）；而禅宗的"悟"，却是悟这个理，这个理是凡圣等一，自心本来清净。

30. 恕

扫一扫，
进入课程

"恕"字在哲学上，是一个很难解说得清楚的字。虽然它只在《论语》中出现了两次，在《孟子》中出现了一次，但在儒家看来它却是一个非常重要的德行。它没有在道家和佛家的文字中出现过，而它却是中国文化里最有特色的德行。它被翻译成英文的"同情""原谅"和"利他"，但是没有一个词能说明它的真义。

1）恕的推己心

孔子的学生子贡问："有一言而可以终身行之者乎？"孔子说："其恕乎！己所不欲，勿施于人。"（《论语·卫灵公》）这是大家都知道的定义，你自己不要别人这样对你，你就不应这样的对人。"恕"和《大学》所讲的"絜矩之道"是一样的作用：所谓"是以君子有絜矩之道也。所恶于上，毋以使下；所恶于下，毋以事上；所恶于前，毋以先后；所恶于后，毋以从前；所恶于右，毋以交于左；所恶于左，毋以交于右；此之谓絜矩之道。"（《大学》）

2）恕是仁的作用

孔子说："参乎！吾道一以贯之。"曾子说："唯。"孔子出去后，学生问他："何谓也？"曾子回答："夫子之道，忠恕而已矣！"（《论语·里仁》）忠诚和恕，是仁的作用，都是孔子德行的基础。

有些学者认为"恕"和仁同义。"恕，仁也。"（许慎《说文解字》）事实上，"恕"不是仁，而是仁的作用。它的作用，是以自己为例子，把内在的感觉转成外在的行为。孔子说："道不远人，人之为道而远人，不可以为道。诗云：'伐柯伐柯，其则不远。'执柯以伐柯，睨而视之，犹以为远。故君子以人治人，改而止。忠恕违道不远，施诸己而不愿，亦勿施于人。君子之道四，丘未能一焉：所求乎子以事父，未能也；所求乎臣以事君，未能也；所求乎弟以事兄，未能也；所求乎朋友先施之，未能也。"（《中庸》）通过人性去追求道，通过自性去治国，由自己为例去对待他人，这是仁道，也是恕道。所以"恕"的意思非常接近仁，它们之间有关联，但它们是不相同的。仁是恕的本质；恕是仁的作用。

孟子虽然不常用"恕"字，却特别善用"恕"的作用。他说"老吾老，以及人之老，幼吾幼，以及人之幼；天下可运于掌……故推恩足以保四海，不推恩无以保妻子。古之人所以大过人者，无他焉，善推其所为而已矣。"（《孟子·梁惠王》）由自己推到他人，转化仁心到仁的作为。这个推己是"恕"，所以，"恕"是仁的作用，仁能包括恕。当孔子和孟子谈到"仁"，他们所指的是仁道，也就是"恕"。因此，他们虽然没有特别用这个字，但"恕"却是他们作为儒家非常重要的德行。

3）恕与忠、诚有关

"恕"是仁的作用，它与所有的德行有关联。其中，有两个德行特别接近。

一个是忠。

"忠"和"恕"像是双胞胎。在孔子那里，"忠"和"恕"是连接的词语。"忠"总是指心中的诚，提供一个"恕"的基础；另一个说法，没有"忠"，"恕"就没有办法表现出来或推己及人。如果一个人有诚在他的心中，才能把"恕"落实下来。子思说："忠恕违道不远，施诸己而不愿，亦勿施于人。"（《中庸》）这是恕。为什么子思（《中庸》的作者）说那是忠恕之事也？朱熹以为，忠和恕不能分割。当你忠你就不能见恕；当你是恕，忠就与你一起。没有忠，一个人就不能做到，"我不欲人之加诸我也，我亦无加诸人"。因此，没有忠，恕也就不完整。当忠和恕相连，它们一起所强调的是"恕"，可见"恕"不能和"忠"分离。

一个是诚。

孟子说："万物皆备于我矣。反身而诚，乐莫大焉。强恕而行，求仁莫近焉。"（《孟子·尽心》）在这段话中，孟子将三个德性——诚、恕、仁连在一起。这里，"诚"类似"忠"，但比较深。"诚"是没有虚假。在《中庸》，"诚"是指天道，是至善。如一个人说："我不要他人爱我，因此，我不爱他人。"这一定不是

"诚"，而且也不是"恕"。所以，"诚"是"恕"的基本，使"恕"可以确实地表达出来。

在宋明儒家思想里，"忠"和"诚"是相同的。这就是为什么程颐和朱熹都把"忠"视为是天道，他们了解"忠"是"诚"。例如，程颐说："忠者天道，恕者人道。"（朱熹《论语集注》）朱熹说："在圣人，忠即诚，和恕即仁。"（朱熹《朱子语录》）

4）恕是中国文化的特性

虽然道家和中国佛学不强调"恕"，但他们用的术语，通常都可以和"恕"相通。例如，老子强调处下，庄子主张万物平等，禅宗思想说平常心是道。所有这些思想的核心都是承认其他人的重要。这些也是基本方面的"恕"。因为这些，中国文化的一个特性，就是不会把自己的观念强加到其他人身上，或强迫其他人同意并跟随自己的主张。例如，孔子的孝道强调你必须孝顺你的父母，强调你的子女要孝顺于你，但它不会要求你孝顺别人的父母。儒家不是宗教，不会坚持让别人要膜拜自己信奉的神。同理，道家的"自然"是每个人自己的"自然"，并不会要求别人跟随你的自然，每个人都跟随他自己的自然就好。同样，禅学也是让每个人去"悟"其自己的本来面目。因此，在中国文化里，任何人都能成为圣人，很多神明，如大禹、关公，都是由他们的德行和功业而为人所崇拜的。

5）恕和慈悲、原谅、利他思想

在印度佛学和西方宗教中，慈悲和原谅是相同的词语，都是指同情他人，怜悯陷入痛苦和罪恶中的他人。因此，当你表现出对他人慈悲和原谅时，这就意味着你是对的而他们是错的，因而可怜他们。这样就把别人看得比自己低和弱。但是"恕"要求从自己推到他人，"我"和他人是在同一层次上的。

利他思想是一个概念，强调为了他人牺牲自己，为了他人的福利献出自己的一切。墨子是标准的利他主义者，墨家是无私地为他人而努力的。他们的思想不是基于人性的本质，因此他们不是恕道。

大多数的世界文明的范例，众所周知的，就黄金律"己所欲，施于人"来说，是以自己为前提，以自己的同情心为基础的，这在儒家书中常有负面的作用。因为"己所欲，施于人"意味着，我们先认为自己的主意是正常的、正确的，然后要求别人也跟自己一样，我们就变成了推销员，我们的价值观似乎只在乎我们自己的产品。这在信仰上是特别危险的，如宗教激进鼓吹自己的教派，导致世界陷入了宗教的战争。因此，如果我们依照"恕"的原理，将不会造成这种后果，因我们是单纯的，不希望别人对自己做的事情，就不会对别人做。例如，在丈夫和妻子之间，如西方的黄金律"己所欲，施于人"，意味着，我对他／她做的，也是我要他／她对我做的。但是"恕"不一样，丈夫把自己放在妻子的位置上，考虑"如果我是她，我要求我做什么"，这是以别人的立场来设想。"恕"的精神就是先要承认别人的存在、了解别人的需要。

怡按

我曾在数篇文章中强调，在21世纪我们如果希望恢复"道"，或推行一种大家都能接受的德行，最适合的就是"恕"。我曾列举十几种理由，此处简约为以下几点：

（1）一般道德的特色，是严肃的，要求人牺牲的，可是"恕"却不要求我对别人做什么，而是一切都不做，何乐而不为。

（2）大至国事，小至个人的一些生活小节，都可以"恕"来推理。如，自己的人民不能吃的受核辐射污染的食物，就不能强卖给他国；自己不喜欢别人以尖酸刻薄的态度对待，自己也不要以尖酸刻薄对人。

（3）以自己为出发点，不避自我，甚至容许人都有私心，这是合乎心理学的原则的。

（4）其他的道德都是有很多的理论，很多的教训，实践起来，也有不少的条件。但"恕"却很简单，只在一念之转。

（5）"恕"是同理心的推理，是基于双方的同等地位，是我与他人绝对而真正平等的。不像有时我们讲的"平等"，只变成一个口号、一种概念或政治上的操作，"恕"在我们一己心中打破了人与人的间隔。

（6）任何坏事，如战争等，都是缺了"恕"。如果没有"恕"的推己及人之心，而要求世界和平，恐怕永远只是一个空想而已。

31. 虚

这"虚"字原本的意思是墟、大山丘，由墟而写成"虚"，有空旷的意思，再转成较抽象的空虚。在中国哲学上，把"虚"当作修养的功夫。

1）空虚

"虚"字在《论语》和《孟子》中各出现两次，都指空虚的意思。当然它也有哲学意义，但是负面的。如孔子说："亡而为有，虚而为盈，约而为泰，难乎有恒矣！"（《论语·述而》）

2）虚心

在道家，"虚"是一个重要的术语，意思是心的修养。如"虚其心"（《老子》第三章），这里，心是指欲望，即从心中除掉欲望。荀子说："不以所已臧，害所将受，谓之虚。"（《荀子·解蔽》）这里，"虚"是在心中心没有偏见，没有欲望。

3）虚己

"方舟而济于河，有虚船来触舟，虽有惼心之人不怒。有一人在其上，则呼张歙之。一呼而不闻，再呼而不闻，于是三呼邪，则必以恶声随之。向也不怒而今也怒，向也虚而今也实。人能虚己以游世，其孰能害之。"（《庄子·山木》）这里，"虚"的意思是放掉或超越自我。

4）无形或空间

"古之至人，假道于仁，托宿于义，以游逍遥之墟。"（《庄子·天运》）这里，"墟"是"虚"，意思是无形的空间。

5）《易经》的爻位

"变动不居，周流六虚。"（《易经·系辞下传》第八章）这里，"虚"是指爻位，因为这六根爻是指天地之中的空间；每条爻像空的容器，等待事物来填满。

怡按

讲虚己、虚心，谈何容易？究竟要如何着手？因为这个"虚"字太虚了，我们无处下手。我认为，要虚不空易在"虚"字上着手，而应在另一个字就是"谦"上着手。我们常常将谦与虚连言作

"谦虚"，不无道理，因为"谦"才能"虚"。"谦"不是普通的客气、礼让，那是行为，而是心中真正的谦。真正的"谦"是在心中把自己看得很低，即使有很大的成就，有很高的才气，比起宇宙的大，又算得了什么？"秦皇汉武今何在？"这样一想，心自然会低，也就自然的会"虚"了。所以要"虚"，首先要能"谦"。在中国哲学史上，把"虚"做得最彻底的是庄子，因为他把自己放得最低，他"不敖倪于万物，不谴是非，以与世俗处"（《庄子·天下》），他自认为"无用"，他真正能"谦"，所以他能以"虚"自处，以"虚"待物。（很遗憾，本书没有写"谦"字，但在拙著《哲学与人生》的散论中，曾有"谦"的专文可资参考）。

32. 理

"理"原本意思是"治玉也"（许慎《说文解字》）。玉石上有纹理和云似的各种颜色，雕刻师必须熟悉掌握这些纹路，随着理念的暗示而雕琢。所以，由于纹类的推寻，"理"渐渐地成为原由或原理的意思。宋朝以前，"理"当作理由解，通常由哲学者的意思是顺着道，或者是实践德性。在宋朝，儒家特别用"理"代替"法"，即取代佛家的"法"。在佛学上，"法"代表所有的事物，而以空为本质。在宋明儒家，"理"也代表所有的事物，但是它是以真实为本质的。在宋明儒家思想中，"理"成为一个关键的术语，比"道"或"仁"更常用。"理"和其他的德性都有密切的关系，甚至成为学派的名称。

1）义理

"理"没有出现在《论语》中，但在《孟子》中出现了七次。这七次里，有五次是单纯的意思，是有理路、合理；另外两次有哲学意思。这两方面，都与公义有关。例如："心之所同然者，何也？谓理也、义也。"（《孟子·告子》）虽然孟子不强调"理"，但很明显，他讲的"义"可以代替"理"，因为它们有同样的性质。

孟子以后，"理"被当作正义来看，和"义"合成"义理"，意思是原理、理性或哲理。

2）礼法

"礼"和"理"同音不同形。"礼"的德行是中国社会的基础。荀子强调"礼"，把它连接到"理"。他说，"礼也者，理之不可易者也。"（《荀子·乐论》）

3）名理

"名"为名家所强调，是讨论名词的逻辑性，但不是指原理。在三国魏（220—265）和晋朝（265—420）有些哲学家讨论名家的"名"的议题，形成名理学派。因此"名理"变成一个术语，意思是指分析名词。例如，"（钟会）精练名理"（《三国志·钟会传》），钟会就是名理派最重要的人物。

4）道理

在道家，"道"是最高的理想和标准。"理"是万物之理。"理"没有出现在《老子》中，但老子讲的"道"，其意亦指万物之理。"理"字常出现在《庄子》中，用来当作道的定义。如，"道，理也。"（《庄子·缮性》）"知道者，必达于理者。"（《庄子·秋水》）这里，"道"和"理"被赋予相同的意义。"道""理"合言，指原理和理性。

5）伦理

在父母和儿女、丈夫和妻子、兄和弟、君主和人民及朋友之间，表现出的正常的伦理关系。"行有伦理，副天地人也。"（董仲舒《春秋繁露》）

6）天理

"人化物也者，灭天理而穷人欲者也。"（《礼记·乐记》）这是天理第一次出现在经书中。宋明儒家采用这一词当成强调"天理"中心的思想。

7）人性

宋代儒家视天理与人性为一，视人性与性为一。例如，"性只是理，万理之总名。此理亦只是天地间公共之理，禀得来便为我所有。"（朱熹《朱子语类》一百一十七卷）因为宋代儒家把"性"和"理"合一，他们的学说被称为"性理之学"。

8）心理

在宋明儒家的心学中，强调"心"即是"理"。"心，一心也；理，一理也。至当归一，精义无二。"（陆象山《与曾宅之书》）

9）物理

"圣人者，原天地之美，而达万物之理。"（《庄子·知北游》）
在庄子的思想中，"万物之理"单纯的意思是万物都有它特别的
理。在宋明儒家，"万物之理"是指心、性、天，所有的"理"
就是一个理。"一物之理，即万物之理。"（《二程遗书》卷二）

10）太极

在朱熹思想中，至理就是太极。如他说："总天地万物之理，
便是太极。"（《朱子语类》）

怡按

在这里，有两点必须一提：

第一，中国的"理"与佛学的"法"有何不同？

（1）中国的"理"来自"道"，是"道"的分身，是"道"
在现象界的作用，所以称"道理"；佛的"法"，是指万事万物的
存在变化，是事物的表现，所以称"法相"。

（2）"理"完全是正面的，是真实的"有"；"法"除了指名佛
法外，都是负面的，是无自性的"空"。由于它的"空"，甚至连
佛法也被空掉了。

（3）由于"理"是"道"的分身，所以中国哲学重视"理"，
甚至中国的禅宗也以"理"代"法"，主张以"禅理"而悟入。

至于"法"，大乘佛学强调要破我执和法执。

第二点，如何求"理"？

"理"本身也是抽象的，不易把握。但"理"有很多复合词，我们可以在另一个字上做功夫。如天理、伦理、心理、性理、情理等。我们可以体认天道，注重伦常，虚其心，重人性，合人情，这样我们自然就能合乎"理"了。

33. 情

"情"在中国文学、哲学、法律和政治上，扮演了一个极重要的角色。它从平常的情感出发，在不同领域而有不同的意义，包括万物的真实到人类的心理现象。总之，中国文化的特色和基础是"情"。

1）诚

在《论语》和《孟子》中，有些例子"情"的意思是"诚"。如："上好信，则民莫敢不用情。"（《论语·子路》）

2）真实

"情"常出现在《庄子》中，一般的意思是真实。如，"若有真宰，而特不得其朕。可行已信，而不见其形，有情而无形。"（《庄子·齐物论》）

3）欲望

在《庄子》中，虽然"情"大多数是指真实，但有两个例外。"吾所谓无情者，言人之不以好恶内伤其身"（《庄子·德充符》），"以情欲寡浅为内"（《庄子·天下》），这里庄子的"情"含有感情（喜怒哀惧）和欲望。接着以后的道家和儒家也都定义"情"为欲望。如许慎解"情"字说，"人之阴气有欲者"（许慎《说文解字》），董仲舒说，"人欲之谓情"（董仲舒《对策三》）。印度佛学带来的术语，像"情尘"（六官六识）、"情有"（执着现象界的一切）、"情见"（以情绪而看物）和"有情"（人类），所有这些都是负面的意思。

4）人性

荀子和法家把情感当成人性或各种人类的本能，"情者，性之质也"（《荀子·正名》）。宋明儒家也认为感情是人性的作用。对他们来说，人性是好的本质，情是人性之动。如朱熹说："性是未动，情是已动。心包得已动未动。盖心之未动则为性，已动则为情，所谓心统性情也。"（《朱子语类》卷五）

5）理性和心理

两个较普通的词语是"情理"和"人情"。"情"因为意思是情理，是"真实"的情操，像父母和孩子、丈夫和妻子以及朋友之间的爱。这是情，也是理。如，所谓"理者，情之不爽失者也。未有情不得而理得者也"（戴震《孟子字义疏证》）。

"人情"意思是人心，在人与人之间能表现好的关系，儒道两家思想都基于人情。相反的，把"人情"看作自私的心理，这是法家所取用的。如，"凡治天下，必因人情。人情者，有好恶，故赏罚可用；赏罚可用，则禁令可立而治道具矣。"（《韩非子·八经》）

怡按

"情"是中国文化的特色，我们什么事情都讲情，做得过分，甚至以情代法，而破坏了法理。在《庄子》中有段故事："惠子谓庄子曰：'人故无情乎？'庄子曰：'然。'惠子曰：'人而无情，何以谓之人？'庄子曰：'道与之貌，天与之形，恶得不谓之人？'惠子曰：'既谓之人，恶得无情？'庄子曰：'是非吾所谓情也。吾所谓无情者，言人之不以好恶内伤其身。'"（《庄子·德充符》）。

可见情有不同的意义，庄子的无情，也还是一种情。我们分析中文用"情"字所构成的许多复合词，先就哲理来说，我们常用"人情""性情""情理"；再就生活上来看，正面的有"感情""情爱""友情""亲情""情意""情义"等，负面的有"情欲""色情""私情""痴情""情绪"等。我们在生活上，每天介于这两种正负的"情"之间，如何由负面的，提升、转化为正面的，这就是修养，就是功夫。

34. 常

"常"是普通用的字，它原本的意思是时常、寻常或平常。道家，特别在《老子》和《庄子》中，"常"字加添了哲学的深意。印度佛学说"无常"，是含有负面意义的，但是中国佛学，特别是道家影响下的禅宗，"常"字有重要的作用，是正面的意义。

1）不变和永恒

"常"第一次用于哲学术语是在《老子》中，是不变和永恒的意思。如"道可道，非常道。"（《老子》第一章）这里，"常"是道的不变，超越了变动和相对性。

2）真实的生命

"复命曰常，知常曰明。"（《老子》第十六章）这里"常"被理解为真实的生命或天命。

3）和谐

"知和曰常，知常曰明。"（《老子》第五十五章）阴阳和谐是不变的天道和地道。所以，这里"常"是指阴阳的和谐。

4）自然或自然的

"无遗身殃，是为习常。"（《老子》第五十二章）这里"常"的意思是自然之道。

5）人性和物性

在《庄子》中，"常"字与老子的思想是一致的，但是庄子用此词的方式更加实用。有时，它是不变的人性，"彼民有常性"（《庄子·马蹄》）；有时，它是正常和普通的自然，是我们生存所需要的，"吾失我常与，我无所处，吾得斗升之水然活耳"（《庄子·外物》）。

6）真常

传统佛学，"常"字有两个意义，即"平常"和"永恒"。前者是否定的，如"常见""常行"和"常道"，是一般相对性的妄想；后者是正面的，如"常静""常智"和"真常"，是真实或真如，这是永恒，是超越相对的理念。

7）平常

在禅宗，"常"字是平常而转化为入道的平常心。"平常心是道。"（《景德传灯录》）这里"平"和"常"在一起，它的意思是心念无欲，没有分别心。

怡按

这个"常"字，本指普通、寻常或平常的意思，但这个"常"字正由于它的普通、寻常，而有自然的意思。也由于它的平常而常常，也有永恒的意思。因此在这个"常"字上兼有这深浅和高下两义。我们如何由下而向上提升，这就是"常"字的转化功夫，约可分为以下三点：

（1）返纯归朴。

普通和寻常的事物，都是非常单纯的、简朴的，但单纯和简朴也是一种理。所以返纯归朴是回到一种平淡的理上。

（2）返于平常心。

受到禅宗口头禅的影响，很多人常提"平常心"，但只注意"平常"两字，而忽略了心的功夫。其实"平常心"的出处是马祖道一的话："道不用修，但莫污染。何为污染？但有生死心，造作趣向皆是污染。若欲直会其道，平常心是道。谓平常心，无造作、无取舍、无断常，无凡无圣。经云：'非凡夫行，非贤圣行，是菩萨行。'只如今行住坐卧，应机接物尽是道。"（《景德传灯录》

卷二十八）在这里，要点是没有分别执着，做了对人有益的事，而不自以为是圣贤。

（3）返于道的自然。

老子的"道"法自然，自然中有道。我们返于自然，但并不是任意而为的自然，而是无欲无求的自然。我们常说的常情、常理，就是道的自然。

35. 术

虽然"术"的普通意思是技术和方法，但它有时却代表了负面意义的权诈。不只孔子，就是老子也不用"术"。孟子虽然用了五次正面意义的"术"，但在他的思想中，"术"并不是重要的术语。《庄子》中，"术"字都作负面词用，含有诡辩的瑕疵。所以后来，在一般哲学文化里，人们尊重道，而轻视方术。在过去的历史上，较少数的知识分子研究"术"。有人会问为什么？因为在哲学上，方法论、认识论不是主体，而科学和科技也不是特别受推崇。

在中国哲学上，"术"有以下三方面的意义。

1）道术

"鱼相忘乎江湖，人相忘乎道术。"（《庄子·大宗师》）在这个引文中，庄子把"道"和"术"连在一起。用"术"使"道"不致太抽象。但是在《庄子》里，"术"的出现也是和"道"相比的。如，"后世之学者，不幸不见天地之纯，古人之大体，道术将为天下裂。"（《庄子·天下》）这里的"道术"是"道"落入了"术"，即方术撕裂了道的整体性。

2）方术

在庄子的思想中，"术"是"道"的一部分，强调"术"，就会忽略了本质，或走到极端，而步入邪途。"天下之治方术者多矣，皆以其有为不可加矣。"（《庄子·天下》）庄子以后，"方术"是用来指称那些研究神秘主义者，如占卜术、巫医等。

3）术数

这里，"数"意思是指变化的关系，这是源于《易经》六十四卦中的爻位的变动。所以，"术"的数目研究是《易经》的方法，用此法说明宇宙的变动是由于爻位的改变。朱熹说："自秦汉以来考象数者，泥于术数而不得其弘通简易之法。"（《伊川易传》）。

怡按

在这里我们把"道"和"术"作一分别：

道	无为	自然	全部	智慧	正道	超时空
术	有为	人为	局部	知识	技巧	有时空

"道"只有一个，虽然我们也称它为"大道""常道""天道"，但仍然只是一个"道"。而"术"却有不同的称呼，如"学术""方术""技术""武术""医术""巫术""占星术""炼金术""术数"等。

36. 弱

在平常的用法，"弱"只有负面的意思，即衰弱。所有中国哲学家，只有老子看到它有正面价值。即使庄子也忽视这个"弱"字。在《庄子》中，"弱"字只出现五次，四次是平常的衰弱的意思，唯一例外的一次是引证老子的"弱"字。

1. 弱的意义

在《老子》中，"弱"不是病人的衰弱。了解老子的"弱"，我们须要明白它相反的"强"的意思。当他说："故坚强者死之徒"（《老子》七十六章），"强梁者不得其死"（《老子》四十二章），"心使气曰强，物壮则老"（《老子》五十五章），则"强"是盲目使用精力和能力，那是违反了自然的。另一方面，实际的"弱"是保藏一个人的精力和能力，不要任意浪费掉。老子认为"弱"就是柔软或谦让。"守柔曰强"（《老子》五十二章）和"柔弱胜刚强"（《老子》三十六章），虽然弱表面看起来弱，但内心却很坚强。

2. 弱是道之用

老子思想中，"弱"不只是保护人的精力和能力的一种技巧，而是道的一种运用，如，"弱者道之用。"（《老子》四十章）但在同一章，老子也说："反者道之动。"因此，"弱"也是用在反和返的一面。又如，"含德之厚，比于赤子。蜂虿虺蛇不螫，猛兽不据，攫鸟不搏。骨弱筋柔而握固，未知牝牡之合而全作，精之至也。终日号而不嗄，和之至也。知和曰常，知常曰明。益生曰祥，心使气曰强。物壮则老，谓之不道。不道早已。"（《老子》五十五章）这段话充分说明了"弱"是"道"的作用。

3. 弱是德性

《老子》中，"弱"也是通向"道"的德性。它有知足和谦虚两方面。

一是要知足。

"祸莫大于不知足，咎莫大于欲得。故知足之足常足矣。"（《老子》四十六章）"知足"，就是少欲。它也是"弱"的一种运用。

二是要谦虚。

"故贵以贱为本，高以下为基，是以侯王自谓孤寡不谷。"（《老子》三十九章）谦虚是"弱"的一种德性表现。

怡按

以上我们举了"弱"的正面意义，但我们生活上所遇到的却是许多"弱"的事实，我们如何面对它们、转化它们，使它们由负面而去往正面呢？我们可以从以下四点着手：

（1）知弱。首先我们要了解这个"弱"是怎样形成的？是外力的影响还是自己的缺点？这个"弱"是天生的还是可以改变的？

（2）处弱。其次要思考如何面对这个"弱"，如何使自己不受"弱"的影响，而保持内心的安定、头脑的清醒。

（3）除弱。接着想方法除掉这个"弱"。例如身体上的"弱"，可加锻炼以强身；愚昧的"弱"，可用勤以补拙增加知识。

（4）用弱。有时弱点可以转化成优点。例如拙于言辞是弱点，但"木讷近仁"，切实的工作反而能赢得他人的信任。《庄子·人间世》便有则故事，一位驼背弯腰的人不能正常工作，但他的弯腰却可以为人淘米，做必须弯腰的工作，反而养活了十口之家。当国家有战事征兵时，他因身体有残疾，反而保全了性命。庄子虽然举的是一个特殊的例子，但我们在实际生活上确实是有许多弱点可以转化而成为优点的。

37. 几

"几"的意思是非常微小，本来没有哲学的含义，但《易经》和《庄子》是例外。在《易经》中，"几"意思是非常微小，但却寓有变化之机。而这个变化的"机"，却是庄子所强调的。

1. 动的微妙

孔子说："知几其神乎？君子上交不谄，下交不渎。其知几乎？几者，动之微，吉之先见者也。"（《易经·系辞下传》第五章）这是"几"最好的定义，实际上，也是最明确的解释。"动之微"是指宇宙、人生和卦爻在变动开始时的微小处。因为在宇宙中，所有事件的变动、人际的关系及卦爻的形成和象征，这三者都是相互作用的。因此，如一个人知道卦爻的预兆，就能处理好人际的关系；由于把握到预兆，也就能顺从天地的变化。所以，在变易中"几"是非常重要的因素。

2. 精微的本质

在《易经》中，"几"是变动的微妙处，它是使我们行正确的德性。在《庄子》中，"几"变作"机"，指微小的自然物质的生机。如"种有机"（《庄子·至乐》），这里的"机"即"几"，在树木生长的微小处。是像一种原生质，而后能形成万物。但庄子的"机"和"几"相同。庄子继续说，"人又反入于机。万物皆出于机，皆入于机。"（《庄子·至乐》）在此处引文中，"几"或"机"意指本原和万物的本质。庄子用这个"机"和其他的字合成复合词，如"气机""天机""心机"和"机器"。前二个是正面的意思，"气机"是指"气"的精微，而"天机"是指智慧；"心机"是指狡猾的心思，"机器"是指人制造的东西，不是自然形成的。

怡按

对于这个"几"字和它演变的"机"，我们从两方面来论，一是"知几"；一是"转机"。

先说"知几"。"几"有四义，如何去知：

（1）知微："几"在《易经》中是预兆，是微小。我们能"知微"便能知道如何发展，如"知微知著"。

（2）知生：易理是生生不已的，在"易"的变化之开端是"几"，也是始生，所以"知几"就是要知道这个生之始。

（3）知因：《易经》的运用讲的是感应。对事物的发展来说，就是因果。而"几"就是因，所以"知几"就是了解事物发展旳初因。

（4）知转：知因之后，不是一味地跟着走，必须要知道如何去转。如知道凶兆，就要懂得如何转凶为吉。

再说"转机"。这个"几"字在《庄子》中是"机"。这个"机"有四个复合词，都和"转机"有关：

（1）危机：在机变中，当然有危有安。因此我们在任何变动之时，要有危机感，知道危机的原因。

（2）转机：有句话所谓"危机就是转机"，这是说我们看到危机时，不要逃避它，危机和转机是同一个"机"，因此我们只要去分析这个"机"，因为这个"机"中就有变化的种子，即"几"。我们就在它的开端处下手，自然就能很容易地转变了。

（3）投机：投机的本意是把握机变或机会，易理上所谓"见几而作"就是这个意思。我们常说把握机会，因为机会是机变之会，即机变之交叉点，稍纵即逝，所以要及时把握。今人用于投机分子，那又是负面的做法了。

（4）禅机：禅宗是以理悟入的，禅理是生命之理。但宇宙中的一切变化是动的，这个"理"显于动中就是"机"。不仅黄花、翠竹有机，就是水滴、鸟声也有"机"。普通人只看到现象，高明的禅宗师徒却因它们而顿悟。

38. 无

"无"（無），在《易经》中是写成"旡"；它们是一样的字，不同的形状。"无"是一个极普通的字，意思是"不"或"没有"。只有在道家书中，特别是《老子》和《庄子》，"无"变成哲学术语，成为一个关键的理念。

1）老子的"无"

"无"第一次被赋予哲学意义是在《老子》中，一共出现在三十五个章节里，最重要的一次出现在第一章。"无名天地之始，有名万物之母。故常无欲以观其妙，常有欲以观其徼，此两者同出而异名。"（《老子》第一章）这里，"无"和"有"是相对的，两个都是形而上的词语，都来自"道"的本原。

2）不存在

在《老子》，有时"无"的意思是不存在。"故有无相生，难易相成，长短相较，高下相倾，音声相和，前后相随。"（《老子》第二章）这段是论述相对的关系，所以这里的"无"和"有"在现象界是相对的，所以应翻译成"不存在"较贴切。

3）道家的德性

"无"连接其他的名词形成各种德性，如"无为""无欲"和"无知"等。可见"无"连到负面的字，"为""欲""知"等，所成的复合词有正面的意义。例如"为无为则无不治"（《老子》第三章），这里的"无为"不是不去做，而是把握要点，有效地去做；不花气力，即顺自然地去做。

4）道之名

在老子思想中，虽然"无"不等于"道"，但在魏晋时期的玄学中，却把"无"看作"道"。如，何晏说："夫道者，惟无所有者也。"（《无名论》）王弼说："道者，无之称也。"（《论语释疑》）他们之后，很多学者也把"无"当作"道"的本质。

5）诸法本无

魏晋时期的很多佛学家受了玄学的影响，也把一切法解作"无"。如，吉藏说："安公明本无者，一切诸法，本性空寂，故云本无。"（《中观论疏》卷二）

6）禅宗的特别用法

在禅宗的公案对话中，为了证入开悟，"无"扮演了一个主要角色。如，无门慧开的《无门关》："赵州和尚因僧问：'狗子还有佛性也无？'州云：'无。'"这是"无"第一次被用在公案中来帮助学生开悟。接着无门说："参个无字，昼夜提撕，莫作虚无会，莫作有无会。"（《无门关》第一则）在禅的公案里，"无"是用于帮助学生"言语道断"，超越相对性。禅宗就是用"无"在坐禅时，使我们的心超越相对。

怡按

这个"无"字，自老子提出后，影响了庄子，也影响了以后的道家、道教，甚至魏晋的玄学家。这个"无"字，自梁武帝问达摩："何谓圣谛第一义？"达摩即回答："廓然无圣"。这个"无圣"的"无"也成为整个禅宗思想的眼目。所以从老庄到中国禅宗，这个"无"扮演了非常重要的角色。中国哲学里的各种主题，如无名、无欲、无知、无我、无心、无念等，都以"无"为主。这个"无"由于都出自《老子》，虽然它和"虚"不同，但却都有老子思想的基础，所以"虚"也和"无"的运用有关，可以看作"无"之用。至于佛学的"空"和"无"虽然表面上相似，而佛学初传的学者，也以"无"来解"空"，但终因中印思想本质的相异，这个"无"还是从"空"中跳脱出来，与"空"分道扬镳。所以在中国禅宗里，虽然用"无"，但不是"空"。在印度佛学里，讲佛性是空，到了禅宗讲自性是"有"，只是妙有而已。

39. 象

"象"是象形文字，是大象的形貌，表示图象和形式的意思。引申而变成哲学的词语，是在《易经》中，有两个意思。

1）天象

"天地变化，圣人效之。天垂象，见吉凶，圣人象之。"（《易经·系辞上传》十一章）在此引文中，这第一个"象"是显示《易经》的图象来自天。所谓"河出图，洛出书"（《易经·系辞上传》十一章），都为占卜者所用。这个图象已经被学术界认为是讲的宇宙变化中的自然现象。占卜者所说也许是超自然或宗教的神秘思想，但后来发展也可进入科学或哲学。图像在易经中能解释这两种途径。在占卜上，六月下雪是一个象；对科学家来说，苹果从树上掉到牛顿的头上，也是一个象。

2）卦的图象

在引文的第二个"象"是出现在卦中的象。《易经》的圣人作者跟着天的图象而画卦和爻，因而，卦中的爻位关系是图象，这个"象"能读出图象所显出的好或坏的时运，告诉我们在生活上该前进或后退，或是悲伤和快乐。正如《系辞传》所说："圣人设卦观象，系辞焉而明吉凶，刚柔相推而生变化。是故吉凶者，失得之象也。悔吝者，忧虞之象也。变化者，进退之象也。刚柔者，昼夜之象也。"（《易经·系辞上传》第二章）

儒家的系辞中，图像学说用卦象来说明古代怎么发明器物和工具而建立了物质文明。"古者包牺氏之王天下也，仰则观象于天，俯则观法于地，观鸟兽之文，与地之宜，近取诸身，远取诸物，于是始作八卦，以通神明之德，以类万物之情。作结绳而为罔罟，以佃以渔，盖取诸离。包牺氏没，神农氏作，斲木为耜，揉木为耒，耒耨之利，以教天下，盖取诸益。……上古结绳而治，后世圣人易之以书契，百官以治，万民以察，盖取诸夬。"（《易经·系辞下传》第二章）这个物质创造的过程说明了卦的图像和原始文明之间的关系。这不是占卜之事，而是实际发展图像和理想的文化。

可惜的是，一直以来学者的《易经》研究窄化了他们收集卦的图象；他们忽视了古代圣人对图像的重视，不明白天地变化之象对现实世界建立文明的重要。后来更多的学者研究《易经》，都走错了方向。他们看图像都被锁定在抽象的符号上，而割断了卦的图像与它的来源，即天上或自然界的联系，他们不能把象用在真实的世界上。因此，《易经》便走入了文字游戏和占卜迷信的路子。

怡按

接着上面所说,《易经》的"象"是指天象,是指自然界的象,这是活的,因此我们运用观象,也应该是活的。譬如《蒙卦》的卦象是山水,卦义是讲教育的,我们就应于山水中去体验教育的意义。甚至我们可以爬到山上去尝尝泉水的清澈;我们也可以走到水边去了解孔子的"知者乐水"及"逝者如斯夫,不舍昼夜"的道理,这样,我们的心中就会有教育的体会。可惜后代的一些解易者,不观天道天象,而在爻辞的文字上拼命用错综复杂的方法,把阴变阳、阳变阴,制造了另一套错综复杂的学说,以求解通爻辞。这是错看了"象",不是真的、活的天象。

40. 道

扫一扫，
进入课程

　　"道"，用作动词，简单的意思是讲述或指导；用作名词，它是中国哲学的灵魂。我们可以说中国哲学的主旨和目标是去学习和实践"道"。"道"的原始意义是："所行道也。从辵从首。一达谓之道。"（许慎《说文解字》）"辵"意思是走路，"首"意思是头。因此，"道"的意思是主要的路。虽然"道"可以被认为是万物的唯一的路，但它有不同的意义和各种不同的路。

1)《易经》及"十翼"的"道"

　　值得注意的是，"道"字在《易经》六十四卦中出现了四次，都是一般意思的"人道"。但它在"十翼"中出现了很多次都涉及"天道"。"十翼"是孔子和他的学生所写。可见这个"道"已由单纯的意义发展到深度的哲学意义。如，"是以立天之道，曰阴与阳。立地之道，曰柔与刚。立人之道，曰仁与义。"（《易经十翼·说卦传》第二章）可见在"十翼"中，"道"是与天（形而上）、地（物质环境）和人（德性）互相关联，而形成一个整体的。

2）先秦儒家的"道"

虽然在"十翼"中，这个"道"有一个超越的意思，但它在《论语》中还是非常简单的，孔子只关注政治和伦理。难怪他的学生子贡自怨说："夫子之言性与天道，不可得而闻也。"（《论语·公冶长》）孔子有性和天道的思想，都是记录在《中庸》和"十翼"里。但在《论语》中，只是记录和学生的对话，他们所讨论的都是有关人道方面的问题。主要有这几项：

一是德性。

孔子说："君子道者三，我无能焉！仁者不忧，知者不惑，勇者不惧。"（《论语·宪问》）

二是治民。

有子说："礼之用，和为贵；先王之道，斯为美。"（《论语·学而》）

三是真理。

孔子说："朝闻道，夕死可矣！"（《论语·里仁》）

四是正道。

孔子说："富与贵，是人之所欲也；不以其道得之，不处也。贫与贱，是人之所恶也；不以其道得之，不去也。"（《论语·里仁》）

3）"道"在道家

一是老子的道。

第一，真实和永恒。"道可道非常道"（《老子》第一章）。

第二，创生。"道生之。"（《老子》五十一章）

第三，动力。"反者道之动。"（《老子》四十章）

第四，无处不在。"周行而不殆，可以为天下母。吾不知其名，字之曰道。"（《老子》二十五章）

第五，理则。"执古之道，以御今之有。能知古始，是谓道纪。"（《老子》十四章）这里，理则的意思是道理，是了解和看清万物的来源和发展。

第六，最高标准。"孔德之容，惟道是从。"（《老子》二十一章）

第七，自然。"道法自然。"（《老子》二十五章）

二是庄子的道。

在《庄子》中，如老子一样，"道"是被用为万物本质的。但是，庄子更关注生命。

第一，自然的生命。"泉涸，鱼相与处于陆，相呴以湿，相濡以沫，不如相忘于江湖。与其誉尧而非桀，不如两忘而化其道。"（《庄子·大宗师》）"道"对于人就像江湖对鱼一样，是生命的自然条件。

第二，生命的本质。"纯素之道，惟神是守。守而勿失，与神为一。"（《庄子·刻意》）这个"道"，被理解为生命的本质，后来的道教要借此以修炼成仙。

4）"道"在中国佛家

因为道家的"道"的性质类似佛教的概念，早期的翻译者用这个术语去翻译印度佛学。

一是路径。

"六道众生，生死所趣。"（《法华经·序品》）"道"是路径，是一个人要通向好或坏的境地的路子；"六道"是地狱、饿鬼、畜生、阿修罗（精灵）、人和天。

二是最高的境界。

早期的佛家用"道"去表达修行最高的涅槃境界。例如，僧肇说："夫涅槃之为道也，寂寥虚旷，不可以形名得。"（僧肇《涅槃无名论》）

三是实性、真如、佛性或自性。

"无二之性，即是实性。实性者，处凡愚而不减，在贤圣而不增，住烦恼而不乱，居禅定而不寂。不断不常，不来不去，不在中间及其内外，不生不灭，性相如如，常住不迁，名之曰道。"（《坛经·护法品》）这个"实性"和真如、佛性、自性都因为这个"道"而可以相通。

5）道在宋明儒家

宋明理学家受道家和禅宗的影响，用"道"在作为天道和人道之间的桥梁。

一是理。"理即道。"（程颢、程颐《二程文集》卷一）

二是性。"道即性也。若道外寻性，性外寻道，便不是。"（《二程遗书》卷一）

三是万物。"道外无物，物外无物，总天地间一道也。"（《二

程文集》卷四）

四是太极。"道即太极。"（《朱熹全集》卷九十四）

五是心。"心体即所谓道心"，"道心即天理。"（王阳明《传习录》卷一）

6）良知

"道即是良知。"（王阳明《传习录》卷四）宋明儒家的推论，一切的观念都包含在"理"中，也不能离开"道"。

怡按

上面我们已把"道"方方面面说了很多，但相信还是有人会问："道究竟是什么？"我的第一句回答是："我不知道。"也就是，我不知"道"。我如果知"道"的话，那已不是"道"了。因为"道"不属于"知"的客体，不是我们用"知"可以定义的。我在美国教学时，很多学生，尤其中国学生告诉我，他们的美国教授说，他们始终抓不住"道"。被他们抓住了的当然就不是道了。有位学者在《老子》中描写"道"是宇宙最高的实体，这是西方宗教的上帝，或西方哲学的真实（reality），而不是中国的"道"。我们的这个"道"就在我们的周围，就在我们的心中。

那么这个"道"究竟是什么？我虽然无法描述"道"的本质，但近年来，我觉得"道"至少有两种作用：一是"道"使万物都能生生发展，"道"使万物都能由小变大地生长；二是"道"给万物以发展的空间，无论小草还是大树都各有它们的空间。前者是老子"道生一"的"生"；后者是老子强调的"无"，所以这两种作用都来自老子讲的"道"。

41. 敬

普通的用法，"敬"是恭敬和尊敬的意思，但在哲学上，它成为很重要的一德。如《尚书》说："王敬所作，不可不敬德。"（《尚书·召诰》）《诗经》说："各敬尔身。"（《诗经·雨无正》）这些都是指"敬"是谨慎自己的行为，后来的儒家把它发展为一种修养的主德。

1）"敬"在孔子思想中

"敬"在《论语》中出现了二十一次，有三种意义：

一是敬其事。

孔子说："道千乘之国，敬事而信。"（《论语·学而》)，无论做任何工作，我们必须以真诚和持敬之心去对待它。

二是对上用敬。

"子谓子张：'有君子之道四焉：其行己也恭，其事上也敬，其养民也惠，其使民也义。'"（《论语·公冶长》）这里，"事上"是指服务上位的人（包括君主和官吏）。同时，"事上"也是指孝养父母，所谓"事父母须敬"。另外也是非常重要的是敬鬼神，如"敬鬼神而远之"（《论语·雍也》）。这里的"鬼神"是祭祀中

136

的祖先。如子张说，"祭思敬"（《论语·子张》）。这里说明了祖先祭祀中须用"敬"。

三是修己以敬。

子路问君子，孔子回答说："修己以敬。"（《论语·宪问》）这里是指，修养自己的德性，先要做到"敬"字。

2）"敬"在孟子思想中

在《孟子》中的"敬"与《论语》中的"敬"没有什么差别。

孟子说："陈善闭邪谓之敬。"（《孟子·离娄》）虽然孟子是指用"敬"以断除君主的邪念，但宋明儒家则把"敬"用在修心时避免邪念的产生。

3）"敬"在《易经》"十翼"中

"君子敬以直内，义以方外。"（《易经·坤卦·文言》）这里，"直"是指诚，"方"是指义。这种"直内"的"敬"就是后来宋明儒家的修心之道。

4）"敬"在宋明儒家

宋代的儒家受《易经》的影响，把"敬"转入心的修养。尤其程朱学派特别"主敬"，以避免走入道家的"静"和佛家的"寂"。程朱学派用"敬"的主要功夫就是专一。程颐说："敬只是主一也。

主一则既不之东，又不之西，如是则只是中。既不之此，又不之彼，如是则只是内。存此则自然天理明，学者须是将敬以直内涵养此意，直内是本。"（程颢、程颐《二程遗书》卷十五）由于宋儒的主敬和持敬，使"敬"在中国哲学上有两点特殊的贡献：

第一，"敬"是内在的德。

在先秦哲学中，孔子和孟子思想里，"敬"是一种道德行为，是表现出对事对人的一种尊敬的态度。在宋代儒家的转变下，"敬"从外向内，成为内心修养的德性。我们对万事万物持敬，不是因为它们比我们高或在我们之上。这个"敬"是存于内心，不是表现于外的，所以是自我的一种修养。

第二，"敬"在打坐中。

宋明儒家和孔孟不同的是，他们受禅宗的影响，也重视打坐。但他们的打坐又与道家（道教）、佛家不同。道教重数息行炁，佛家主无念无我。宋明儒家则在打坐时，内心涵养"诚""敬"二德。所以"敬"字是宋明儒家打坐时非常重要的一德。

怡按

这里我要根据"修己以敬"提出一个"敬"字的新看法，就是"敬己"。一般来说"修己以敬"还是被解作修养对天、对人、对物的"敬"，而我这里的"敬己"却是敬重自己、尊重自己。这不是自大也不是自傲，而是承担责任，期许自己。宋明儒家在打坐时，要涵养"诚敬"。这"诚敬"两字连言的"敬"就是对自己的敬。"自敬"和自尊有点相似，能敬己自然能敬天、敬人、敬事。

42. 义

"义（羲）"的原意是个人的表现或个人的态度，因为它的字形部首是"我"。意思是指以"我"为仪表。在孔子和孟子的思想中，"义"成为重要的德行。

1）"义"的两个重要表现

由于"义"和"我"的关系，它太容易用"我"的观点去裁判他人。墨子说："一人一义，十人十义，百人百义，千人千义。逮至人之众，不可胜计也，则其所谓义者，亦不可胜计。此皆是其义，而非人之义。"（《墨子·尚同下》）为了避免这种现象，需要强调以下两个条件：

一是利。

"利者，义之和。"（《易经·乾卦·文言》）"义，利之本也。"（《春秋左传·昭公十年》）"义，利也。"（《墨子·经上》）所有这些引言的共同点，都是认为，"义"必须有利于所有的人。

二是宜。

"义者宜也。"（《中庸》）"义者，谓各处其宜也。"（《管子·心术》）这里，义是指正好，也是指一个人做任何事都应该在对的时间，对的地方，和适宜的关系。

2）"义"在孔子思想中

"君子义以为质。"（《论语·卫灵公》）"君子之于天下也，无适也，无莫也，义之与比。"（《论语·里仁》）因此，"义"是君子的标准。孔子没有告诉我们标准是什么，但他确实说过："君子喻于义，小人喻于利。"（《论语·里仁》）这里，"义"是利的相对，但同时也是利的基础。因此，"义"是一个大利，是一个人为大多数人做的事，而不是只为自己做的事。君子强调的"义"是这个大利，而绝非小利。

3）"义"在孟子思想中

孟子使"义"成为中国哲学里最关键的字，后来发展成三个重要的解释。

一个是合"义"于"仁"。

孟子联结"仁"和"义"成一个词，被公认为儒家思想的本质。孟子用"义"为桥梁把"我"从内在的"仁心"转为外在的行为，所以"义"是在仁和礼之间。孟子说："仁，人心也。义，人路也。"（《孟子·告子》）"夫义，路也。礼，门也。"（《孟子·万章》）这里，孟子视"义"为一条路，是由"仁心"通向"礼"之门，通过"义"而付之于实践。所以孟子的"义"就是"仁"的实践。

同时，很多的君主不在乎"礼"，也无视于孔子的"仁"，他们几乎不会用"礼"和"仁"去规范自己的行为(孟子也表示"仁"的特色只是恻隐之心而已)。孟子强调"义"因为它比"仁"有力量。"义"是人道;假如人不义,就不能成为人。虽然"义"是外在行为的规范,但孟子又把"义"转化为内在的德性,和"仁心"连结。比如他说:"仁义礼智根于心。"(《孟子·尽心》)

第二个是"义"和"利"的区别。

虽然孔子说,"君子喻于义,小人喻于利"(《论语·里仁》),但他并不认为"利"是绝对不好的。他要人们避免一心追求"利",并建议当有利的机会出现时,应该想到"义"。但是在孟子那里,"义"和"利"似乎是完全不相容的。在他的书中,所有言及"利"之处,都是负面的意思。"鸡鸣而起,孳孳为善者,舜之徒也。鸡鸣而起,孳孳为利者,蹠之徒也。欲知舜与蹠之分,无他,利与善之间也。"(《孟子·尽心》)可见,孟子是以"义"取替了"利",作为行动的动机。

第三,培养义气。

在孟子把"义"转化为内心后,接着他把"义"与"气"相连。如,他说:"其为气也,至大至刚,以直养而无害,则塞于天地之间。其为气也,配义与道,无是馁也。"(《孟子·公孙丑》)这里,孟子把"义"通过了气,而涵养成充满天地的浩然正气。

怡按

上面所讲的"义"都从孔孟的思想来说的,当然都是正面的,但在老子的思想中,却是负面的。如,老子说:"上德不德,是以有德。下德不失德,是以无德。上德无为而无以为,下德为之而有以为。上仁为之而无以为，上义为之而有以为。"(《老子》三十八章）在老子那里，"上德"是较高的玄德，不自以为有德。"下德"是指一般的道德，或儒家的道德，是相对的、有为的，如仁、义、礼等。"上仁"是无条件的爱，所以尚能无为。而"上义"即使是最高层次的"义"，仍然是有为的，即有目的、有欲望，所以老子把它列入"下德"。不过在这里要注意，老子此处的"义"是指是非的判断，即使公义、正义也是以己见判人，所以是负面的。如果我们把"义"解作"宜"，也许老子对"义"的看法就会不一样了。

43. 诚

在孟子之前，"诚"不是一个哲学词语。它偶尔出现在《尚书》《诗经》和《论语》中，也都是用作助动词。到了战国时代（公元前403—公元前222年），在《中庸》中，"诚"字有了很深的哲学意义，也建构了"诚"的整个思想体系。"诚"字普通的意思是真诚、诚实、忠诚和诚信。所有这些词语都是由"诚"的普通意义发展出来，以至成为精神的最高境界。如《中庸》上就很清楚地说："诚者，天之道也，诚之者，人之道也。"（《中庸》）

1）天道

"诚者，天之道也"，是把"诚"看作天道，也就是说，是自然之道，即也是圣人之道。"诚者，天之道也。诚之者，人之道也。诚者，不勉而中，不思而得，从容中道，圣人也。"（《中庸》）

所谓天道有以下二义：

一是至诚如神。

"至诚之道，可以前知。国家将兴，必有祯祥；国家将亡，必有妖孽。见乎蓍龟，动乎四体。祸福将至：善，必先知之；不善，必先知之。故至诚如神。"(《中庸》)在这段话中，虽然提到占卜，但没有牵涉到迷信。相反地，是以"诚"代替迷信。事实上，"至诚"是顺乎天道，和宇宙中的人事变化是相通的。

二是至诚无息。

"故至诚无息，不息则久，久则征，征则悠远，悠远则博厚，博厚则高明。博厚，所以载物也。高明，所以覆物也。悠久，所以成物也。"(《中庸》)如此，"诚"的作用是和天地万物生生不已之道相合的。

2）人道

"诚之者，人之道"，是指人道、德行。所谓"诚之者，择善而固执之者也。"(《中庸》)这里有两条路可付诸实践：

一是自成。

"诚者，自成也。而道，自道也。诚者，物之始终；不诚，无物。是故君子诚之为贵。"(《中庸》)一个人的实践德行和增进知识和智慧，就必须先修己以诚，也就是说要健全自己的人格。

二是成物。

"诚者，非自成己而已也，所以成物也。成己，仁也；成物，知也。性之德也，合外内之道也。"(《中庸》)"成物"就是帮助其他的人和事能好好地发展，也就是说，让所有人和事能和谐地生存，而且都能依据他们的自性而发展。

3）"诚"在道家中

在道家，"诚"并不是一个被强调的字。在《老子》中，它只出现了一次，是当作助动词。在《庄子》中，出现了十六次，但只有八次有哲学意义，而这八次的"诚"没有一次出现在庄子的内七篇中；这八次也许是受了《中庸》影响，是后来的道家学者拿来运用的。表面上，它们和《中庸》有类似用法。但重要的不同是，"诚"在儒家是本于"仁"和"义"上；但在《庄子》中，"诚"是心的真实本质，它超越了"仁"和"义"。"夫仁义之行，唯且无诚。"（《庄子·徐无鬼》）这里，可见"诚"是道家修心的特别功夫，和儒家的道德中的"诚"无关。

4）"诚"在宋明儒家中

一般来说，诚在宋明儒家是受《中庸》影响的。多数的宋明儒家一味地赞扬它，给予三种新的意义：

第一种，诚是所有德行的根本。

周濂溪使"诚"成为所有德行的本源。如，他说："诚者，圣人之本。"（周敦颐《通书》）又说："诚，五常之本，百行之源也。"（《通书》）这里，"诚"是"仁"的基础。在周濂溪的眼中，"诚"是比"仁"更重要了。

第二种，诚是心性的修养。

这是受道家和禅宗的影响，程明道（程颢号明道先生）的心性修养就是实践诚。他说："识得此理，以诚敬存之而已，不须防检，不须穷索。"（程颢《识仁篇》）这个方法像是道家和禅宗的打坐，唯一不同的是程明道在心中存养于"诚"和"敬"。

第三种，真实无妄。

这个说法把"诚"当作真实无妄是程颐所创，后来为朱熹所强调。"真实无妄之谓。天理之本然也。"（朱熹《中庸章句》）这个思想是从"诚者，天之道也"（《中庸》）而来，它的定义是真实无妄，是把"诚"提升到形而上的境界。宋明儒家的思想，用"诚"取代了佛家的"真如"，避免了太过抽象的问题，而落实在心的修养上。

怡按

在儒家，甚至整个中国哲学里，"诚"字的哲学源头来自《中庸》一文，也可说《中庸》建立了整个"诚"的思想体系。我们读《中庸》往往注意到"诚者，天之道；诚之者，人之道"一语，好像《中庸》自这两句话展开了对"诚"的讨论。我们忽略了开宗明义第一句"天命之谓性"，已经伏下了"诚"的基础。因为"天命之谓性"已说明了这个"性"是天道之所禀，所以"性"也是天道，而这个"性"来自天道，所以是至诚的，也即天之道。而我们有了这个"性"，再根据这个"性"发展就是"择善固执"的"人之道"。"择善"的"善"，一般都以为是指的善德，这是通解。但我认为另有一个意思也值得考虑，就是庄子的"善者机"（《庄子·应帝王》）和《易经·系辞传》的"一阴一阳之谓道，继之者善也，成之者性也"（《系辞上传》第五章）。这两个"善"

都是指生生之善，也就是说使这个天禀之性，能生生的发展，是
人性就好好地发展人性，至于善之德也是这个生之善发展的第二
步。所以"诚之者"就是把握这个善的"生机"，把我们的"性"
充分的发展出来，以不负天之所禀。

44. 数

原本"数"是指数字和算数。在象数学家的手中，它变成了哲学术语。

1）"数"在古代教育中

在周朝（前 1111—前 249），教育包括"六艺"：礼、乐、射、御、书、数。"诸侯保氏，有六艺以教民者。"（《周礼·天官》）"六艺"出自《周礼·保氏》，如"养国子以道，乃教之六艺：一曰五礼，二曰六乐，三曰五射，四曰五御，五曰六书，六曰九数。"

2）"数"在道家

老子似乎是第一位用"数"来说明宇宙的生成变化的，他说："道生一，一生二，二生三，三生万物。"（《老子》四十二章）但是老子只是强调"一"，他不是真对"数"有兴趣，"数"这个字也并未出现在他的书中。庄子常用"数"这个字，但意思只指数目很多。只有在最后一篇中，出现了哲学的意义，如"明于本数，系于末度"(《庄子·天下》)，这里的"数"与"度"对称，是指法的意思。《易经》影响了以后的道家和道教，使"数"与宇宙变化及人身的气息产生了关联。

3)"数"在后代儒家和法家中

在《论语》和《孟子》中，"数"字都只是数目的多寡，没有哲学的意思。

后来的儒家，像是荀子，还有法家，"数"变成实际的数学计算、经济、统计，以及所有那些与"法"有关的事。"众庶百姓则必以法数制之。量地而立国，计利而畜民，度人力而授事，使民必胜事，事必出利，利足以生民，皆使衣食百用出入相掩。必时臧余，谓之称数。"(《荀子·富国》)这里，荀子的"数"是与法有关，成为法家的术语。《庄子》在这方面的定义也相同，但是含有负面的意思，如"礼法度数刑名比详，治之末也"(《庄子·天道》)。

4)"数"在《易经》

在《易经》的理论中，"数"是一个重要的字，有两个意思：

一是天和地的"数"。

"天一地二，天三地四，天五地六，天七地八，天九地十……天数五，地数五。五位相得而各有合……天数二十有五，地数三十。凡天地之数，五十有五。此所以成变化而行鬼神也。"(《易经·系辞上传》第九章）在这一段话中，"十翼"的作者用"数"去说明天和地的变化的图像。虽然我们不能确切地知道这一系列的数字代表什么，但它影响后来的学者，形成象数学派。有些宋朝哲学家画了很多图表试图去说明和发展这一系列。

二是占卜的爻数。

"大衍之数五十，其用四十有九……分而为二以象两，挂一以象三……揲之以四以象四时。归奇于扐以象闰。五岁再闰，故再扐而后挂。……是故四营而成易，十有八变而成卦。"（《易经·系辞上传》第九章）这里，"十翼"的作者用"数"去创造出占卜的方法。

5）"数"在汉朝的学者中

在汉朝（前206—220），为哲学家所批评的象数学派，他们夸大了《易经》的"数"，发展成一套包括了星象、历法的神秘学说，他们企图以"数"去控制天地的变化。他们认为人与天地能够互相感应，这些感应的关系就在于"数"。董仲舒是最有名的研究"数"的学者，他说，"天地之符，阴阳之副，常设于身，身犹天也，数与之相参，故命与之相连也。天以终岁之数，成人之身，故小节三百六十六，副日数也；大节十二分，副月数也；内有五藏，副五行数也；外有四肢，副四时数也。"（《春秋繁露·人副天数》）

6）"数"在宋明儒家中

宋明儒家受"数"影响有两个方面。

第一个方面，"数"在宇宙的次序。

邵康节（邵雍谥康节）把汉代的象数之学，加以推衍，而成为一套由天数来解释宇宙运转和人事历史变迁的"皇极经世"之学。他说："日经天之元，月经天之会，星经天之运，辰经天之世。"（邵雍《皇极经世·观物篇》）这是说元当日，会当月，运当星，世当辰。十二会为一元，这象征一年有十二个月；三十运为一会，这象征一月有三十日；十二世为一运，这象征一日有十二个时辰。所以一元统十二会，一会有三十运，即一元统三百六十运，而一运有十二世，因此一元就统四千三百二十世。康节这个时间的数字再推衍下去也就是十二与三十交相为用，最后一元就有十二万九千六百年。这是一元的终始一个数的宇宙哲学。

第二个方面是"数"在气的表现。

朱熹说："气便是数，有是理，便有是气，有是气，便有是数。"（《朱子语类》卷六十五）这里用"数"来表达"气"，是指出"气"的变动有"数"的多样性。

怡按

这个"数"在周代，本是小学教育上的算数、算术，可是后来的发展便很复杂。我们举一些和"数"结合的复合词来看，如法数、象数、天数、运数、气数、术数、理数等等，这些复合词中，虽然有"数"字，但重心都转到前面的字那里了，如法、象、天、运、气、术、理上，而发展都在前面一个字中，至于"数"本身却没有系统的发展。所以在中国，我们的"数"只局限于算术，今天小学中所习的仍是算术，至于几何、代数、微积分等数理课程，都是舶来品。西方的科学是由他们的数理学而来，这也是中国科学发展不如西方昌盛的一个主要原因。

45. 德

本来，"德"有升和得两个意思。"德，升也。"（许慎《说文解字》）又，"登读言得。"（段玉裁《说文解字注》）后来，从原本的定义，发展成为德性或道德，在哲学上和普通用法上都含有人格提升和内心有得的意思。各种学派都分别对这个字充实了他们各自的见解和内容，而有他们各自对道德的解释。

1）"德"在先秦儒家

在儒家，"德"只是道德。在《论语》中，它的意思和作用都是一致的。孟子和荀子都是用道德，修养自己和治理国家。孔子说："据于德，依于仁。"（《论语·述而》）在这个引文中，我们注意它强调人的行为必须依据"德"。但孔子把"德"和"仁"分开。虽然"仁"也是德行，但是这里解释是仁心和理念；"德"是善的社会行为，包括义、敬、礼、孝、和等等。如果我们分析《论语》和《孟子》中的"德"，将会发现，所有和"德"有关的句子都是用在政治上的。"为政以德""道之以德"（《论语·为政》），"德何如，则可以王矣"（《孟子·梁惠王》），"以德服人者，中心悦而诚服也"（《孟子·公孙丑》），可见"德"在先秦儒家还是偏于外在的道德，多用于政治上。

2）"德"在道家

在《老子》中，"德"有两个层次的作用：一是上德，是指超越的玄德；一是下德，指一般的道德。如，"上德不德，是以有德。下德不失德，是以无德。"（《老子》三十八章）在另一章，"上德"的描写是："是谓玄德。"（《老子》第十章）在其他几章，"孔德之容"（《老子》二十一章），"常德不忒"（《老子》二十八章），"广德若不足，建德若偷"（《老子》四十一章），都有共同的特征，是不占有、不自是、不争名。

"下德"是指一般的道德和社会的仁、义、礼等等。《老子》的"德"是至德，借修心通过无为和无欲，达到与"道"相合的境界，而不是相对性道德的"下德"。王弼注解《老子》的"德"是："德者，得也。常德而无丧，利而无害，故以德为名焉。何以得德？由乎道也。何以尽德？以无为用。"（王弼《老子注》三十八章）这里，"得"的意思是内心有得，因为德在道家是内在的德性。

通常，"德"在庄子的思想和老子是一样的。因此庄子描述它的特质和作用大约有以下各端：

一是超越名望。"德荡乎名。"（《庄子·人间世》）

二是和谐。"而游心乎德之和。"（《庄子·德充符》）

三是无为。"无为也，天德而已矣。"（《庄子·天地》）

四是静。"静而与阴同德。"（《庄子·天道》）

五是超越道德。"夫孝悌仁义，忠信贞廉，此皆自勉以役其

154

德者也。"(《庄子·天运》)

六是超越情欲。"恶欲喜怒哀乐六者，累德也。"(《庄子·庚桑楚》)

七是智慧。"知彻为德。"(《庄子·外物》)

八是无心。"贼莫大乎德有心。"(《庄子·列御寇》)

3）"德"在禅宗

"德"在一般佛学中只是一个行善的普通用语，在戒律上只是行为上的律法。中国禅宗受道家的影响，却给"德"一个详细而有深度的内容。如，慧能说："见性是功，平等是德；念念无滞，常见本性，真实妙用，名为功德。内心谦下是功，外行于礼是德。自性建立万法是功，心体离念是德。不离自性是功，应用无染是德。若觅功德法身，但依此作，是真功德。若修功德之人，心即不轻，常行普敬。心常轻人，吾我不断，即自无功。自性虚妄不实，即自无德。为吾我自大，常轻一切故。善知识！念念无间是功，心行平直是德；自修性是功，自修身是德。善知识！功德须自性内见，不是布施供养之所求也。"(《坛经·决疑品》)在这段引文中，"德"是内在的，无分别心、无执着、直心和修身等。这些和庄子的"德"也没有明显的不同。这和一般佛教僧徒的重布施和持戒却大异其趣。所以中国禅宗的师徒们因慧能的教言而专重修心，由顿悟而明心见性。

后来的禅师，尤其在宋朝，他们发现顿悟的方法走上了极端，而变成空谈的文字禅，他们为了纠正此偏差，因此采用儒家的思想用之于日常生活。如妙喜禅师说："且圣贤深戒去利，尊先仁义，而后世尚有恃利相欺"，"尽礼津遣，其爱人恭孝如此"（妙喜、竹庵《禅林宝训》）。这里，可见禅师们在他们的讲法中，也用儒家的仁义恭孝的道德之言。

怡按

"德"是一个总名，是统言外在和内在的德性的。这个"德"和"道"有极密切的关系，老子讲"道"和"德"，"道"是主，"德"是从，如，"孔德之容，惟道是从。"（《老子》二十一章）其实"道"是天道，是普遍的、无为的，而"德"是个人的、有为的。所以"道"根本没有意念，只照自己的路子走。而人，或发挥他的性分，或修正他的行为，使他的所作能合乎"道"的，就是"德"。这是老子把"道"和"德"分开来说的用意。可是后来把《老子》一书称为《道德经》，"道""德"连言成为复合词以后，"道德"变成一个概念的名词，而成为形式的、外在的道德的概念，而失去"德"能顺乎"道"的实质内容。这也就是为什么会造成"道"的所以失落，"德"的所以迷失了。

46. 静

　　"静"是描述静止不动。在中国哲学里，它是用来表达宇宙和人心的本体，也成为修心的一种方法。它在不同的学派有不同的意义，在中国思想史上扮演着重要角色。

1）"静"是"动"的相对

　　"静"没有出现在《论语》和《孟子》中，原因可能是这两本书关注于伦理和政治，不处理宇宙论或形而上的观念。在《易经》六十四卦中也没有"静"字，因为它不谈抽象概念的动静，却常用到"居""出""来""入"等行动的字语。无论如何，"静"和"动"常出现在《易经》"十翼"中。例如，"动静不失其时，其道光明。"（《易经·艮卦·象辞》）合理的解释是，在占卜的卦辞中，运用具体的词语是适当的，但"十翼"成为哲学的研究时，当然会涉及抽象概念的"静"和"动"。

2）"静"是"动"的根本

　　在"十翼"中，"静"字出现了六次，但是有六十次是"动"字。

很少有人去探索这二者之间的关系。道家看"静"的意义比"动"更基本。任何事情都会回到它的根本，回到根本就是回到"静"，意思是回到真正的生命本体。如老子说："夫物芸芸，各复归其根。归根曰静，是谓复命。"(《老子》十六章) 又老子说，"重为轻根，静为躁君。"(《老子》二十六章) 王弼更引申说："动息则静，静非对动者也。"(王弼《周易注疏·复卦》) 王弼不认为"静"字只是简单为"动"的反义词；它们不是在同一层次。"静"是永久，"动"是暂时的，"静"是"动"的根本。

3) "静"是无欲或心的本质

庄子使"静"成为心的一种境界。他说："圣人之静也，非曰静也善，故静也。万物无足以铙心者，故静也。"(《庄子·天道》) 这里，"静"的意思是指无欲。

孔子和孟子以后的儒家重视"静"，把它当作心性。荀子说，"人何以知道? 曰: 心。心何以知? 曰: 虚壹而静。"(《荀子·解蔽》)《礼记》说："人生而静，天之性也。感于物而动，性之欲也。"(《礼记·乐记》) 这两段话中，"静"是心的本质或本性，而心之动是欲望造成的。很难说他们不是受到庄子的影响。

宋朝儒家把"静"转为修心的功夫。周濂溪说："圣人定之以中正仁义，而主静，立人极焉。"(周濂溪《太极图说》) 这个"静"也出现在《荀子》和《大学》里。如，"大学之道，在明明德，在亲民，在止于至善。知止而后有定，定而后能静，静而后能安，安而后能虑，虑而后能得。"(《大学》) 这个"静"是心的状态或心的发动的第一步。在儒家和宋明儒家的解释，"静"为实践德的方法。尤其宋明儒家，强调"静坐"，似乎是受到道家和佛家的打坐或禅坐的影响。

4）"静"与佛家的关系

在印度佛学中，有两个重要的术语：涅槃和禅那（dhyana）。涅槃是佛法的本质；禅那是修心的方法。而与涅槃的特质有关的是寂灭，与禅那有关的是禅坐。这两种的特质都是在一个"静"字。

怡按

周濂溪在他的《太极图说》中，替他的"而主静"的"静"字自注说："无欲故静。"为什么周濂溪要以"无欲"来注"静"？因为"静"的本身就是"静"，一有作为就动了，就不是静。所以，求静的方法不在静，而在欲，欲是动之源，无欲则自然静。但是否也可把"静"当作方法来使用呢？老子曾这样用过："孰能浊以止，静之徐清。"（《老子》十五章）这里所指的，譬如一杯浊水，我们要使它变清的，只有把它放在一边，静止不动，它自然会逐渐地变清。老子此处是指修心，这个"静"就是放在一边，不要躁动。"躁"也是欲之动，所以能放在一边，也必须先无欲。

47. 朴

"朴"原意是未雕琢的一块木,"朴,木素也"（许慎《说文解字》）。一般用法是表示简单、纯净或朴素。老子使"朴"成为哲学术语,而有各种不同的用法。

1）纯净的心

"敦兮其若朴"（《老子》十五章）,"见素抱朴,少私寡欲"（《老子》十九章）和"我无欲而民自朴"（《老子》五十七章）,在每句中,"朴"的意思都是纯净的心,那就是无欲。引申而为我们的心性是真诚的和社会的风俗是素朴的。

2）以简驭繁的管理

"知其荣,守其辱,为天下谷。为天下谷,常德乃足,复归于朴。朴散则为器。圣人用之,则为官长,故大制不割。"（《老子》二十八章）"守其辱"的意思是指君主以谦虚治国,而不显耀他的才能。这里,是指以"朴"的无为政道治国,即是顺着自然,避免用规则制度干扰人民的生活。所以说"大制不割"是指政治是保全人性的完整，而不任意把人性割裂得支离破碎，这就是"朴"。

3）"朴"是道之"一"

"道常无名。朴虽小，天下莫能臣也。侯王若能守之，万物将自宾。天地相合，以降甘露。民莫之令而自均。"（《老子》三十二章）"朴"是小到像这个"一"，"朴"是"道"的化身，它的作用像"道"一样，是使万物顺着自然而发展。

4）"朴"是少欲以解纷

"道常无为，而无不为。侯王若能守之，万物将自化。化而欲作，吾将镇之，以无名之朴。无名之朴，夫亦将无欲。不欲以静，天下将自定。"（《老子》三十七章）老子在这里提出一个有趣的问题。如果"无为"的意思是不干扰，让人民走他们自己的路，但是在自然发展中，人民的欲望也会自然地升起，我们要怎么应付？通常，我们用法律、道德和礼制来控制欲望。但老子认为，法、德和礼是表面的，只能暂时解决问题，一定会产生更多、更大的欲望。有野心的人士常会利用法规自利。老子说："天下多忌讳，而民弥贫。民多利器，国家滋昏。人多伎巧，奇物滋起。法令滋彰，盗贼多有。"（《老子》五十七章）至于强调礼和德，也会造成虚伪的心态，使问题更为复杂。"大道废，有仁义；慧智出，有大伪。"（《老子》十八章）"夫礼者，忠信之薄，而乱之首。"

（《老子》三十八章）因此，老子强调"朴"替代法、德和礼，去减少欲望，以为这是圣人自然的方法，使人民生活简朴。"不尚贤，使民不争。不贵难得之货，使民不为盗。不见可欲，使心不乱。是以圣人之治，虚其心，实其腹，弱其志，强其骨。常使民无知无欲。使夫知者不敢为也。为无为，则无不治。"（《老子》第三章）用"朴"减少人民的欲望，是强调简朴的生活，让人民跟随自然之道。注意，这并不是要真正使我们进入无知的状态，暗示要回到像动物一样的无知无识的存在；它的意思是使我们的精神生活不受物质的控制，能借简朴的生活与"道"相合。

怡按

这个"朴"字是老子所专用，主要是用在政术上。这个"朴"是个象征的字，本来是少、简、纯的意思。但它可以包含老子所有重要的思想，如"无为""无欲""无名""知足""知止""少私寡欲"等。这些德性和方法有不同的名称和不同的对象，而"朴"却始终是一个字。

48. 儒

"儒"是一个指代学者的普通名称，也是指儒家的特别称呼。它虽然是平常的字，但却有很深的含意，有特别的理念和行为准则。

1）温文儒雅

"儒，柔也。"（许慎《说文解字》）这里，"柔"的意思是温文，用来描述那些博学的温文儒雅之士。如："宽柔以教，不报无道，南方之强也，君子居之。"（《中庸》）

2）"六艺"的学者

"儒，柔也。术士之称。"（许慎《说文解字》）"儒"是对那些有特别技艺的学者和教授"六艺"的老师的称呼（"六艺"是礼、乐、射、御、书、数）。在孔子之前，"六艺"是周朝的教育内容。《周礼·天官》曰："儒以道得民。"郑玄注："儒，诸侯保氏，有六艺以教民者。"（郑玄《周礼注》）

3）君子儒

虽然"儒"在《论语》和《孟子》中只出现两次，但它却因孔孟的精神而有了新的含义。在《论语》中，"儒"字是连在"德"上的。孔子对子夏说："女为君子儒，无为小人儒。"（《论语·雍也》）虽然，君子和小人不同，但孔子以为不同之处在于道德，就是儒者必须负起伦理教育的责任。孟子的看法与孔子是相同的。他说："逃墨必归于杨，逃杨必归于儒。"（《孟子·尽心》）这说明，儒者还有匡正学术风气的抱负。

4）儒家学者的称呼

在孟子的时代，很多哲学家和他们的徒弟兴起，各自形成学派并提出他们的主张。孟子在与他们辩论中，建立了儒家学说和学派的基础，他选择"儒"为其名称，并且以"六经"代替"六艺"，也确定了儒家的理念和奋斗方向。

怡按

这个"儒"由周朝教授"六艺"的老师，到孔子时教学生以君子为模范，这是君子儒，是君主治国的顾问。在《礼记》中有《儒行》篇，详细记载了儒者的高度行为规范。如："儒有席上之珍以待聘，夙夜强学以待问，怀忠信以待举，力行以待取。""儒有不宝金玉，而忠信以为宝。不祈土地，立义以为土地。""见利不亏其义，劫之以众，沮之以兵，见死不更其守。""儒有可亲而不可劫也，可近而不可迫也，可杀而不可辱也。""儒有上不臣天子，下不事诸侯，慎静而尚宽，强毅以与人。"

这里只是选录《儒行》篇的一小部分，也许有点过分理想，但作为一个儒者，应有这样的期许。到了宋朝，张载曾写了四句话："为天地立心，为生民立命；为往圣继绝学，为万世开太平。"言简而意赅，为宋明儒家及今天的学者所推崇、所期许。

49. 禅

"禅"最早的意思是封禅，即君王的祭天；及禅让，即圣君让位于贤者。当印度佛教传入中土，梵文的 dhyana 中文音译是"禅那"，后来省略为"禅"字。因"禅那"的原意有打坐、禅坐的意思，这与中文原意的封禅与禅让已经无关了。

1）封禅

"禅，祭天也。"（许慎《说文解字》）在古代，当君主登基，便要去山东的泰山祭天。这个祭礼好像是一个认证书，由天授予王国，得到天的祝福，验证君主的权力。这个仪式基于中国天人相互影响的学说。

2）禅让

"子曰：'唐虞禅，夏后殷周继，其义一也。'"（《孟子·万章》）这是说，从圣王尧到禹是一种禅让制度，每位圣王在让位时，把王位交给另一位有德性、有资格的继任者。很多现代学者怀疑这个制度的存在，他们认为这是孔子创造出的一种理想。但无论如何，它也出现在《墨子》和《庄子》中。可见"禅让"制度有它的可能性，也有可信度，是被中国人高度重视的，这是因为谦让在中国哲学和文化里是一个重要的德性。

3）中国印度佛教的打坐

梵文"dhyana"原本翻译成中文为"禅那"，简化为"禅"。"禅那"，意思是"打坐"或"冥想"，在所有的佛教学派中是一个共法。通过它，可以得到"三摩地"（samadhi），在中文里也称作"三昧"或"定"。"禅"经常联结"定"，形成一个复合词"禅定"。

印度佛教进入中国是在汉朝末期，带来的佛经都关注于打坐的"止观"，涉及由呼吸而控制意念。如安世高传来的《安般守意经》，"安般"即呼吸。该经重视四点：即数息、相随、止观、还净，从而达到意念纯净。这种打坐的方法又称为"止观"。

大乘佛教传入于魏（220—265）和晋（265—420）而带来的佛经强调"般若"（即智慧）。他们的主张是通过禅坐，可以得到智慧。

4）中国佛教和禅宗的禅坐

佛教从印度传入中国后，少数佛家使佛学融入了中国哲学。佛教带来的深奥的"禅"到中国的梁朝（502—577）时，菩提达摩因而创立了第一个最有影响力的学派，即禅宗。以"禅"为它命名，并作为它的中心思想。"五传"之后，北方有神秀的北禅，南方有慧能的南禅。北方学派继续去教基本的印度形式的禅坐，后来经过了几传，而逐渐衰落。南方学派把印度禅的种子播入肥沃的中国思想中，而发展成本土的佛教。禅的法统一直很盛，传到韩国和日本，日本的禅也是偏重禅坐的。

5）"禅"的不同类别

圭峰宗密说："禅则有浅有深，阶级殊等。谓带异计，欣上厌下而修者，是外道禅。正信因果，亦以欣厌而修者，是凡夫禅。悟我空偏真之理而修者，是小乘禅。悟我法二空所显真理而修者，是大乘禅。若顿悟自心本来清净，元无烦恼，无漏智性本自具足，此心即佛，毕竟无异，依此而修者，是最上乘禅，亦名如来清净禅，亦名一行三昧，亦名真如三昧，此是一切三昧根本。若能念念修习，自然渐得百千三昧。达摩门下，展转相传者，是此禅也。"（圭峰宗密《禅源诸诠集》）这里，叙述了各种不同的禅，最后强调了最高境界的禅定，当然也是中国的禅宗。

6）"禅"的标准定义

慧能建立禅宗的标准定义中，对坐禅的意见是，"此门坐禅，元不著心，亦不著净，亦不是不动"，又"此法门中，无障无碍，外于一切善恶境界，心念不起，名为坐；内见自性不动，名为禅。"（《坛经·妙行品》）这里，"禅坐"是不执着内心的念头和外在的事物。慧能的思想中，"禅"不仅是坐禅得定，而且要能见自性

（真性，即本来面目）。这种说法影响到他以后的禅师们，经常批判禅坐或打坐。在中国禅宗，打坐是帮助我们的心地能归于宁静，但它不是根本的智慧，要紧的是觉悟。也就是说，通过禅坐，使我们能觉悟，能见性或本来面目，也就是佛性。

怡按

今天我们用这个"禅"字，都指禅宗的禅。而提到这个"禅"字，又经常会与禅坐、禅定混在一起。其实唐宋的学禅者，跑来跑去，拜师拜祖，并不是为了学禅坐的方法、修禅定的功夫。因为禅坐和禅定已有一个模式在那里了。而他们要参禅，在参禅之前、参禅之时，根本不知道"禅"是什么，甚至也不知道自己要什么。他们的心中只有一团迷茫，使自己不安。虽然这个"禅"字来自印度 dhyana 的翻译"禅那"的简称，但"禅那"是打坐冥思，而参禅绝不是参这个"禅那"。那么，究竟什么是"禅"？如果我们用这个问题去讨教禅师，保管要吃棒喝。本书对任何字义都有比较具体的解释，唯独对这个"禅"字，在上面已有定义，但在这里不想多说，留给读者自己去"参"好了。

50. 礼

扫一扫，
进入课程

"礼"，是礼仪或礼制，在中国文化、哲学和历史上发挥了核心的作用。所以中国人自称为"礼义之邦"。《礼记》一书记录了礼制和礼仪的具体细节和精神，"礼"在古代中国是标准的社会行为。从礼制和礼仪可以看出"礼"对中国文化和哲学的作用。

1）"礼"在中国文化

一是在宗教方面。

"礼，履也，所以事神致福也。从示从丰。"（许慎《说文解字》）"丰"是祭祀时的一种器皿，所以"礼"是祭祀祖先或神明的仪式。例如："礼有五经，莫重于祭。"（《礼记·祭统》）祭祀通过了"礼"的系统化的仪式，表达了对神明和祖先的诚意。

二是在社会方面。

"是故夫礼，必本于天，肴于地，列于鬼神，达于丧祭、射御、冠昏、朝聘。故圣人以礼示之，故天下国家可得而正也。"（《礼记·礼运》）这里，"礼"扩充影响到人民每日的生活上，所以它是社会的规范。

三是在教育方面。

"礼"是"六艺"之一，是古代教育的重要部分。孔子说，"不学礼，无以立。"（《论语·季氏》）"礼"是所有社会行为的规范，如果一个人不知"礼"，就不能顺利生活在社会中。正如《礼记》所说，"道德仁义，非礼不成，教训正俗，非礼不备。分争辨讼，非礼不决。君臣上下父子兄弟，非礼不定。"（《礼记·曲礼》）

2）"礼"在中国哲学

第一，"礼"在儒家。

在中国古代，"礼"是通向伦理、政治和宗教的门户，也是整个社会、道德和人心的基石。

在《论语》中，"礼"字常常伴随着"乐"字，这是因周公制礼作乐，所以"礼"和"乐"成为周代教育的最重要的课题。

孔子赞美周公的礼乐制度。在他的思想中，礼仪和礼制也负起最重要的两大作用：第一个作用，他以"礼"为一切生活行为的规范。当他的学生颜渊问"仁"，孔子回答："'克己复礼为仁。一日克己复礼，天下归仁焉。为仁由己，而由人乎哉？'颜渊曰：'请问其目。'子曰：'非礼勿视，非礼勿闻，非礼勿言，非礼勿动。'"（《论语·颜渊》）这就是说，一切要以礼为准则。第二个作用，他把"礼"和礼制作为管理的基础。"道之以政，齐之以刑，民免而无耻。道之以德，齐之以礼，有耻且格。"（《论语·为政》）这即是以"礼"治国。

"礼"，在《孟子》和《论语》之间有点不同。在孟子那里，"礼"常与"义"连成一个复合词，即"礼义"，成为心中的一德。所谓"君子所性，仁义礼智根于心"（《孟子·尽心》），可见"礼"也是根于心的内在之德。

在《荀子》的思想中，"礼"是关键的理念，与孔子的"仁"和孟子的"义"一样重要。《荀子》的"礼"有三种。第一种是至德："礼者，人道之极也。"（《荀子·礼论》）第二种，修心之道："凡治气养心之术，莫径由礼。"（《荀子·修己》）第三种是法的基础："礼者，法之大分。"（《荀子·劝学》）注意这里，荀子和孔子的思想是不同的，孔子是强调以"礼"代替法的。

第二，"礼"在墨家。

墨子批评孔子对"礼"的看法。他说，"而儒者以为道教，是贼天下之人者也。且夫繁饰礼乐以淫人，久丧伪哀以谩亲。"（《墨子·非儒》）作为一个实用主义者，墨子以为复杂的仪式是不切实际的。

第三，"礼"在道家。

"故失道而后德，失德而后仁，失仁而后义，失义而后礼。夫礼者，忠信之薄，而乱之首。"（《老子》三十八章）这个对"礼"的严厉批评好似与历史的记录不符。因为老子是一位周朝的史官，当然精通周朝的礼制，而且有记载说孔子到周朝去是向他问礼的。假如这是事实，合理地说明了也许是因为老子了解"礼"是心中的信念，如果人们只注意到"礼"的形式和外在的仪式，就会变成死板的和没有生命的制度了。

3）礼的作用

一是实践。

"礼，履也。"（许慎《说文解字》）"履"是实践或付诸实践的意思。没有实践，"礼"只是一个空虚的字。

二是和谐。

孔子的弟子有子说："礼之用，和为贵。"（《论语·学而》）这里，"礼"维持了人与人之间的和谐。

三是谦让。

"辞让之心，礼之端也。"（《孟子·公孙丑》）

四是分别。

"人之所以为人者，非特以其二足而无毛也，以其有辨也。……夫禽兽有父子，而无父子之亲，有牝牡而无男女之别。故人道莫不有辨。辨莫大于分，分莫大于礼。"（《荀子·非相》）这里所谓"别""辨"和"分"，是指在社会伦理上，每个人的角色不同，如父母和子女、丈夫和妻子，以及其他人与人之间的关系，了解这个分别和不同，就会知道自己的义务和责任。

五是满足。

"先王恶其乱也，故制礼义以分之，以养人之欲，给人之求。使欲必不穷乎物，物必不屈于欲。两者相持而长，是礼之所起也。故礼者养也。"（《荀子·礼论》）这里，荀子像现代社会学家一样，定义"礼"是合理的平衡，会满足人民的欲望和需要，而不致伤害到他人，或滥用物资。

173

怡按

"礼"在中国历史文化中，比"法"还重要。法虽严密，我们如不违反法律记载的罪错，便与法无关。但"礼"却是我们日常生活的规范，而且还变成风俗习惯，再通过舆论，时时刻刻与我们息息相关。它的重要，司马光写《资治通鉴》时，第一段便开宗明义地说："臣光曰：臣闻天子之职莫大于礼，礼莫大于分，分莫大于名。何谓礼？纪纲是也；何谓分？君臣是也；何谓名？公、侯、卿、大夫是也。"可见"礼"在治道上的重要性了。这是就政治上来说"礼"。

接着，我们在中国哲学上，再分析一下"礼"的作用。有如下几点：

（1）原始儒家，即汉以前的儒家，都是以"礼"来表现他们作为儒家的特色；到了宋明儒家，除了生活上不违"礼"之外，他们通过"理"来表现他们的特色。

（2）"礼"有内外两面：内，本之于德，孔子已特别加以强调；外，在于礼制。

（3）"礼"的本源来自宗教，所以"礼"都和祭祀有关；礼的运用，在于社会规范，都和"法"相表里。

（4）礼制由于时间的变迁，会变成不合时宜，而成为呆板的条文，以致被淘汰。至于"礼"的精神，却仍是活的，它活在人心中，否则社会必大乱。

附录 1：谈中国哲学术语的生命力

一、前言

对中国哲学术语作系统性的研究，这在中国哲学史上，并没有显著的地位。虽然在哲学文献里，也有陈淳的《北溪字义》，戴震的《孟子字义疏证》等书，但这些书都是非常简略的陈述一家之言，还谈不上对哲学术语，作历史性、综合性，以及客观性的研究。

真正对中国哲学术语作有系统的研究，还是在民国以来，受到西洋知识方法的影响，不过这种研究的成果仍然不大显著，就拿《中国哲学辞典》的编著来说，还是近十年来的事。这说明在国内学术界，虽然大家都在运用着先哲留下来的术语，或采用西方哲学概念，创造了许多术语，但却并没有反刍的来研究这些术语，使它们变得有条理一点，易懂一点，实用一点。

正是由于国内哲学界对中国哲学术语的研究并没有特别的注重，因此在国外介绍中国哲学思想时，它们就变得非常重要。因为对于思想方法和生活观念完全不同的西方人士来说，他们没有中国学术文化的全盘背景，要想深入地了解中国哲学，也只有首先把握住那些重要的术语。所以在西方有关中国哲学的杂志上，经常看到许多专门对某一两个术语做详细分析的论文。在中西哲学比较研究的会议上，也常就一两个重要术语做比较研究。对研究中国哲学的西方学生来说，最有兴趣，也最容易产生问题的，就是这些术语。由于对这些术语的了解，可以使他们比较容易地进入中国哲学的天地。可是也往往由于他们对这些术语的一点错解，而差以毫厘，失之千里，以至于最后不知所云。

基于这一事实和需要。使笔者不得不对这些术语另眼看待，结果发现他们不仅都拥有自己的王国，而且又错综复杂地构成了整个中国哲学的发展脉络。

二、中国哲学术语在过去所扮演的角色

中国古代的哲学家们虽然都是面对真理，解决人生和社会的实际问题，而无心去刻意的制造术语，但许多术语在他们的思想和著作中，仍然扮演了极重要的角色。

孔子的中心思想是一个"仁"字。他自己说："道一以贯之"（《论语·里仁》）。这个一贯之道自然就是"仁"了。虽然孔子没有给"仁"字下过一个确切的、一成不变的定义，但他对学生们的问"仁"，答以各种不同的行"仁"的实际方法，却正是孔子"仁"字的特色。这个"仁"不仅在概念上涵盖了儒家一切德行，同时，在实际上，它与一切德行发生了密切的关系，成为一切德行的原动力。所以孔子的"仁"不只是一个简单的术语，而是他

整个思想的结晶。

到了孟子，虽然仍尊崇孔子的"仁"字，但代表他整个思想精神的，却是一个"义"字。在孟子眼中，"仁"是恻隐之心。但这个恻隐之心比较微妙、柔软。谁都有恻隐之心，可是遇到外界的种种情境，不能完全发展出来，也就等于没有"仁"的存在。所以孟子特别强调这个"义"字。他说："义，路也。"（《孟子·万章下》）"义"就是把恻隐之心发展出来的路，也就是人们必须遵循的路。不能行义，非但不是仁人，而且也不能配称为万物之灵的人了。可见义有转内为外的力量，有强制的规范作用，这是孟子思想的特色。

以上，限于篇幅，笔者仅举孔孟为例，来说明"仁"和"义"两个术语在他们思想中的地位。其他的哲学家，如老子的"道"、庄子的"化"、荀子的"礼"、韩非的"法"、六祖慧能的"明心见性"，以及程朱学派的"理"与"气"，陆王学派的"心性"与"良知"等，他们所用的这些术语，不仅都关系着他们整个思想，而且彼此间的相互影响着和前后相承，基本构成了整个中国哲学思想的发展脉络。

然而在这里，千万不要误会，中国古代的哲学家们好像与西方的某些哲学家，以及现代的某些中国学者一样，只知刻意的制造术语，以标新立异或虚构体系。其实，情形正好相反，中国古代伟大的哲学家们都是直接面对真理，希望寻求一种理论，来解决社会人生的问题。可是当他们陈述如何解决问题时，很自然地形成一套有系统的学理；而在运用上，也就很自然地精简为几个重要的术语。以孔子的思想来说，他对政治、社会、伦理、教育和人生的看法，当然有一套详细的内容和方法。但在运用上，以及后人的传述上，不能动辄原原本本地详述他的整套思想，于是便拿他的几个重要术语作为他思想的代表。这就是孔子之所以要拿"仁"字来作为一贯之道。一提到这个"仁"字，我们很自然地就会了解孔子在政治上、社会上、伦理上、教育上和人生修养上的基本看法和做法了。所以孔子并不是无中生有地创造了一个"仁"字，来架搭他整个思想的空中楼阁，而是在他实际解决问题时，很自然地将自己解决人生实际问题的经验归结为一个"仁"字。这一点，和老子的运用道字相同，老子说：

　　有物混成，先天地生。寂兮寥兮，独立不改，周行而不殆。可以为天下母。吾不知其名，字之曰道。(《老子·第二十五章》)

　　可见老子的"道"虽然也是个名词，但却是拿来描写天地间那永恒不易，又无所不在的作用的。也是实有所指的。同样孔子的"仁"，更是从经验中提炼出来的，有历史的渊源，有人性的基础，更有其能解决人生问题的实际功效。

　　尤其重要的是，当这些一术语被哲学家们提炼出来，运用以后，它们就好像一个生命的诞生，是活泼的、有机的、整体的。这些术语并非只在学者们作观念游戏时的一些棋子，而是投入了活生生的社会中，成为每个人口头上常谈到的，心中常想到的许多原则和信念。试看从古到今的社会中，并非每个人都熟读孔孟的著作，都精研孔孟的思想体系，可是又有几个人没有在口头上提到"仁义"两字，没有在心中想到过"仁义"两字？纵然由于现实的环境，使他们未必能完全照着"仁义"去做，甚至有时还会违反了仁义的原则，但当他们听到或提到"仁义"两字时，却也知道这是孔孟的思想。而他们深夜扪心自问，感觉悔意时，他们用"仁义"两字来自责，也正表明了他们的内心是趋向于孔孟之道的。

在这里，我们可以看出中国哲学上的这些术语，并非只是一套概念游戏中的符号，而是在中国历史文化、社会人心方面，产生了实际和深远的影响。

三、中国哲学术语在西传上的重要性

在中国哲学向西方发展的过程中，这些术语更是扮演了举足轻重的角色。

西方哲学偏重知识概念，注重逻辑体系。只要把握住推理的原则，便可了解其论说的旨趣，可是中国的哲学却不然。我们注重生命的理境、实践的经验，而欠缺逻辑的推论。这对习惯于知识训练的西方人士，便不易豁然而贯通。

以《论语》一书来说，都是孔子和门人对答的语录。根本不是一部有计划的著作。如果我们把握不住它的整个思想精神，那么它与坊间的那些格言选粹便没有什么区别了。尤其那些对中国哲学文化本来很生疏的西方人士，更无法依据其他方面的知识和体验，把整个《论语》的思想贯穿起来。可是这一点对中国人来说便不成问题。因为整部《论语》共有四百八十二章，一万一千七百零五个字，其中五十八章是论"仁"，有一百零五个"仁"字。因此中国人读《论语》时，一看到这些"仁"字，便很自然的把它们贯穿起来，去理解《论语》的整个思想。

再就西文翻译的《论语》来说。在翻译中国哲学经典方面最有贡献的，首推李雅各（James Legge）。就他所译《易经》《书经》《春秋》《左传》《四书》《老子》《庄子》等书来论，他对中国哲学文化的了解，是有广博而深厚的功力的。可是就《论语》一书的翻译来看，他对于作为该书中心思想的"仁"字，便没有一贯的译法，如：

"孝弟也者，其为仁之本与。"《学而》的"仁"字，译为"benevolent action"。

"巧言令色，鲜矣仁。"《学而》的"仁"字，译为"true virtue"。

"泛爱众而亲仁。"《学而》的"仁"字，译为"good"。

"人而不仁，如礼何？"《论语·八佾》的"仁"字，译为"virtues proper to humanity"。

"不仁者，不可以久处约。"《里仁》的"仁"字，译为"virtue"。

"回也，其心三月不违仁。"《雍也》的"仁"字，译为"perfect virtue"。

这种把同一个"仁"字，翻成不同的含义，对于不能阅读中文原著的西方人士，是很难把这些一思想贯穿在一个"仁"字上的，也无法用统计的方法来了解孔子的仁道思想。

另一方面，在前面我们曾强调过，当孔子思想贯穿在一个"仁"字上之后，这个"仁"字便活现在中国人的生命精神里，日常生活中，我们无须去重复的详述孔子思想的细节，只要一提到"仁"字，便和孔子的精神联结起来了，便凸显出人之所以为人的特色。李雅各的翻译文本却失去了这种功能。即使他把极大部分的"仁"字译为德（virtue）或至德（perfect virtue），但德和至德都是一种泛称的名辞，其本身并无所规定，道家和其他各家也都用这个德或至德来描写他们修养的境界。可是这个"仁"却不一样，它虽然一方面是道德的总和，但却是实有所指，所谓"仁"民而爱物，所谓"己立立人，己达达人"这完全呈现出儒家特有的精神与理想。

以上，只是借李雅各的翻译来说明中国哲学术语在中国哲学西传方面的重要性。这些术语就像一把把的钥匙，只有凭借它们，西方人士才能打开中国哲学的大门，才能和中国人的生活信念相互沟通。

四、中国哲学术语的特色

笔者由于深感到这个重要性，因而尝试着去做点基础的工作，于是完成了《中国哲学关键词50讲》。该书主要是为了帮助西方读者能通过这些主要的术语，去了解儒、道、佛（禅宗）的思想及中国文化的精神。由于对象是一般读者，因此内容重在简明扼要，深入浅出。该书共选辑了五十个单字：一、人、天、仁、心、化、中、反、丹、玄、名、志、忘、孝、命、和、直、易、物、忠、知、法、性、勇、真、神、时、气、悟、恕、虚、理、情、常、术、弱、几、无、象、道、敬、义、诚、数、德、静、朴、儒、禅、礼。在起初挑选这些单字时并没有什么特别的标准，只是集合儒、道、禅，以及其他学派中主要的和常用的术语而已。可是等到完稿后，替该书写导论时，再把这些单字在中国哲学上的作用加以综合的研究，却发现这些单字术语几乎都具有三个特点。这三个特色不仅和西方的哲学术语截然不同，而且集中体现了中国哲学文化的特殊精神。这三个特点如下：

（一）普通用语

这五十个单字几乎都是最普通的用语，经常出现在我们日常生活中。在中国这些字即使小学生都认得。大部分的人对这些字虽然不一定能了解各门各派中的特殊作用，但他们都不自觉地加以运用，而又不失其哲学的意义。这和西方哲学术语大不相同，譬如西方的几个重要术语：质料（matter）、形式（form）、理念（idea）等，虽然也为普通用语，但在哲学上的意义和普通用语的意义却截然不同，完全是两个世界。一般人用到 idea 时只是泛泛地指"想法""看法"而已，完全和柏拉图或者亚里士多德所指的 idea 的没有一点点关系。而中国人一谈到仁、孝、恕、义等字，都会牵连到孔孟的思想；一谈到中、和、命、理等字也都很自然地呈现出中国特有的那套人生哲学。

关于中国哲学术语的这一特色，我们可以从三方面来了解其形成和作用：

1. 普通字语的提升

中国哲学术语都是从普通字语中加以提升的。先以这个"仁"字来说，在孔子之前，它本是指君主的爱民而已，可是经孔子的运用，把它提升了上来，具有了形而上的意义，而能一统诸德，一贯诸行。再说这个"道"字，本是指的道路，孔子把它提升上来，作为人生必须遵循的道德准则，便成为人道。老子把它提升得更高，用它来代表宇宙人生的总原理，而成为天道。

除了"仁"和"道"之外，其余如"一""命""气""理""常"等都是极普通的常用字，可是经过中国古代哲人的点化之后，都纷纷飞上枝头作了凤凰了。

2. 还归于日常生活

当这些普通用语变成了哲学术语之后，它们便带着被赋予极深刻的意义，又返回到日常生活之中，就像"仁"与"道"两字，当它们被哲学化之后，并没有被关在象牙塔内，供哲学家们玩赏；而是在实际生活中去指导人生。今天，当一个人未能尽到做人的本分，或对别人没有同情心时，我们就说他不仁。当一个人做事乖戾，违反常情时，我们就称他为无道或不讲道理。所以"仁"和"道"便成为社会生活的一种规范。

3. 两栖的性能

所谓两栖性能是指这种哲学和普通的性能交织在这些字中，非但没有相排相斥，反而是互相补充互相成就的。哲学的深意，丰富了它们的内涵，使它们的境界更高；通俗的意义，使他们易于实践，传得更广。譬如这个最普通的"人"字，本来只是指那个圆颅方趾、用两脚走路的人罢了，可是自孔子"仁者，人也"《中庸二十章》，把整个仁道注入了人字之中后，使这个"人"不再是那个与物性为伍的人了。同时，由于这个"人"字的通俗意义，也使得被深度化了的"人"，不致钻入形而上的牛角尖，而是能活生生地顾及人情、人欲。

这种两栖性能使得不懂中国哲学，或无意去作哲学思考的人，也会不自觉地触及中国哲学的精义。譬如当我们一提到"做人"时，都知道我们并不是只做个会用两脚走路，会说话的人而已，而是做一个合情、合理的人。至于如何才算是合情、合理呢？在这里，很自然地就会牵涉到儒家那套忠孝信义的思想了。因为那是中国哲学里"做人"的标准。再说这个"志"字，本是指的意志或愿望，这是每个人都懂的。可是当我们一提到立志，便把这个志立在儒家的那套人生哲学上。所谓志气便自然地灌注了孟子的"贫贱不移，威武不屈"的精神。

（二）内交于心

这些术语大部分都和心发生关联。这与西方的哲学术语不同。西方哲学术语即使和心有关的，西方哲学家们也会把它们从心中提了出来，像解剖家一样去研究、去分析。中国哲学术语和心发生关系的，有以下三个特点：

1. 转外在为内在

虽然有很多字语本来都是指外在的事物，可是经过中国哲学家们的运用后，却转向内心，和心发生关系。譬如这个"物"字，明明是指外在的物，可是中国哲学家们把它和理或欲连在一起，成为物理或物欲，于是这个物也因此而被搬入了心中。

2. 转知识为智慧或德行

术语本身的功能就是传达知识，可是当这些术语转为内在，与心沟通之后，便由知识而转为智慧或德行。譬如当中国哲学家们把"物"搬到了心中之后，明心中之理，就是明物性；除心中之欲，就是除物累。这已不是科学性的对外物的了解，而是变成内心的一种修养功夫。再如，这个"礼"字，最早是宗教的仪式，后来变成社会的制度，这都是属于外在的知识。可是到了孔子手中，这个"礼"便转向于内心，本之于"仁"。到了孟子，更认为"礼"是四端之一，而植根于心，成为仁义礼智的德行。又如，这个"虚"字，本是指外界的空旷，可是老子把它转向内心，由虚其心，而变成无欲或谦逊的德行。

3. 易于实践

当这些术语转向内在，和心发生关联之后，也就是把复杂的，难以控制的情况，转化为易于实践的行为。譬如这个"化"字本是指外在的变化而言。可是宇宙和人生的变化又是何等的复杂，何等的难以控制？但当道家把这个"化"字转向内在，而成为心中之化时，一切便可操之于心了。例如庄子要"齐万物"，可是万物参差，又如何使它们齐？于是庄子便由心中下功夫，打消分别心，以达到物化的境界。再如佛学中的"悟"字，依照印度佛教，虽然悟本是内心的作用，可是要启悟却必须研读不少佛教烦琐的经典，了解佛所说各种不可思议的法门。显然这些寄托于经典言教的研究，并不是一蹴能就的。可是中国的禅宗却把它完全转向内在，而成为明心见性的顿悟。这种不立文字，当下即得的功夫，显然把佛学的义理变得更容易实践了。

（三）沟通天人

在西方的哲学文化中，天人常是对立的。他们不是尊天贬人，便是重人抑天。可是从中国哲学术语中，却可以看出天人互成的这一特色，如：

1. 本体和现象合一

在西方哲学上，本体和现象往往被分成两截。可是在中国哲学里，本体和现象都共存于同一个术语中。在"人"之中有天，所谓"天命之谓性"（《中庸》）就是指人性中禀有天道。而在"天"之中也有人，所谓"诚者，天之道"（《中庸》）就是指天道也有人道之至诚。譬如同一个道字，一面是天之道，一面又是人之道。同一个常字，一面是永恒之道，一面又是平常之心。同一个理字，一面是太极的总原理，一面又是事物个别之理。这都说明了中国哲学术语里的体用不二的特色。

2. 人性的向上一路

寓天于人，这表示了人性中有天道、天理。只要我们在人性中下功夫，自可下学而上达，与天地合其德。中国哲学中的这些术语可以说都不是封闭式的，每个术语都开着一扇向上的天窗。譬如诚字，本是指对人的诚信，可是"诚者，天之道"（《中庸》），只要我们择善固执，便能金石为开，至诚如神。再如"忘"字，在普通用语上并不是一个讨人喜欢的字，可是庄子为它注入了道家哲学的精神，由忘己、忘物，而同于大通，让它为我们开出了一条逍遥适性，快乐无忧的通天之路。

3. 日常生活的永恒化

由于这些术语都沟通了天人，使它们在通俗意义上，成就了其永恒的一面。譬如"易"字、"化"字，都是指外在事物的变化，这本是通俗的常识，可是中国哲学家们却为它们注入了不易和永恒的血液。再如"孝"字本是指个人对父母的一种报恩的行为，但"孝"的哲学意义，却显示了生命延续的不朽性，我们在日常生活中对父母所表达的一点爱、一点敬，都只是稍纵即逝的现象而已，可是这些现象一连在"孝"字上，却都成为天地之间生生不息的永恒之道了。

五、哲学术语的传入与输出

在中国哲学的园地上，自汉末以后，传入了许多外来的哲学术语。这些术语不仅丰富了中国的思想，也改变了中国人的许多生活信念。关于它们的传入，第一次是印度的佛学；第二次是西方的哲学。它们传入的经过，正可作为中国哲学术语输出的借镜。在它们传入的过程中，大约有三种情形值得我们注意。

（一）梵文的音译

在印度佛学初传时曾经用老庄的名词来翻译佛学术语，如以道代佛，以无释空等，这称为格义之学。但到后来发现这样的翻译偏差很大，于是便产生了唐玄奘大师所谓的五种不翻，就是：秘密不翻、含多义不翻、此方所无不翻、顺于古义不翻、为生善不翻。由于这五种条件不能意译，因此只有保留梵文的音译，如佛陀、涅槃、般若、三昧、菩提、菩提萨埵（简称菩萨）等。

（二）共用中国字

玄奘大师的译例不能适用于全部的印度佛学名词。仍然有很多佛学名词合于以上五种不翻的条例，可是却被翻成了中文的意义，如法、业、戒、色、空、识、相、性……这些本来都是通俗的字语，当佛学家们借用了这些字来表达特殊的意义后，这些字便同时具有两种性能：一是中国的原意；一是佛学的意义。它们共存于一个字中，彼此并不排斥。有时候，它们同床异梦，各诉各的情；有时候也有互补的作用。譬如这个"法"字，原意为法律的法；佛学上是一切法相的法。这两层意义各有天地，而不互相排斥。再如这个"色"字，本是指颜色和美容，后来佛家借用了它去当作一切物质的代名。这两层意义本不相关，但在后来的运用上，却有相补的作用。如色相两字在佛学上是指一切物质的形色；通俗却是指美色，而美色也是佛学色相中的一种。

（三）另创新词

中国文字的衍生，为了适应广大的需要，往往由简单的字连接成复合的词。佛学的翻译家为了使印度佛学变成中国的信仰，便创造了许多新词。如解说、境界、轮回、意识、真如、因缘、无漏、烦恼、有情、众生、苦海……这些词语都是由两个单字组成，都保持了它们原来的意义，经佛学家们把它们结合成新词后，便表现了佛学的观念。这种观念可以由这两个单字的原意中获得。这种观念虽不见于佛学未传入以前的中国思想里，但在它们被运用之后，却完全融入了中国的文化和语言中，以致密不可分。

分析以上三种翻译，第一种梵文的音译，除了极少数重要的专有名词，如"佛陀""菩萨"等专有人称名词外，都不能流行于中国文化里。如"涅槃"和"般若"两词本是佛学里最重要，也最常用的术语，但它们除了在专门学术性的佛学研究及佛教上的讲经外，并没有变成纯粹的中国哲学术语而为一般人所接受，它们始终被当作印度哲学的术语。至于第二和第三种翻译，由于它们是中国原有文字的意义，因此它们都能很快和普遍地被接受，而成为中国哲学思想中的一环，直接影响了中国人的生活信念。

再看西方哲学的传入也是一样。今天除了极少数的几个音译之词如"逻辑"外，几乎都是采取第三种翻译的例子，另造新词。如哲学、本体、一元、观念、归纳、演绎、质料、形式……这些术语都是利用复合词表达西方哲学的意义。它们之中，有的仍然只用于哲学的园地如一元、本体等；有的却融入了中国的思想生活里，如观念、归纳等。

由以上的分析可以看出，在外来哲学术语的翻译中，音译始终格格不入，而由中国原来文字意义所组成的复合词却能很快融入中国哲学，甚至变成了日常用语。如"智""慧"两字，在佛学传入以前都只是指聪明而已，可是佛学家们用智慧两字去翻译般若。结果般若只用于印度学，而智慧一词却因此加深了它的意义，不仅流行于中国佛学界，而且也融入了中国人的思想信念中。

关于中国哲学术语的输出，也只是近百年来的事，由于东西思想的不同和语言文字性能的差异，在早期的翻译中，对于中国哲学术语都采取比较自由的意译。前面我们曾谈过李雅各对孔子仁的多种翻译。这一点连早期的中国学人辜鸿铭的《论语》翻译（把"仁"译为 moral life）都是如此。

最近，许多中国学人发觉这样过分自由的意译往往会错失了中国哲学的原意，所以对于重要的哲学术语纷纷保持音译，如译道为 Tao、仁为 Jen、德为 Te、气为 Ch'i、义为 I 等。

音译虽然比过分自由的意译较能不失原意，但它们和梵文的音译一样，只能用于专门学术研究的场合，而很难融入西方文化语言中，去影响他们的思想生活。

最近也有许多学者，采取比较严谨的意译，把"道"译为Way，"仁"译为Humanity等，如陈荣捷教授的《近思录》译本，《中国哲学资料》（*A Source Book in Chinese Philosophy*）等书。但这仍然都限于学术性的著作，尚未能把这些一术语推广到西方的文学、社会及日常生活中去。

六、瞻顾中国哲学在西方的发展

前面我们已经谈过在中国哲学在西传的过程中，这些一哲学术语的重要性。但还需指出的是，这些哲学术语都是生命的有机体，它们生命的泉源就是整个中国的社会文化。如果这些术语不能为社会大众所接受，不能影响他们的日常生活。它们便失去了活泉，便会老化、枯死。例如这个"孝"字，它在中国历史上是和整个中国社会文化连成一体的。但今天，我们的社会形态正逐渐在改变中，如果我们不能研究出一套方法或制度来使得孝道能继续成为我们生活之道和文化的特色，那么孝就将变为历史的名词，成为学者们概念游戏中的一颗棋子！

至于中国哲学传播到西方，这根本是一种横的移植。西方自有它们一套不同的社会文化。中国哲学的这些术语到了西方，就像飘零的花果，早已离开了根和土，又如何能生长、发展？试看中国哲学被正式介绍到西方来，也已有多年的历史了。虽然近几十年来，西方人士对中国哲学的热爱，曾一度把中国哲学的研究推上高潮。但分析他们的成就，不外于两方面：

（一）限于学术性的研究

在众多研究中国哲学的西方学者里，不能说没有杰出的人士。但他们的贡献，多属于学术性的研究。在这方面最有成就的，当然是中国哲学经典的翻译。但这些经典除了《易经》和《老子》之外，都被锁在学术的象牙塔内，而不易流行。这在中国已是如此。在民国初年就曾提倡所谓的读经运动，正是表明了大多数人的不愿研读经书。但在中国，这些经书毕竟影响了中国社会文化，因此民众虽然不能读经，但在生活信念中仍然受到这些经书的影响，同时，还有许多学者文人做了很多深入浅出的推广工作，使得多数民众仍然可以从报章杂志中接触到这方面的影响。可是这些经书翻译到了国外，便无异成为天书。因为这些经书与他们的历史、社会和文化根本不相连。他们没有生活和知识方面的基础去了解这些经书的内容。所以这些经书最多只能作为研究中国文化的学者们撰写论文的参考资料而已。这样一来，学术研究，便和社会人生脱了节。

（二）限于个人特殊的兴趣和发挥

也有一些西方人士是真正醉心于中国哲学，而用之于人生的。不过他们的兴趣多半在于《易经》、道家和禅宗方面。至于禅宗，又多半是受日本的影响。他们之中真正能契合中国哲学精神的，不能说没有，可是大多数的却是由于好奇而研究，或因一知半解而任意的发挥。举一个《易经》的例子来说，卫礼贤（Richard Wilhelm）翻译的《易经》英译本，在美国是被公认为《易经》翻译的经典之作，凡是研究《易经》的，几乎人手一册。就该书的翻译来说，除了少数错误外（如《易经·乾卦》中"大人"与"君子"的解释不分），尚称确切。但他在解释中，却常附加自己的意见而加以发挥，并没有说明"十翼"中的许多基本原理。这就现代人注解《易经》来说，也是常有的事。可是许多不明就里的《易经》读者，却用了三个铜钱卜了一卦，便依据他的解释去盲目的信从，既不能知其然，更不能知其所以然。

以上两个例子只是说明今天中国哲学在西方的发展，仍然徘徊在纸上的研究和好奇性的探索而已，尚未能真正走上极高明而道中庸的康庄之道。

今后，要如何做才能使中国哲学能够进一步地、有深度地活现在西方文化中，为大多数人所乐于囊行？显然这是一件复杂而艰巨的工作。但依笔者的看法，第一步功夫，还须在这些一重要的哲学术语上做一大转变。

这一转变，在观念上来说，就是转被动为主动。以笔者的感受，历来许多西方人士对于中国学的研究，多半都出自好奇心。十年前，中国热之所以热，是由于好奇；而今中国热似乎变冷了，也是由于好奇心的冲淡了。中国哲学在西方的发展，绝对不能只寄托于这点好奇的热心，这完全是被动的。今天我们要转被动为主动，要积极地把中国哲学融入西方文化之中。

这一转变，在实际做法上，就是先要把这些重要的中国哲学术语，转变成他们生活思想中的活语言、活文字。关于这一点，笔者有亲身的经验。笔者在美国研究所中教《老子》一课已有好几年，以前每次讲授《老子》时，对于"道"字都沿用音译"Tao"，而学生们都把这个"Tao"看作老子所专有的，因此所有的问题都是关心老子说什么。今年，笔者在老子一课中，特别用"Way"字去翻译老子的"道"字，并强调老子的"道"也是他们的"Way"。很有趣的，学生们的问题都集中于运用老子的"道"去解决他们生活中切身的问题。在这里可以看出，对他们来说，这个"Way"字远比"Tao"字更为亲切，因而更易于把握。

基于这一经验，笔者以为在西方研究中国哲学的学者们有必要共同研究出一套中国哲学术语的标准翻译。如译"道"为"Way"，"仁"为"Humanity"等。当然这样的翻译在起初的阶段也会有许多困难。如："仁"字的含义深，而 Humanity 的意义浅，把"仁"译成"Humanity"后，便容易失去"仁"字那种统摄诸德的特性。

对于这点，我们的工作不只是翻译字义而已。我们仍须致力于阐述这些术语所代表的意思，去丰富这些翻译的内容，使西方人士在 Humanity 一字上，也接触到人之所以为人之道。这也就是说把中国的这个"仁"的精神，移植到英文的 Humanity 上，使他们在 Humanity 上活现了中国仁道的思想。这样一来，在 Humanity 与仁的沟通上，他们将受到中国哲学思想的灌注，而在 Humanity 一字的反省与自觉上，他们是对他们自己生活的体验与提升。这两层意义的相融，对中国哲学来说，是完全主动地走入他们的生活中，并对其产生了指导作用。对西方文化来说，却是吸收和消化中国哲学，走上了他们自己的路子。

把中国哲学术语翻译成一种标准的英文术语，这是具体而切实的工作，只要大家同心合力，这并不困难。至于如何再进一步把中国哲学的精神注入这些术语中，使大多数人都受到影响，却有待于学者们不断地从各方面作深入浅出的推广工作。哲学术语正如花朵，必须有耐心的灌溉和培育，才能使它们永远的鲜艳和芬芳。当然这种工作不是一蹴而就的，但这总不失为一条路。中国的"道"是路，西方的"Way"也是路。只要是路，总是可以彼此沟通的，总是可以走出活路来的。

附录 2：谈中国哲学的术语与翻译

问：吴先生，您认为中国哲学在西方是否容易被接受，术语是个关键。能否请您深入分析其原因。

答：我在台湾地区教书时，并未感觉这个问题的重要，我博士论文是《〈中庸〉"诚"字的研究》，一些旅居国外的中国教授却对这篇论文产生了兴趣，像陈荣捷先生。可见在美国的中国学者常感到在其传达中国哲学的过程中，术语就像开启中国哲学之门的钥匙一样。到美国教书后，才体会到当地学生常问及中国哲学术语的关联及比较，因为他们在阅读有关中国哲学的书籍时，简直没有其他可供参考的背景，而且他们大都不认识中国字。我们读到"仁"，大约知道孔子说些什么，但此字常被译为"德"，或其他内涵极为接近的字，西方学生如果不是下过许多功夫，无法立刻加以归纳，从而得到一个较具体的概念。而中文书籍又相当难译成外文，困难之一是中国字常具多义，"仁"字有"爱""孝""悌"等相当多的内涵，所以通常是被认为是至德，统有诸善德，这样一个字如何用外文字来译呢？很多学者因此就主张用罗马拼音，我认为这当然可免去西方学者误解原意，但罗马拼音不能令人直接了解，例如"仁"拼成（jen），西方学者看到

195

这个字必须阅读过其他许多相关书籍，才知道它是什么意思。依我的看法，还是尽量译成外国字，也许这样做可能失掉一些意义，但我们可以不断予以解释、阐扬、发挥、塑造，使这个字的内涵较为接近原意，例如，"仁"译成"Humanity"，我们可以用许多文章介绍这个术语属于中国哲学中的含义，然后西方人才能在这个字中体认出一个新的、属于中国哲学内涵的意义，知道这个字代表了中国做人的道理，这个字可以说在这点上活了过来。西方人能一看就了解，这个字才能影响他们的生活，中国哲学就能进入其思想中。换句话说，我们不只是要进行重新定义的工作，还要借着大量的介绍，塑造文字的内涵，使这个字的意义更为丰富。

例如，"孝"（Filial Piety），西方通常不用，只在宗教的场合出现，本来只代表了宗教上要求对父母的敬爱，但"孝"在中文却代表了一套制度，展现出一套儒学的系统，孔子所界定的孝，在《论语》中可以找出许多含义。在西方除了一些深入研究中国哲学的学者外，一般人是不懂这个字的，这个字在西方已经逐渐失去了它的地位，甚至已毫无影响力，成了一个死字，一个只具形体毫无内含的死字。以后有可能成为大辞典上相当冷僻的字，不是学者根本没有机会接触到了。我们就可以用此字来译中文的"孝"字，这个字等于借尸还魂，成了我们的字。许多外国学生是由于我介绍中国哲学，介绍儒家思想，才知道英文中有这个字，但这时他们对这个字的了解已经是属于中国式的了，这样他们就很快能了解中国哲学的内涵。

我本打算写一部简单的、定义性的字典，来介绍中国哲学中的术语，起先当然是最简单的字："一"，然而我发现这个字没有那么简单。陈荣捷先生将此字以罗马拼音英译，并说明这是老子思想中的重点，就等于道。西方哲学术语中没有较接近的字，有一个"one"，是柏拉图、天主教中对至高无上者的称呼，中西双方的意义当然相差很大。"一"就等于道，这实在翻译得太简单，如果"一"等于道，为什么不直接说道？"天得一以清"说"天得道以清"不就可以了吗？可见"一"一定有另外的作用，不完全同于道，这些就该详细地加以解释：道是产生作用，是本体，而"一"还代表了少、无欲，"一"某方面是道，有产生的作用；另一方面表示了化至最简的作用。"一"在庄子那里，在许多其他中国古代思想家那里也都成为重要论题，如此把各家说法详细解释，就不只是单纯的定义而已。因此，可以通过对术语的解释，给西方学者归纳出一个轮廓性的概念，他们多半不可能看完中国各家各派的书，但通过这个管道，却能很快地有所了解。我计划中只是很简单的字典，后来却成为一部书，讨论五十个重要中国哲学术语。

问：从您这个想法中，中国哲学在西方可能有哪些进一步的发展，或者是否可能造成某种融合？

答：术语的英译及解释如果做得好，我相信中国哲学在西方的传播是很容易有所突破的。至于融合，就不光是学者写几本书而已，必须让内涵深入人心，影响及西方的社会、习惯、想法等各方面。写一篇关于"孝"的论文，长篇大论，影响又如何呢？必须让大多数外国人发现中国的孝有用，并且也实践了，这才算融合。我教过一位对中国哲学相当景仰的女学生，西方社会一般都是在父母年老时，将其送至养老院，这位女学生却重新将父母接回家里奉养，她说是中国哲学慢慢影响了她，这样会生活得更好。西方人也知道要爱父母，但不谈孝顺父母，中国人说"孝道"，"孝"已经成了一个大系统，所以加了一个"道"字，如果我们说这位女学生像中国人一样地爱她父母，这句话完全没有意义，西方人一定不赞同，为什么说西方人就不爱他们的父母呢？他们还写卡片、买礼物，花了很多精力呢！但如果我们说她像中国人一样地孝顺父母，能恪尽孝道，这就不同了，明显分出了东西方文化中的差异。

简单一个术语就显明其差异，可见术语影响之大。我认为中国大学的哲学系应该合作，举办一次大规模的中国哲学会议，集合大家的智慧，合力编一部《中国哲学辞典》，好好讨论其内容。目前，韦政通先生编有两部辞典，以开创的眼光而言，算是不错了，但过于简略，缺少佛学的术语，而且由于是许多学者合编，体制上的默契也不够。中国的哲学界应该像韦先生一样，重视这个问题。还要再进一步讨论英译的问题，当然总有人持不同意见，但只要参加的学者是公认优秀的，又经过大多数学者的共同讨论，这些术语的译法就具有权威性了，慢慢就能普遍化，接下来还有阐述的工作，这些学者就可以系统地介绍这些术语在各家中的发展。

问：西方有自己一套哲学思想，当我们定义中国哲学术语时，是否要完全避免引用其术语，或者少用，以免引起歧义？

答：还是可以用的。我们现在所用的西方哲学术语，例如，一元论、观念论、归纳等都可看出中国文字约略可译出其内涵，然而，如果不了解西方哲学，这些字一般人是不容易了解的。我认为外文译成中文，并不太困难，问题在译名不统一，这应该也是当务之急，我们也可以召开一次大规模的会议，讨论外国哲学术语中译的问题，集合所有学者的智慧，讨论出定译，大家就可以用同样的术语，而且也知道这个术语的内涵，不会造成类似字的混淆，如概念、观念等字。在没有统一译语之下，许多人各自用自己认可的译语，这样我们加以引用时，可能由于译语的内涵未定，而造成该术语有多重含义乃至引起歧义的可能。而如果有统一的外国哲学术语译名，这种现象就可避免。

（本访问记录是作者参加 1985 年台湾大学哲学系举办的国际中西哲学会议时由《哲学文化》杂志社所访问，原载于《哲学文化》第 139 期）

CHINESE
PHILOSOPHICAL
TERMS

PREFACE

Chao-chou Ts'ung-shen, a great Ch'an master of the T'ang Dynasty, once asked a monk, "How many sutras do you read each day?" The monk answered, "Eight or ten volumes." Chao-chou said, "You do not know how to read sutras." The monk then asked, "How many do you read?" Chao-chou replied, "I read only one word each day" (*Five Lamps Meet Together on the Source*, Chao-chou). The one word, of course, is the key word by which one can open the sutra's lock and enter the door of wisdom.

In this book, I am like a locksmith making two keys for Western readers: one is for opening the doors of Chinese philosophy and culture, and the other is for opening their minds. To make the first, I have selected fifty important Chinese philosophical terms and discussed their various meanings in the different Schools. To make the second, I have used transliterations, but only as aids to translation; *Tao*, for example, is translated as 'the Way' .

When I read this book's introduction at the Conference of Asian and Comparative Philosophy last summer, several American scholars encouraged its completion; they thought that such a work would be very useful to Western readers. Some Chinese professors considered it too difficult an undertaking for one person; however, someone had to start it. Everything is difficult in the beginning, but no beginning is nothing.

Also, some favored transliterating rather than translating words to remind readers that the terms have depths unrecognized in commonplace English equivalents, that *Tao*, for example, is more effective than 'the Way'. In discussions of this point with students, however, I remind them that even if they have a deep understanding of Lao Tzu's thought and appreciation of the mystery of *Tao*, the *Tao* is still Lao Tzu's; it cannot be internalized as the Way of their own lives. In the Ch'an School there is the story of a monk who asked Ma-tsu Tao-i, a T'ang Dynasty master, "How can I be in accord with the Way (*Tao*) ?" Ma-tsu replied, "I have already not been in accord with the Way" (*Records of Transmission of the Lamp*, Ma-tsu). The act of wanting union with the Way externalizes it; the one is made two. Thus, by translating *Tao* into 'Way', I hope that students can interpret the *Tao* of Lao Tzu as the Way of themselves. Each of the fifty single-character terms of this book opens a different door to Chinese philosophy and culture. But inside each door is simply the Way. Some understanding of this Chinese approach to Reality is my goal.

In the research and preparation of this book, I would like to thank my teacher, Professor Constant C.C. Chang, my friend,

Professor Huang Ching-hsuan, and my wife, Fang Shu, for their encouragement. Professor Ralph Metzner, Academic Dean of the California Institute of Integral Studies, has been most helpful in arranging a grant from the Kern Foundation to support the writing. And Professor Elgin Heinz, as editor, has helped to provide a bridge between the Chinese and American world views that can enable Americans to understand what Chinese philosophers meant when they used these terms and what I mean in discussing them.

EDITOR'S NOTE

Selection of terms.

A primary task in a project of this kind is selection of the terms to be discussed — a task that can be paralyzing because of the sheer numbers from which to choose. Starting with the 2,600 philosophical terms he defined recently for a comprehensive Chinese dictionary, Yi Wu first eliminated foreign terms (mostly from Indian Buddhism) that had retained their original meanings. From the remaining indigenous Chinese items, he selected, for this volume, 50 single−character terms that are conceptual keys to the ideas of major philosophers and the schools that emerged from their teaching; explication of some multiple−character terms will follow in a second volume.

Style of explication.

Chinese Philosophical Terms is unique in that the commentary on each term is written as an English analogue of a classical Chinese treatise. In its format and use of questions and quotations, it is an illustration of Chinese epistemology, not simply an expanded glossary.

Translation and transliteration.

Translation from any language into another is perilous. Words are not mathematical symbols; they are cultural symbols, each with a whole spectrum of connotations conditioned by the intersection of purpose in using the word, the user's background and emotional state, and the context in which the word is being used. Chinese is particularly difficult to translate into English because of substantially different cultural assumptions as well as multiple meanings ascribed to single terms.

Under these circumstances, many scholars carefully refrain from translating key terms. Instead, they transliterate the characters into Roman letters, assuming that frequent use in various contexts will foster the emergence of an understanding that will be more faithful to the original than specific English terms chosen as approximate equivalents. Chinese, however, is full of homonyms; use of the same transliteration for different characters can confuse the unwary. A glance at the index, for example, will show that *chih*, *i*, *shu*, and *wu* appear three times each, representing different characters with different meanings. Therefore, as explained in his introduction, Yi Wu has chosen to deal with the problems caused by translation rather than opt for transliteration which, initially easier, leaves lasting barriers to assimilation.

All translations, both of terms and illustrative quotations, have been made by Professor Wu from primary sources. Many, of course, have coincided with those of other scholars.

Procedural use of translation or transliteration.

1. In the explanatory text, translations are used for all terms except the one being discussed. Here, transliteration is used to reinforce comprehension of the term as originally understood. For example, *hsiao* is used throughout the discussion of the term translated as 'filial piety'; when there is reference to it in the discussions of other terms, it is given in translation — filial piety. All transliterations are printed in italics.

2. Similarly, in each quotation, the topical term is transliterated; other terms are translated. This encourages sensitivity to the shades of meaning within the translation finally adopted.

3. Where, for any translated term, the character or its transliteration might be in doubt, they are included parenthetically.

Elgin Heinz

CHRONOLOGY OF QUOTED PHILOS-OPHERS

Pre-Ch'in Creative Origins（722–222 B.C.：Spring & Autumn, Warring States）

Kuan Tzu 管子（Kuan Chung 管仲, d. 645 B.C.）. Legalist.

Lao Tzu 老子（Lao Tan 老聃, Li Erh 李耳, 6th cen. B.C.? and 4th cen. B.C.?）.

Central figure in Taoism.

Confucius（K'ung Fu Tzu 孔夫子, K'ung Ch'iu, 孔丘, 551–479 B.C.）. Founder of Confucianism.

Tzu Ssu 子思（492–431 B.C.）. Grandson of Confucius.

Mo Tzu 墨子（Mo Ti 墨翟, 479–381 B.C.）. Founder of Moism.

Chuang Tzu 庄子（Chuang Chou 庄周, 399–295 B.C.?）. Taoist.

Mencius（Meng Tzu 孟子, Meng K'o 孟轲, 371–289 B.C.）. Confucianist.

Hsün Tzu 荀子（Hsün Ch'ing 荀卿, fl. 298–238 B.C.）. Confucianist.

Han Fei 韩非（d. 233 B.C.）. Legalist.

Han-T'ang Continuity and Change（206 B.C.–907 A.D.）

Tung Chung-shu 董仲舒（176–104 B.C.）. Confucianist.

Yang Hsiung 杨雄（53 B.C.–18 A.D.）. Confucianist.

Wei Po-yang 魏伯阳（fl. 147–167）. Taoist（Immortalist）.

Ho Yen 何晏（195–249）. Taoist（Mystery）.

Chung Hui 钟会（225–264）. Taoist（Mystery）.

Wang Pi 王弼（226–249）. Taoist（Mystery）

Ko Hung 葛洪（Pao-p'u-tzu 抱朴子, 250–330?）. Taoist（Immortalist）.

Chih Tao-lin 支道林（314–366）. Buddhist.

Tao-sheng 道生（372–434）. Buddhist.

Seng-chao 僧肇（384–414）. Buddhist.

Bodhidharma（P'u-t'i-ta-mo 菩提达摩, arrived 520?–d.536?）. Indian Buddhist.

Hui-k'e 慧可（487–593）. Ch'an Master.

Tao-hsin 道信（580–651）. Ch'an Master.

Fa-jung 法融（594–657）. Ch'an Master.

Shen-hsiu 神秀（606–706）. Ch'an Master.

Hui-neng 慧能（638–713）. Ch'an Master.

Shen-hui 神会（668–760）. Ch'an Master.

Chao-chou 赵州（Ts'ung-shen 从稔, 778–897）. Ch'an Master.

Kuei-fêng 圭峰（Tzung-mi 宗密, 780–841）. Ch'an Master.

Sung-Ch'ing Integration（979-1912）

Shao Yung 邵雍（Shao K'ang-chieh 邵康节，1011-1077）. Neo-Confucianist.

Chou Tun-Yi 周敦颐（Chou Lien-hsi 周濂溪，1017-1073）. Neo-Confucianist.

Chang Tsai 张载（Chang Heng-chu 张横渠，1020-1077）. Neo-Confucianist.

Ch'eng Hao 程颢（Ch'eng Ming-tao 程明道，1032-1085）. Neo-Confucianist.

Ch'eng I 程颐（Ch'eng I-chuan 程伊川，1033-1107）. Neo-Confucianist.

Chang Tzu-yang 张紫阳（?-1082）. Taoist（Immortalist）.

Chu Hsi 朱熹（Chu Yuan-hui 朱元晦，1130-1200）.

Neo-Confucianist.

Lu Hsiang-shan 陆象山（Lu Chiu-yuan 陆九渊，1139-1193）. Neo-Confucianist.

Wu-men 无门（Hui-k'ai 慧开，1183-1260）. Ch'an Master.

Wen Tien-hsiang 文天祥（1236-1282）. Neo-Confucianist.

Wang Yang-ming 王阳明（Shou-jen 王守仁，1472-1529）. Neo-Confucianist.

Chu Yün-yang 朱云阳（Ch'ing Dynasty; commentary published *circa* 1725）.

211

Taoist（Immortalist）.

Tai Chen 戴震（Tai Tung-yüan 戴东原，1723-1777）. Neo-Confucianist.

INTRODUCTION

Rationale.

To write an explication of Chinese philosophical terms, even in Chinese, is a challenging project. There are scholarly analyses of particular terms, such as *jen* (仁, humanity)and *i* (义, righteousness), but there has been a gap between these and the compressed generalizations of conventional dictionaries. To try to fill the gap in English rather than in Chinese requires not only a charting of unexplored territory but the additional hazards of dealing with a second language. Words that have one-to-one equivalence in denotation, for example, may have positive implications in one language and negative implications in the other.

I first became aware of the need for such a dictionary fifteen years ago when writing my dissertation on 'sincerity' in the *Doctrine of the Mean*. Although 'sincerity' played a very important role in Confucianism, no systematic explication existed. The profound insights of some philosophers into this and other terms were only hinted at in cryptic commentaries. I resolved to select key terms from major texts for analysis and explanation. The present project is the result, stimulated and modified by the needs of students in my classes in the United States.

Since coming to the United States in 1977, I have been teaching courses on Lao Tzu, Chuang Tzu, Confucianism, and the *Book of Changes*. The translations available as texts present three problems to students who cannot read the originals:

1. Translations vary widely (sometimes, wildly). Students have no way of knowing which translations use terms recognizably related to the original and which reflect personal idiosyncrasies of the translators.

2. The nature of the Chinese language is such that any given term can have several valid meanings, even in the same context. For instance, Lao Tzu said, "The *Tao* that can be talked about is not the *ch'ang Tao*" (*Lao Tzu*, Ch. 1). *Ch'ang* has several common meanings, such as 'often', 'regular', 'ordinary', and 'constant'. In philosophy, it refers to 'eternity', 'true life', 'harmony', 'natural', 'human nature', 'nature of all things', 'true substance' and 'ordinary mind'. It has been translated as 'eternal' (John C. H. Wu), 'enduring and unchanging' (James Legge), 'permanent' (J. J. L. Duyvendak), 'absolute' (Lin Yu-tang), 'infinite' (Bhikshu Wai-tao and Dwight Goddard), 'everlasting' (Men-jan Cheng), 'unvarying' (Arthur Waley), 'all-embracing' (Edward H. Parker), 'true' (Walter Gorn Old), 'itself' (Chang Chung-

214

yuan), and so on. Each of these expresses a meaning of *ch'ang*, but no translation can include all of its meanings; accuracy of choice depends on the translator's understanding of what the term meant to the philosopher who used it.

3. Often, translations are inconsistent. Where *ch'ang* appears in several places in the Chinese text, each time with the same meaning, it may be translated in one place as 'eternity', as 'constant' in another, and omitted entirely in a third. It is impossible for a Western student to make comparisons, statistical analyses, or even frequency counts that are simple in Chinese.

The final inducement to work on this project of explaining essential Chinese philosophical terms in English came last year, when I was invited by a publisher in Taiwan to edit the Chinese philosophy and Buddhism sections of a large Chinese dictionary. To make them reasonably comprehensive, I selected and defined about 2600 entries. Although all are useful to Chinese readers, direct translations would be too terse and take too much for granted to serve the needs of Western students.

Approach.

My original intent was to provide a succinct definition of each term, followed by a few illustrative quotations. However, the inadequacy of this procedure soon became evident. What would Western readers really understand when told only that *i* (一, one) is produced by *Tao* or is equal to *Tao*, even if they are given the quotations, "*Tao* brings forth one. One brings forth two. Two bring forth three. Three bring forth all things" (*Lao Tzu*, ch. 42), and "Those of ancient times attained *i*. Heaven attained *i* and became clear; Earth attained *i* and became calm; spirits attained *i* and had divinity; the valley attained *i* and became full; all things attained *i* and had lives; dukes and kings attained *i* and became the models of the world. All was achieved by *i*" (*Lao Tzu*, Ch. 39) ? After reading these quotations, they would wonder why *Tao* produced *i* and what the relationship is between them. If *i* is equal to *Tao*, why did Lao Tzu not use *Tao* directly without substituting *i*? If they looked in a Western dictionary of philosophy, such as that edited by Dagobert D. Runes, they would find that there also is a 'one' in Western philosophy that was used as "the Supreme Idea (Plato), the absolute first principle (Neo-Platonism), the universe (Parmenides), Being-as-such and divine in nature (Plotinus), God (Nicolaus Cusanus), the soul (Lotze)" (Runes, *Dictionary of Philosophy*, 15th ed., p. 219) . Questions about relationships between *i* and 'one' would be compounded. It is impossible to make even simple comparisons unless the various meanings of *i* to different philosophers and in different schools are explained. Therefore, I have tried to provide a context for each of the selected terms.

In general, the definition of each character has included four elements:

1. The recognition of various meanings ascribed not only in different schools but by different philosophers in the same school. For example, the character *te* (德, virtue) has different meanings in Confucianism and Taoism. In the former, it refers to morality, ethics, and good social conduct; in the latter, it refers to desirelessness of mind. *Jo* (弱, weakness) is a key idea in the *Lao Tzu*, but it is not mentioned in the *Chuang Tzu*. In the definitions, meanings cited most frequently are from Confucianism, Taoism, and the Ch'an School.

2. The treatment of each character as a living idea that has developed from simple to complex and from common to philosophical usage. For instance, *li* (理, principle) originally meant to work on jade. Pre-Ch'in Confucianists such as Confucius, Mencius, and Hsün Tzu used it in reference to reason or to a principle that meant the right way or the correct action. Neo-Confucianists, however, made it a fundamental idea. They not only enriched its connotations, they used it as a defense against Buddhist thought.

3. Comparisons and couplings with other terms. Although each character can be defined individually, its usage in compound terms and comparisons clarifies both meaning and function. A typical example of this is *shu* (恕, empathy) . It is always connected with *chung* (忠, loyalty) as a compound word, *chung-shu*, in which it is *shu* that is emphasized. Comparison with 'compassion', 'forgiveness', and 'altruism' not only shows the inadequacy of the English terms as synonyms but also suggests that the concept of *shu* can enrich Western interpersonal relationships.

4. The term in its cultural context. Rather than being abstract formal statements, definitions tend to become brief informal essays, because it is only in a context that terms come to life. For example, explanation of *li* (礼, propriety/rite) involves not only an analysis of its different meanings in Con-fucianism, Moism, and Taoism and its social functions, but also a discussion of the relationships between *li* and religion, education, and society.

Characteristics shared by the selected terms.

At the outset, the fifty single-character terms of this volume were selected solely on the basis of their importance in Chinese philosophy. However, review of the completed definitions reveals an interesting byproduct — major characteristics of the individual terms are also the essential characteristics of Chinese philosophy in general and, in fact, of Chinese culture itself. There seem to be three reasons for this: the terms have retained a relationship with the vocabulary of common usage, they are internalized and interrelated, as shown by the idea of 'mind', and they concern the interlinking of Heaven with humankind:

1. Unlike Western philosophy, in which terms frequently are given meanings unrelated to those of common usage, most Chinese philosophical terms not only are derived from the language of everyday life but simply elevate the words conceptually without losing their ordinary meanings. For example, in English we commonly use 'idea' as an aspect of thinking, whereas Plato, Aristotle, Berkeley, and Kant used it as a construct in their theoretical systems. The Chinese process can be illustrated by reference to the key ideas of *jen* (仁, humanity) and *Tao* (道, Way) . Before Confucius, *jen* was a common word that referred to love for people. Confucius made it the paramount virtue of his philosophy, and Mencius established a theory of human nature for it. *Tao*, too, was a common word, referring to the road or the way. Confucius made it the "proper" way that we must follow, and Lao Tzu took it into the realm of metaphysics, making it the key idea of Taoism. Other terms that were philosophized in the same way include *i* (一, oneness), *ming* (命, life), *ch'i* (气, energy), *li* (理, principle), *ch'ang* (常, constancy), and *jo* (弱, weakness) .

Terms can move in both directions. Conceptually enriched, they return to everyday use with general recognition of their new significance. There is no discrimination or mutual exclusivity between the two realms. For example, the character *jen* (人, human being) commonly refers to people in general; philosophically, it refers to an ideal of humanity and is regarded as the same as *jen* (仁, humanity) . Both meanings are in common use; the idiom *tso jen* (做人) refers to man in the ideal sense. Thus, if a man is unkind or without compassion, we say that he is not *jen*. In this way, *jen* became the standard of social behavior. In a sense, the term is amphibious, equally at home in the water of common usage and the atmosphere of philosophical thought.

This "amphibian" characteristic has a significant by-product: whenever one of these terms is used in ordinary communication, its philosophical meaning is present as an enriching overtone. *Jen* (人, human being) is a common word, but when we talk about being a man, we become involved with such basic Confucian virtues as humanity, righteousness, loyalty and filial piety. The common meaning of *chih* (志) is will, purpose, or ambition; but its overtones are altruistic rather than selfish. Talk of establishing *chih* always implies a great goal for helping people or the duty of spreading the thoughts of ancient sages. The ordinary sense of *jo* (弱, weakness) is negative, but Lao Tzu's "The soft and weak can overcome the hard and strong" (Ch. 36) has become a familiar saying.

2. A second shared characteristic of these terms is their relationship to 'mind' (心, *hsin*) . Western terms seem to be abstracted from reality much as the Western study of anatomy separates organs from the living organism. In the West, 'mind' is a convenient term for cerebral storage or function. In China, however, *hsin* is the fusion of intellect, spirit, and feeling or 'heart' — qualities that, in the West, are categorically separate and compartmentalized. To think of *hsin* as one's 'heart-of-hearts' helps us to understand the Chinese meaning of mind. Even terms that originally concerned only external aspects of reality have been internalized and interrelated by Chinese philosophers. For example, the character *wu* (物, thing) that typically refers to objects was internalized by thinking of things as made of the same substance as human beings or relating them to desire or principle.

Internalization was aided by the distinction between knowledge and wisdom, between data accumulation and insight developed through 'cultivation of mind'. When ancient Chinese philosophers connected things with principle or desire, then, knowing the principle of things became wisdom, and purification of desires became a way of cultivating the mind.

Internalization of terms often transformed them into virtues. *Li* (礼, propriety/rite) originally referred to the rules of society; after Confucianists related it to mind, it became a principle of morality. *Hsu* (虚) originally meant emptiness or void; after Taoists internalized it, it became the virtue of humility or desirelessness.

Internalizing such terms was equivalent to humanizing them; they became amenable to understanding and practice. *Hua* (化) originally meant the changes of the universe, impossible for us to control. But the Taoists internalized *hua* and made it a transformation of mind. Thus, Chuang Tzu's "equalization of all things" means that one's mind is beyond things or is not attached to relativity, not that all things are caused to be equal. *Wu* (悟), in most Buddhist thinking, means to awaken the *dharma*, a complex process of textual study and ritual activity; so, it is difficult to become a Buddha. In the Chinese Ch'an School, however, *wu* was internalized and became the direct seeing of original mind (sudden enlightenment) . Therefore, one's original mind or nature is enlightened, and one becomes a Buddha immediately.

3. The third characteristic these basic terms seem to have in common is the assumption that there is a complementary relationship between Heaven and humankind as parts of a single reality. In much of Western philosophy and culture, Heaven and human beings seem, if not actually in opposition, to be separate entities in an either–or relationship: either respect Heaven and subordinate man, or make man primary and control Heaven.

In Western philosophy, metaphysics and phenomena occupy two different categories; but, in Chinese philosophy, they coexist. For example, in *jen* (人, human being) there is the nature of Heaven, and in *t'ien* (天, Heaven) there is the virtue of man. In the *Analects*, Confucius did not talk about Heaven because, in his thought, *jen* (仁, humanity) is the way of Heaven. Neo–Confucianists emphasize the Heavenly principle, *t'ien li* (天理), which is in the mind of man and pervades everything.

With Heaven in human nature, if one cultivates one's mind, one will attain the supreme state. For example, *shen* (神, spirit) means both the spirit of man and spiritual beings such as God and the gods as well as immortality. Only by cultivating one's own spirit can one become immortal. Again, *ch'eng* (诚, sincerity) includes two Ways, the Way of Heaven and the Way of man. By practicing the Way of man, which requires sincerity in learning, working, and dealing with others, one would naturally attain the Way of Heaven. With Heaven existing in man, with the highest state abiding within the ordinary, cultivation begins in common activities. Although *jen* (仁, humanity) is the highest state of Confucianism, its practice begins in the activities of daily life.

As an extension of seeing Heaven and humankind as one, all things and all persons become everlasting. Although *ch'ang* (常) refers commonly to the ordinary, in the *Lao Tzu* it acquired the meaning of constancy or eternity, with the implication that only the ordinary can be everlasting. In the same way, *i* (易, change) and *hua* (化, transformation) are common ideas, but Chinese philosophers made them changeless and the essence of the universe.

Planting the seeds of Chinese philosophical terms in Western culture.

In bringing Chinese philosophical terms to the West, it may be instructive to review the introduction of Sanskrit Buddhist terms to China. Both the ideas and the language of Indian Buddhism were completely alien. In the beginning, translators simply substituted Taoist approximations for Buddhist terms. Thus Buddha became *Tao* and *nirvana* became *wu-wei* (无为, non-action). This was a facile solution but as confusing to the Chinese as when Christian missionaries tried the same tactic sixteen hundred years later, substituting *Shang-ti*（上帝）for 'God'.

The greatest translator of Indian Buddhist *sutras*, the T'ang Dynasty monk Hsüan-tsang, established a rule that there were five kinds of terms that should be transliterated rather than translated: the esoteric, those with several meanings, those without Chinese equivalents, old and established terms, and those that would arouse feelings of faith or goodness in the minds of those who heard the sounds of Sanskrit. There are, therefore, many transliterations in Chinese Buddhist literature, such as *nirvana*, *samädhi*, *bodhi*, *bodhisattva*, *Buddha*, *sangha*, *and prajña*.

Many Buddhist terms, of course, did not fall into Hsüan Tsang's categories, and were translated. For words that did not have direct equivalents, one procedure was to select Chinese terms that already had clusters of related meanings and add Buddhist meanings without attempting to usurp or disturb the existing Chinese interpretations. Examples include *dharma*（法，*fa*），*karma*（业，*yeh*），*sila*（戒，*chieh*），*rupa*（色，*se*），*sunya*（空，*k'ung*），*vijnana*（识，*shih*），*laksana*（相，*hsiang*），and *svabhava*（性，*hsing*）.

The other device most frequently used was to create new terms that were compounds of two existing characters. These include *chih-hui*（智慧，wisdom），*chieh-t'o*（解脱，liberation），*ching-chieh*（境界，State），*lun-hui*（轮回，transmigration），*i-shih*（意识，consciousness），*chen-ju*（真如，truth），*yin-yuan*（因缘，cause，condition），*wu-lou*（无漏，pas-sionless，'non-leaking'），*fan-nao*

（烦恼, trouble）, *chung-shen*（众生 all beings）, *yu-ch'ing*（有情, sentient being）, and *k'u hai*（苦海, ocean of misery, this world）. Such new creations enriched the Chinese language. Translation of Western terms in this century has followed the same system of compounding. "Philosophy" was translated into *che hsüeh*（哲学, wise learning）, "metaphysics" into *hsing-shang hsüeh*（形而上学, beyond-form learning）, "ontology" into *pen-t'i lun*（本体论, original substance discussion）, "monism" into *i-yuan lun*（一元论, single be-ginning discussion）, "idea" into *kuan nien*（观念, contemplation）, and "induction" into *kuei na*（归纳, merging, acceptance）. Although some of these terms, both Buddhist and Western, are used only in philosophical discourse, some have become part of the common vocabulary.

Examining these three methods of introducing Sanskrit terminology, we find, first, that transliterations, with the exception of a few important categorical terms such as *Buddha*（佛, *fo*）, *bodhisattva*（菩萨, *p'u-sa*）, and *sangha*（僧, *seng*）, have not been popular. *Nirvana* and *prajña*, for instance, although key ideas, were and are used only in academic studies of Buddhism. Chinese Buddhists and philosophers have used *chih hui*（智慧）for *prajña*, even though it is not a precise equivalent; they added connotations of wisdom to differentiate the term from the pre-existing Chinese meaning of *chih hui* as "intelligence". Although, in Chapter 18 of the *Lao Tzu*, *hui* and *chih* occur together as benevolence and intelligence, but with negative connotations, Indian Buddhism can be credited with intro-ducing a new concept with the *chih hui* compound. This and the other translated terms, whether single character or compound, have been completely assimilated into Chinese literature, philosophy, culture, and daily life.

Can Chinese philosophical terms be introduced to and assimilated by the West in the same way that China assimilated Sanskrit and Western terms? A serious barrier exists in the difference between Western and Chinese conceptualizations of philosophy. Western philosophy is expressed in systematic theories. Epistemology, for instance, deals with knowledge as abstractions explained by logical reasoning. Translated into Chinese, it is easy to understand because of this precision. However, Chinese philosophy deals with the "cultivation of mind" and practice in daily life. Terms are defined, not as abstractions, but as experiential activities. They are culture-bound, requiring not only shared experience for understanding, but shared interpretations of experience.

Introduction of Chinese philosophy through its termin-ology requires, I think, two approaches that have been guiding principles in writing this book, (1) standardization of translations and (2) seeing terms as they have been used in their living cultural context.

All Chinese and Western scholars concerned with transmission of philosophies across cultural boundaries should collaborate to construct a list of standardized translations. Although some scholars might not agree with all of the translations, a consensus would provide enormous benefits of clarification (if in no other way, by requiring dissidents to justify their variant versions). This, after all, is simply a conscious replication, on a small scale, of the process of arriving at the commonly agreed−on meanings of all words that enables us to communicate with each other. In establishing the list, I suggest translating the Chinese terms into single or compound English words, subordinating transliteration. There are at least three reasons for this:

First, although some of the translations will lose some of the meanings of the original, transliteration would not solve the problem. For example, *ch'i* is difficult to translate into English but, except for scholars, most Westerners who use the transliteration understand only the Taoist yoga or Chinese medical meaning of *ch'i*, overlooking its meaning in Confucianism. *Tao* is another term that presents the same problem.

Second, it is difficult to differentiate between words that have the same pronunciation but different characters and meanings such as *li* (礼, propriety) and *li* (理, principle), *i* (一, oneness) and *i* (义, righteousness), and *jen* (仁, humanity) and *jen* (人, human being).

Third, as the Chinese experience with Sanskrit has shown, it would be difficult to merge transliterations with English in a way that would be acceptable and comfortable for most people. The transliterated word is like an immigrant who insists on using only his native language, refusing to communicate in the language of his adopted country. Even if there are differences of meaning between the Chinese term and the English word into which it is translated, the meanings will coexist and both will be enriched, just as the translation of *dharma* as *fa* added new meaning to *fa* without interfering with its original usage. If we translate *jen* into 'humanity', even though 'humanity' cannot encompass all of the meanings of *jen* in the beginning, its continued use by scholars will gradually enrich it with connotations of *jen*.

Even more important than agreeing on definitions is to understand the terms in their living cultural context. A standardized word list is merely a heap of dry bones, however carefully articulated. The bones must be suffused with marrow and surrounded by blood and flesh. I have long felt that any real meeting of Western and Chinese cultures must be through living ideas and the people who practice them; otherwise, linguistic and academic studies are empty discourse. If Chinese philosophy cannot be introduced in a way that will encourage people in general to understand and practice it, our efforts will result only in word games.

An example of a term that could be a model of the cultural approach is *shu* (恕, empathy). Western scholars have given little attention to *shu*, knowing it only from translations of the *Four Books* and a brief explanation in Fung Yu-lan's *History of Chinese Philosophy*, not recognizing it as the foundation of Chinese thought and behavior.

Shu resembles the compassion of Buddhism and the forgiveness of Christianity, yet differs from both. Comparison of *shu* with compassion and forgiveness will help us to understand and accept all three concepts. Immediately and experientially applicable to the solving of social problems, *shu* could be a pragmatic aid in dealing with the generation gap, social alienation, and ideological controversy. Professor C. C. Chang, my mentor at the National Normal University in Taiwan, initiated a movement toward universal harmony through the practice of *shu*. I hope that this explication of basic terms can lay some of the groundwork for support of this new development.

1. 一 (*i*) ONE/ONENESS

I means 'one', which, in Chinese philosophy, is used to describe the essence, the function, and the practice of the Way (道 *Tao*) . In Taoism, the Way is formless and transcendental; it cannot be described or manipulated; therefore, Chinese philosophers always have taken *i* as symbolic of the Way. For example: "Those of ancient time attained *i*. Heaven attained *i* and became clear; Earth attained *i* and became calm; spirits attained *i* and had divinity; the valley attained *i* and became full; all things attained *i* and had lives; dukes and kings attained *i* and became the models of the world. All was achieved by *i*... Therefore, the superior has the inferior as its root; the high regards the low as its foundation. Therefore, dukes and kings call themselves 'the helpless one', 'the little one', and 'the worthless one' . Is this not regarding the inferior as the root? Or is it not? Thus, those who seek honor have no honor. We prefer to be not so rare as jade or hard as rocks" (*Lao Tzu*, Ch. 39) .

In the first lines of the chapter, Lao Tzu used *i* as equivalent to the Way. We can change *i*' into 'the Way' . Why, then, did Lao Tzu use *i* instead of the Way? It was because, in the last part of the chapter, he wanted to emphasize humility and freedom from desire. The word 'Way' symbolizes the highest statement of a principle; but the implications of humility and desirelessness are not immediately apparent. Lao Tzu used *i* because, on one hand, it symbolizes the Way by connotations of beginning, unity, and wholeness and, on the other hand, connotations of low or few, symbolizing humility and desirelessness.

Oneness plays many roles in Chinese philosophy, most notably in conceptualizing creativity, unification, and fund a−mental principle.

1) Bringing forth

"The Way brings forth *i*. *I* brings forth two. Two bring forth three. Three bring forth all things" (*Lao Tzu*, Ch. 42) . " The Way brings forth all things" (*Lao Tzu*, Ch. 51) . "All things in the world are brought forth in Being, and Being is brought forth in Non−Being" (*Lao Tzu*, Ch. 40) . But how could the Way produce all things? How could Being be produced by Non−Being? Lao Tzu used *i* to resolve this paradox, because *i* is the bridge between Being and Non−Being. Thus, in the Way's productivity, the first step is *i*. Through *i*, there are two — the relative principles or energies of dark (阴, *yin*) and light (阳, *yang*) .

2) Unification

"…Because of this, whether a beam or a pillar, a leper or the beautiful Hsi-shih, or things exaggerated or strange, the Way makes them *i*. Their apparent dividedness is their achievement; but this achievement is their destruction. Things are neither differentiated nor destroyed; they return to *i*" (*Chuang Tzu*, Ch. 2) . Thus, all of the different things are *i*. "…Who takes in ten thousand ages and becomes pure *i*" (*Chuang Tzu*, Ch. 2) . Thus, all time is *i*. "Be content with what has been arranged and go along with change; then we can enter infinite Heaven and become *i*" (*Chuang Tzu*, Ch. 6) . Thus, Heaven and man are *i*.

3) Fundamental principle

"The movements of everything under the sky are constantly made firm (properly coordinated) by *i*" (*Book of Changes*, "Great Appendix", Sec. 2) . Here, *i* is the principle which is the supreme and basic rule that permeates all movements, becoming many different rules. This *i*, in the *Book of Changes*, is called the Supreme Ultimate (太极, *T'ai Chi*) . For example, "Therefore, in The Change (the Way of Changes) there is the Supreme Ultimate which produced the Two Forms. Those Two Forms produced the Four Images which produced the Eight Trigrams" (*Book of Changes*, "Great Appendix", Sec. 1, Ch. 11) . The Neo-Confucianists of the Sung Dynasty always took the Supreme Ultimate as *i*. For example, "The Supreme Ultimate is *i*, which is un-moving tranquility. It brings forth two which have creative power" (Shao Yung, *Treatise on the Contemplation of*

Things) .

In the practice of the Way, *i* is used in at least six ways by various Chinese philosophers:

1) Embracing *i*

"Both spirit and body embrace *i*; can they be separated from it?" (*Lao Tzu*, Ch. 10) Here *i* means the Way. Lao Tzu used the word "embrace" to mean making yourself one with the Way. In other words, whatever you do, you must follow the Way.

2) Uniting *i*

"Heaven and Earth were born at the same time with me; the ten thousand things are one with me" (*Chuang Tzu*, Ch. 2) . "If you look at them from the standpoint of their differences, even the liver and gall in your own body are as different as the states of Ch'u and Yüeh. But if you look at them from the viewpoint of their sameness, even the ten thousand things are *i*" (*Chuang Tzu*, Ch. 5) . Chuang Tzu thought that the Way permeates all things, and all things live in the Way. Therefore, if we are able to understand that all things are one with us, we really live in the Way.

3) Performing all actions in *i*

Confucius said, "Ts'an, my way is to perform all actions in *i*." Ts'an Tzu said, "Yes." After Confucius went out, the disciples asked him, "What did he say?" Ts'an Tzu answered, "The way of our master is only loyalty (*chung*) and empathy (*shu*) (*Analects*, IV, 15) . Confucius did not emphasize *i* as the Taoists did, and he did not tell us what *i* is. But, according to his thinking, humanity (*jen*) is the key virtue or central idea, equivalent to *i*. He emphasized that those who practice humanity will be filial to their parents, loyal to their superiors, kind to others, and sincere in all things with which they are concerned.

4) Concentrating on *i*

"To renounce evil is to live naturally in *i*. If you concentrate on *i*, then you do not need to pay attention to renouncing evil. Some think that *i* is difficult to see and inaccessible to practice. What do you think? In my opinion, *i* is simply seeing clearly with an attentive mind. *I* is without wrong or evil. If you cultivate it in your mind for a long time, you will naturally manifest the heavenly principle" (Chu Hsi, *Reflections on Things at Hand*, Ch. 4, Ch'eng I) . Ch'eng I, a Sung Dynasty Neo−Confucianist, emphasized the method of concentrating on Oneness, by which your mind, whatever you do, is constantly focused on goodness and follows the principle without deviation. Most of the Neo−Confucianists, particularly the philosophers of the School of Principle, used concentration on *i* as their central method of cultivating the mind.

5) Desireless *i*

"Can we learn to become sages? The answer is, 'We can'. Is there any best method? The answer is, 'There is'. What is it? The answer is, '*I* is the best method. *I* is desireless'" (Chou Tun−i, *Book of Penetration*) . Chou Tun−i, a Sung Dynasty Neo−Confucian, took over this concept from Taoism, in which *i* meant purification from desire.

6) To what does *i* return

A monk asked, "It is said that the ten thousand *dharmas* return to *i*; to where does *i* return?" Chao Chou answered, "When I was in Ching−chou, I made a robe of cotton cloth that weighed seven *catties*" (*Records of the Trans-mission of the Lamp*, Chao Chou) . Chao Chou, a T'ang Dynasty Ch'an master, answered the monk's question with an irrelevance to indicate that the question was meaning−less. *I* is beyond all things and cannot be attributed or subordinated to something else. What is the *i* to which all *dharmas* return? We cannot get an answer because this is a question that we cannot ask. Generally speaking, in Buddhism *i* symbolizes the true−suchness which is the ultimate *dharma*; in the Chinese Ch'an School, it always means the True Mind. It is not necessary to discuss the True Mind at this point. What we emphasize here is that the Ch'an masters always use the puzzle, "The ten thousand *dharmas* return to *i*; to where does *i* return?" as a device to prod students toward enlightenment.

2. 人 (*jen*) HUMAN BEING/MAN/ PEOPLE

The character *jen*, meaning "human being" is derived from a picture of the human body. In Chinese philosophy, its meaning varies with the school in which it is used.

1) Jen in Confucianism

The human being always is regarded as the center of the universe. "*Jen* is the expression of the virtue of Heaven and Earth, the intersection of dark (*yin*) and light (*yang*), the meeting place of ghosts (demons) and gods (spirits), and the vital energy (*ch'i*) of the five elemental movements or agents of all phenomena (*wu hsing*)" (*Record of Rites*, The Move−ment of Rites) . "The virtue of Heaven and Earth" means that the *jen* was given the responsibility to produce or give life to all things. "The intersection of dark and light" means that the *jen*, in the harmony of dark and light, begins the development of the universe. "The meeting of ghosts and gods" means that the *jen* has a soul, and his spirit can be immortal. "The vital energy of the five movements" means that *jen* is the best product of the five elemental movements and is the most intelligent of creatures. From these state-ments, we find that, in Confucian thought, *jen* is different from the animal and can cultivate himself to be in accord with Heaven. Confucianists know that *jen* has desires that are not good, but they face these desires and try to resolve them harmoniously or convert them to constructive purposes. Thus, in Confucian thought, *jen* is crucially important; only through his nature can the development of the universe be forwarded.

2) Jen in Taoism

Jen is regarded as one element or stage in the changes of the universe. The *Chuang Tzu*, especially, emphasizes the difference between the Heavenly and the human in the passage, "That the ox and the horse have four feet is called Heavenly; that the horse's head is put in a halter and the ox's nose is pierced is called *jen*" (*Chuang Tzu*, Ch. 17). Here, Chuang Tzu means that the natural is Heavenly and the man-made or artificial is human. Thus, in Chuang Tzu's thought, if *jen* follows nature, he will be a perfect or true man; otherwise, he will suffer from being limited by his physical body and bounded by his desires.

3) Jen in Chinese Buddhism

Especially in the Ch'an school, *jen* is generally defined as in Taoist thought. "All *sutras* and all words of the Mahayana and

Hinayana Schools as well as the twelve sections of the Classics were written for *jen*... Common people are Buddha, and feeling troubled is enlightenment. A confused passing thought makes one a common person, while an enlightened second thought makes one a Buddha" (*Platform Scripture by the Sixth Patriarch*, hereafter, *Platform Scripture*, Ch. 2) . Thus, there is no difference between *jen* and a Buddha — *jen* can become a Buddha by his sudden enlightenment.

From these quotations, we find that *jen* is a conceptual foundation in Chinese philosophical systems. Although schools differ, they all agree that human nature has elements of goodness and virtue that, if developed, can make one a sage, a true man, or a Buddha. For this reason, Chinese say "be *jen*." Although we are now *jen* which are incomplete, by cultivating our mind and practicing morality, we could be ideal *jen*.

3. 天（*t'ien*）HEAVEN/SKY

"... the top; the highest point, without anything above it; constructed from *i*（one）and *ta*（great）"（Hsü Shen, *Explanation of Script and Elucidation of Characters*, hereafter, Hsü Shen, *Explanation*）. *T'ien* is that which is the highest and greatest in the universe. But *t'ien* takes both form and meaning from humanity(*jen*); so, Heaven has a relationship with mankind that results in many special usages. Besides the common meaning of sky, *t'ien* has at least six connotations in Chinese thought:

1）Ultimate Authority

"I, Duke Chou, am but a small man and dare not issue commands in place of God. *T'ien* blesses King Wen and helps our small State to rise"（*Book of History*, Vol. 13, The Great Announcement）. Here, *t'ien* is interpreted as a God that has ultimate authority and can control people's fates. This conceptualization of *t'ien* was the norm up to and during the Chou Dynasty. After Chou, many philosophers considered *t'ien* to be supreme or ultimate virtue, but the popular belief in an authoritarian *t'ien* persisted. Depending on the context, the popular *t'ien* was interpreted as God, personified gods, the Creator, or the highest Spirit.

2) **Greatest Virtue**

"The greatest virtue of *t'ien* and Earth is productivity —— the giving of life" (*Book of Changes*, Great Appendix, Sec. 2, Ch. 1). Productivity originally meant the function of creation by *t'ien*; but, here, the author has converted it into the virtue of *t'ien* — which gives life to all things everlastingly.

3) **Material Nature**

"The movement of *t'ien* has its regular way. It does not exist for the sake of sage−king Yao nor does it cease to exist because of the evil king Chieh. If you respond to it with good government, you will get good fortune; otherwise, you will meet with misfortune" (Hsün Tzu, *On Heaven*) . Hsün Tzu, living at the very end of the Warring States period (480−222 B.C.), before the establishment of the Ch'in empire, was one of the few Confucianists who emphasized the importance of material nature and urged people to participate in its functions.

4) **The life of Nature**

"He who knows how *t'ien* acts and man acts is perfect. He who knows how *t'ien* acts will live according to *t'ien*" (*Chuang Tzu*,

Ch. 6) . Although, in the thought of Chuang Tzu, *t'ien* sometime meant nature, more often it was seen as transcendental, having an existence beyond our knowledge. We can act in harmony with this transcendental Nature by the cultivation of mind.

5) The highest standard

"*T'ien* displays its image, showing us what is fortune or misfortune. The sages took it as a model" (*Book of Changes*, Great Appendix, Sec. 1, Ch. 11) . Thus, *t'ien* is the best model for us. We, too, should follow it.

6) The unknown destiny

Confucius' disciple, Tzu Hsia, said, "I have heard that life and death have their determined appointment; riches and honors depend on *t'ien*" (*Analects*, XII, 5) . Here, *t'ien* is seen as determining our fates and arranging our lives; we are powerless to change its decisions.

4. 仁 (*jen*) HUMANITY/HUMANENESS/ THE WAY OF MANKIND

The character *jen* is particularly difficult to translate into English because of the number of its connotations in Chinese philosophy and the number of Chinese philosophers who have used it in individualistic ways. Generally, it means benevolence, love, goodness, kindness, charity, and compassion. But each of these is only a partial meaning, and each has a separate identification with its own ascribed ideogram or character. We cannot accept a word such as 'benevolence' as an adequate definition. 'Humanity' can be used if we think of it as a quality that encompasses all of the social ideals rather than as a collective noun for all human beings.

In etymological studies, *jen* is equivalent to "a close relationship", constructed of 人 (people) and 二 (two) (Hsü Shen, *Explanation*) . It is built upon the relationship between two persons; there is no humanity without this rela—tionship or without the two individuals. This, however, is a Han Dynasty Confucian explanation that does not include the original metaphysical meaning.

Before Confucius, *jen* was simply a rule of moral behavior

involving love or consideration. *"Jen* is to protect people."
(*Conversations of States*, "Conversation of Chou"), or "... showing
them benevolence and love in order to lead them to *jen*" (*ibid.*,
Conversation of Ch'u) .

Confucius, however, chose *jen* as the key concept on which to
base his whole system of philosophy. In his thought, *jen* is sometimes
the virtue of love, but more often it is an ideal of perfection that has
six aspects:

1) The meaning of *jen*

Confucius did not ascribe a definition to *jen* because, to him,
it was not an item of knowledge. In the *Analects*, when asked about
jen, he responded by telling his students how to act. The closest we
come to finding a definition is in the *Doctrine of the Mean*, where
Confucius is quoted as saying, *"Jen* is man" (Ch. 20) . Here, 'man'
means "humanity" or the "way of mankind" . So, *jen* is the ideal
man or the norm of what a man should be.

2) The essence of *jen*

Confucius did not talk about the essence of *jen* in the *Analects*.
However, if we agree that the "Ten Wings" of the *Book of Changes*
was written by Confucius or recorded his thought, we find the essence
of *jen* in "The great virtue of Heaven and Earth is productivity (giving
life)" (*Book of Changes*, Great Appendix, Sec. 2, Ch. 1), and

"The great man is he whose virtue is in accord with Heaven and Earth" (*Book of Changes*, Hexagram 1, *Ch'ien*) . From these two quotations, we find that the great man, having the same virtue as Heaven and Earth, is productive. For man, produc−tivity means, on one hand, to activate the potential of Heaven and Earth and, on the other, to keep a good relation−ship between individuals and help the development of other people. For example, "Only those who are perfectly sincere can fully develop their human nature. If they can fully develop their own nature, then they can develop the nature of other people. If they can fully develop others' nature, then they can develop the nature of all things. If they can fully develop all things' nature, then they can assist in the transforming and nourishing of heaven and earth" (*Doctrine of the Mean*, Ch. 22) . Both the development of other people's nature and assisting in the transforming and nourishing of heaven and earth are the essence of *jen*.

3) The function of *jen*

"Confucius said, 'Ts'an, my way is to perform all actions in Oneness.' Ts'an Tzu said, 'Yes.' After Confucius went out, the disciples asked him, 'What did he say?' Ts'an Tzu answered, 'The way of our master is only loyalty (忠, *chung*) and empathy (恕, *shu*)'" (*Analects*, IV, 15) . Here *chung* means to be sincere, to reflect often on whether, when you act for others, you are doing your best. *Shu* means to consider others in whatever you do. These two virtues represent the function of extending the inside (the mind of *jen*) to the outside (all things) .

4) The content of *jen*

Jen is the key virtue of all virtues. In the *Analects*, when the students asked about *jen*, Confucius told them to act according to their individual characters. Thus, there are many ways in which to practice *jen*. For example, when Yen Yüan asked about it, Confucius said, "To restrain oneself and return to propriety is *jen*" (*Analects*, XII, 1) . When Fan Ch'ih asked about *jen*, Confucius said, "It is to love people" (*Analects*, XII, 22) . When Fan Ch'ih asked again, Confucius said, "In private life, be serious; in managing affairs, be respectful; in dealing with others, be loyal. Even if you are living among barbarians, these virtues may not be neglected" (*Analects*, XIII, 19) . And when Tzu Chang asked, Confucius said, "One who is able to practice five things can be a man of *jen*." Tzu Chang asked what they were, and the master replied, "Seriousness, generosity, sincerity, earnestness, and benevolence" (*Analects*, XVII, 6) . All of these virtues are aspects of *jen*. We may say that *jen* is to love people and to respect others, but we cannot say that to love people or to respect others is *jen*; *jen* is not any one virtue.

5) The practice of *jen*

Confucius said, "Is *jen* far from us? If I wish to be a man of *jen*, *jen* will be at hand" (*Analects*, VII, 29) . Although *jen* is the perfect virtue, its practice is in everyday life. If you are motivated to be a *jen* person and you feel that you need to be a *jen* person, you can practice it everywhere. The place to begin the practice of *jen* is in the family. So, filial piety is the foundation of the practice of *jen*.

6) The effect of *jen*.

Ordinary morality always places restrictions on us or wants us to perform some sacrifice. *Jen* is different. *Jen* is natural; its expression is joyous and beautiful. For example, "Men of *jen* have no sorrow." (*Analects*, IX, 28), and "Men of *jen* live long" (*Analects*, VI, 21), which mean that one who practices *jen* is in harmony with all things and always will be happy.

After Confucius, all Confucianists followed his inter-pretation as representing the highest standard but, because of their individual philosophical systems, they constantly extended its implications or added new ideas to it.

For example, Mencius developed the theory that *jen* is the mind (*hsin*) of man and righteousness (*i*) is the road of man (*Mencius*, Book 6, Part 1, Ch. 11) . From emphasizing the mind of man as good, he formed the hypothesis that human nature is good. Extending *jen* as mind to humaneness in behavior and government, Mencius always coupled it with righteousness, because he believed that righteousness was the way with which to practice *jen*. To Mencius, the mind of *jen* was the mind of love or compassion. Thus, as Mencius developed his system, he narrowed Confucius' interpretation of *jen*.

Neo−Confucianists of th Sung and Ming Dynasties emphasized the metaphysical aspects of *jen*. "*Jen* is the substance of all things" (Ch'eng Hao, *Writings of Sung and Yüan Philosophers*, On Understanding *Jen*) . "*Jen*'s most impressive aspect is the spirit of life in all things. This is what is called, in the *Book of Changes*, the origination of goodness as a primary quality. This is *jen*" (Ch'eng Hao, *Selected Sayings*) . "*Jen* is just, complete, and gentle. Its energy is the spirit of Spring in Heaven and Earth; its principle is the productive mind of Heaven and Earth" (Chu Hsi, *Reflections on Things at Hand*) . "That the great man can take Heaven, Earth, and all things as one body is not because of his imagination; he does so because the *jen* of his mind does so" (Wang Yang−ming, *Complete Works*, "An Inquiry on the Great Learning") . Ch'eng Hao, Chu Hsi, and Wang Yang−ming expanded the concept of *jen* from the *jen* of mind to the essence of all things.

5. 心 (*hsin*) MIND/HEART

In ancient China, *hsin* usually meant "mind" (brain/ spirit) *and* "heart" (emotion); in rare situations, when discussing sickness, it meant the physical heart. In Chinese philosophy, the character always has meant mind, a concept that poses two problems for Westerners. One is the need to recognize its various shades of meaning in the different schools. The second, and more difficult, is the need to remember that, in almost all situations, mind is the interaction and mutual refinement of intellect, spirit, and feeling — qualities that, in the West, usually are categorically separate and compartmentalized. To think of *hsin* as one's "heart-of-hearts" may help to avoid equating it with cerebral function alone. Of the shades of meaning, eight are most firmly established:

1) *Hsin* as a general, value-free denotation of emotion or thought

In the *Analects*, there are only six references to mind; all have this general meaning. For example, Confucius said, "At seventy, I could follow what my *hsin* desired without transgressing the principles"

(*Analects*, II, 4).

2) *Hsin* as spirit or life-force

"In the hexagram of Return one can see the *hsin* of Heaven and Earth" (*Book of Changes*, Hexagram 24, Fu). In his old age, Confucius studied the *Book of Changes* and extended the general meaning of *hsin* to include philosophical connotations and recognized the *hsin* of Heaven and Earth, by which he meant the spirit of life.

3) *Hsin* as the origin of goodness

"The *hsin* of feeling commiseration is the beginning of humanity; the *hsin* of having shame and dislike is the beginning of righteousness; the *hsin* of knowing modesty is the beginning of propriety; the *hsin* of judging right and wrong is the beginning of wisdom" (*Mencius*, Bk. 2, Pt. 1, Ch. 6). Mencius emphasized the goodness of human nature; but, in his thought, *hsin* is good just as nature is good.

4) *Hsin* as intelligence

"How can man know the Way? The answer is, 'By his *hsin*.'"... "The *hsin* is the ruler of the body and the master of the spirit" (*Hsün Tzu*, The Removal of Prejudices). Hsün Tzu's premise was that human nature is inherently bad — but educable. People can be virtuous because the mind has an intelligence that can control human desires.

5) *Hsin* as desire

"By not displaying desirable objects, people's *hsin* will not be disturbed" (*Lao Tzu*, Ch. 3) . *Hsin* is discussed in six chapters in the *Lao Tzu*. The general meaning in each case is emotion and desire; but, in Lao Tzu's thought, desire is bad. Therefore, Lao Tzu urged that people's minds should be empty — i.e., emptied of desires (*Lao Tzu*, Ch. 3) .

6) *Hsin* as spirit and true self

"Through his wisdom, he gets his *hsin*; through his *hsin*, he gets his constant *hsin*" (*Chuang Tzu*, Ch. 5) . *Hsin* appears frequently in the *Chuang Tzu*, usually with the general meaning of emotion/ desire. In the quotation above, however, Chuang Tzu first stresses the concept of *hsin* as spirit, and second, constant *hsin* as the true self.

7) *Hsin* as Buddha, *dharma*, self-nature, including all virtues

"This *hsin* is Buddha; this mind is *dharma*" (*the sutra of Amitabha*). Tao−shen said, "All the hundreds and thousands of *dharma*−doors return to the single *hsin*. All the myriad virtues are in the *hsin*. All the doors of discipline, meditation, wisdom, spiritual power, and transformation are in you without leaving your *hsin*" (*ibid.*, Vol. 4, Fa−jung) . "The self−nature of Bodhi is pure by origin. One just uses this *hsin* to become a Buddha directly" (*Platform Scripture*, Ch. 1) . These quotations from the Ch'an masters illustrate the primacy of *hsin* and its uses in their teaching of direct transmission from *hsin* to *hsin* (Note, by the way, that the Ch'an/Zen School originally was known as the Sect of Mind — not to be confused with the Neo–Confucian School of Mind) .

8) *Hsin* as principle, Nature, the Supreme Ultimate, that includes all things

Sung and Ming Dynasty Neo–Confucian philosophers, influenced by the Ch'an School, made 'principle' all–inclusive and expanded the concept of *hsin* to include all things through principle. "*Hsin* is the Supreme Ultimate" (Shao Yung, *Treatise on the Contemplation of Things*) . "Principle and *hsin* are one" (Ch'eng Hao, *Literary Remains of the Two Ch'engs*, Ch. 5) . "The universe is my *hsin*, and my *hsin* is the universe" (Lu Hsiang–shan, *Complete Works*, Ch. 22) . "*Hsin* and principle are one. Principle is not another thing beside *hsin*" (Chu Hsi, *Classified Conversations*, Ch. 5) . "There is no principle outside *hsin*; there is no thing outside *hsin*" (Wang Yang–ming, *Records of Instructions and Practice*, Sec. 1) .

6. 化 (*hua*) TRANSFORMATION/ CHANGE

Here we have a term that is particularly important in Chuang Tzu's thought. In his opening chapter we find, "In the northern darkness there is a fish named K'un. It is so huge that we do not know how many thousands of *li* long it is. It *hua* (changes) into a bird whose name is P'eng" (*Chuang Tzu*, Ch.1). Here it is easy to understand *hua* as having the general meaning of change, as a tadpole is transformed into a frog or roe into a fish. But K'un is a fish and P'eng is a bird. How can a fish become a bird? Apparently, the meaning of *hua* is not as simple as it first seems.

Analyzing all of the examples of in the *Chuang Tzu*, we find three categories of meaning:

1) Temporal *hua* in things

These are the temporary changes in the world as we observe it, the random successions of birth, aging, disease, and death, of honor, meanness, calamity, and good fortune. "These are the *hua* of all things" (*Chuang Tzu*, Ch. 4).

2) The great cycles of nature

These are the never−ending cycles of the universe, all−inclusive, inexorable, and eternal. "Be content with what has been arranged and go along with *hua*; then you can enter infinite Heaven" (*Chuang Tzu*, Ch. 6) .

3) The way of *hua* through effort

The effort is that of cultivation or discipline of the mind. As one strives to achieve the highest state of spirit or true self, one's nature will be sublimated to enter the essence of the Way. One transcends the changes of the physical body and *hua* oneself with Nature (2, above) . "Forget both sides (relative ideas) and *hua* into the Way" (Chuang Tzu, Ch. 6) .

Now, if we look again at the story of K'un the great fish in he northern darkness becoming P'eng the bird, we can read it as a parable of transcending the physical self and sublimating the spirit. Thus, *hua* in the *Chuang Tzu* probably is better translated as "transformation" rather than "change" . It involves constant practice and discipline of the mind to transcend the temporal body, its knowledge and experience, and move in accord with Heaven and Earth. This discipline or "cultivation" is what Chuang Tzu called Sitting−Forgetting, which we would consider a form of meditation. It is the "forgetting" of the world of temporal activity that is the gateway to *hua*.

7. 中 (*chung*) MIDDLE/CENTER/ INSIDE

Chung is most familiar in the name for China (*chung kuo* is middle kingdom or nation), reminding us of its historically central position in East Asian civilization, surrounded by satellite states and tribes that looked to it for both material and ideological culture. In Chinese philosophy, however, *chung* is used in several special ways that imply essence rather than centrality. For example:

1) The proper way

"Sincerely hold firmly the *chung*" (*Book of History*, Vol. 4, Tai Yu Mo; *Analects*, XX, 1) . "How great is the virtue of the Ch'ien hexagram! It is tough, strong, *chung*, correct, and pure, unalloyed essence!" (*Book of Changes*, Hexagram 1, *Ch'ien*) These quotations imply that the original meaning of *chung* in Chinese philosophy was "proper" or "right" . There are many uses of *chung*, especially in the *Book of Changes*, that mean the proper or right time or position. Generally speaking, this usage was common among Confucianists by the Sung Dynasty.

2) The essence or substance of Nature

"Before the emotions of pleasure, anger, sorrow, and joy are aroused, it is called *chung*" (*Doctrine of the Mean*, Ch. 1) . Here *chung* means the essence of Nature, which is in equilibrium and without emotional implications. The meta–physical possibilities of this definition influenced Sung Dynasty Confucianists.

3) The emptiness of mind

"Too much talk always comes to a dead end; it is better to keep to the *chung*" (*Lao Tzu*, Ch. 5) . In other words, keep the mind free from desires. A common analog is a valley which is empty, yet can produce all things.

4) The unmoved mind

"Just go along with things and let your mind roam freely. Abide by what cannot be avoided and nourish the *chung*" (*Chuang Tzu*, Ch. 4) . Here *chung* means the mind which is in harmony with one's nature and is not moved by outside things.

5) From the unbiased, the perfect, to the Way or Supreme Ultimate

Sung Dynasty Neo–Confucianists ascribed great importance to the *Doctrine of the Mean* and speculated about *chung* as the middle

Way. At first, Ch'eng I explained, "Being without bias is called *chung*" (*Doctrine of the Mean*, Commentary by Chu Hsi) . Later, he said, "*Chung* is the perfect [principle]" (*Literary Remains of the Two Ch'engs*, Ch.19) . Chu Hsi wrote, "Ch'eng I said, '*Chung* is the Way', and 'Being without bias is *chung*. What the Way does is not without *chung*; so, manifest the Way by *chung*'" (*Collected Writings of Chu Hsi*, Letter to Lin Tse-chih) . Hsiang-shan said, "*Chung* is the Supreme Ultimate" (*Complete Works of Lu Hsiang-shan*, Letter to Chu Hsi) .

8. 反（*fan*）REVERSAL/RETURN

Fan, a word in common usage meaning reversal or return, has philosophical connotations in two books, the *Book of Changes* and the *Lao Tzu*.

1) *Fan* in the Book of Changes

As the English translation of the *I Ching*'s title indicates, the entire subject matter of the *Book of Changes* is the flows and counterflows, the movements and returns of the universe and mankind; reversal is part of the process as revealed in the hexagrams.

（a）*Fan* in the lines of the hexagrams. Each hexagram has two groups of three lines. The lower three lines form the inner trigram, so called because it generally concerns thought, family, and other subjective or internalized matters. The upper three lines, the outer trigram, generally symbolize objective activities, such as government, which are overt expressions of inner changes. In each hexagram, there are two lines especially related to reversal, the third and sixth (note that lines are always counted from the bottom up) . When a man is on the third line, about to enter the fourth, he is in the position of one who must turn his idea into action or move from security in his family into governmental responsibility. Therefore, the hex−agram's judgment on this line always enjoins return−ing or reflecting, pausing to examine oneself. For example, the judgment for the third line of *Ch'ien* (The Creative) hexagram is, "The superior man is in *Ch'ien* all day; in the evening he still needs to be cautious as he faces danger. Then he will have no trouble" (*Book of Changes*, Hexagram 1, *Ch'ien*) . The commentary adds, "'In *Ch'ien* all day' indicates that he is involved in *fan* and returning," i.e., engaged in the moral activity of self−examination.

The other line that has a particular relationship with reversal is the sixth, at the top of the hexagram. When anything goes to an extreme or reaches its limit, it reverses or becomes its opposite. So, this line, at the hexagram's limit, always refers to changing position or returning to the original point. For example, the sixth line of The Family (*Chia Jen*) reads, "He has sincerity and majesty; in the end there will be good fortune," and its commentary states, "The good fortune of majesty refers to his knowing to *fan* himself" (*Book of Changes*, Hexagram 37, *Chia Jen*) . "*Fan* himself" means that he reflects on and examines himself in order to become virtuous.

(b) *Fan* **between hexagrams.** All of the sixty−four hexagrams are interrelated, but there are twelve that are paired as opposites: Standstill (12, *P'i*) and Peace (11, *T'ai*), Return (24, *Fu*) and Splitting Apart (23, *Po*), Deliverance (40, *Hsieh*) and Obstruction

(39, *Chien*), Decrease (41, *Sun*) and Increase (42, *I*), The Caldron(50, *Ting*) and Revolution(49, *Ko*), After Completion(63, *Chi Chi*) and Before Completion (64, *Wei Chi*) . Each member of a pair has its lines arranged in reverse order to the other and has a contrasting meaning. If we reflect on their oppositions and differences and understand the principles of alternation between dark (*yin*) lines and light (*yang*) lines, we will know how to deal with our problems.

(c) **The hexagram of reversal.** The hexagram Return (24, *Fu*) has the same meaning as *fan*, but is a different character (复) . In Return, the first (lowest) line is light and the five above are dark, indicating that light energy is beginning to increase gradually and dark energy to decrease. In nature, light begins to replace darkness, indicating that spring is coming. "*Fan* and return (复, *fu*) are the Way. In seven days there is return. This is the movement of Heaven. There will be benefit in going forward because the hardness (the light line) is growing. Through return, is one not able to see the mind of Heaven and Earth?" (*Book of Changes*, Hexagram 24, *Fu*) This passage is a Confucian commentary which emphasizes that the production of light energy and the movement of all things shows the mind of Heaven and Earth. This contrasts with Taoism's emphasis on the mind of Heaven and Earth being shown by tranquility. Although movement and tranquility are inseparable, movement or returning receives the greater emphasis in the *Book of Changes*. Reversal refers to the alternation of dark and light energies, but in the philosophical purpose of the *Book* *of Changes*, reversal becomes a moral term telling us that everything becomes good through change.

2) *Fan* in the Lao Tzu

As a specific term, *fan* occurs several times in the *Lao Tzu*. Examples are, "To be great is to go on, to go on is to be far, to be far is to *fan*" (Ch. 25), "*Fan* is the movement of the Way" (Ch. 40), "The mystical virtue is deep and far. It *fan* with all things till they attain the great natural path" (Ch. 65), "True words sound like their *fan*" (Ch. 78) . However, the whole *Lao Tzu* is suffused with the idea of *fan*, for it is a function of the Way. In the *Lao Tzu*, *fan* has two meanings: 'reversal' and 'return' .

(a) **Reversal.** Everything that goes on will eventually become its opposite. This produces a variety of relative relationships. Lao Tzu described them in phenomena, in the principles of all things, and in politics and daily life.

(1) **Reversal in phenomena.** "Existence and non-existence give birth to each other. Difficult and easy complement each other. Long and short contrast with each other. Sound and voice harmonize with each other. Front and back follow each other" (*Lao Tzu*, Ch. 2) .

(2) **Reversal in principles of all things.** "The bright Way looks dim. The advancing Way appears to be retreating. The level Way looks rough. High virtue looks like a valley. Great purity looks soiled. Abundant virtue looks deficient. Established virtue looks like cowardice. True essence looks changeable. The great square has no corners. The great vessel is completed late. Great sound is voiceless. The great image has no shape" (*Lao Tzu*, Ch. 41) .

(3) **Reversal in politics and everyday life.** "Banish sagacity and abandon cleverness, the people will be benefited a hundredfold. Banish humanity and abandon righteousness, the people will return to filial piety and paternal kindness. Banish craftiness and abandon sharpness, robbers and thieves will no longer exist" (*Lao Tzu*, Ch. 19) .

(b) **Return.** After using *fan* as reversal, one cultivates one's mind and returns to one's true self or Way by returning to life, to simplicity, and to enlightenment.

(1) **Return to life.** "Everything returns to its root. To return to the root is to return to tranquility. This means to return to its (true) life. To return to its life means the eternal" (*Lao Tzu*, Ch. 16) .

(2) **Return to simplicity.** "Knowing the glorious and keeping to the lowly, one will become the valley of the world. Being the valley of the world, one's constant virtue will be completed and one will return to the state of simplicity" (*Lao Tzu*, Ch. 28) .

(3) **Return to enlightenment.** "To know the subtle is called insight. To keep to the soft is called strength. Use the light(intelligence) to return to enlightenment" (*Lao Tzu*, Ch. 52) .

Not only was *fan* the central theory of Lao Tzu, it also influenced other schools and later Taoists. Both the Militarists and Legalists used the principle in strategy and government, and the Immortalists used it in refining cinnabar (see *tan*, 4), but only with the meaning of reversal, ignoring the element of return. By neglecting Lao Tzu's emphasis on return, they went to extremes and, in the end, were acting contrary to the Way.

9. 丹 (*tan*) ELIXIR/CINNABAR

Tan is the character for cinnabar, the red ore from which mercury is smelted. Later Taoists combined it with other minerals in an alchemical process called "refining cinnabar", by which they hoped to create an elixir that would enable them to achieve immortality. It has been hypothesized that their experiments were the foundations of European alchemy, having been transmitted through the Arabs. The cinnabar refiners used the thought of Lao Tzu and Chuang Tzu as their guiding principle; thus, *tan* became a special term that combined aspects of magic, science, religion, and philosophy. As a group, the alchemists became known as the School of Immortality.

1) Definitions of *tan*

In the School of Immortality, *tan* acquired three meanings: first, true energy, which is man's original nature; second, the cultivations of mind and body that bring a person into accord with the true energy; third, golden *tan* or returning *tan*, the medicine or *tan* created by combining cinnabar, refined mercury, alum, and other minerals. Chu Yün-yang said, "The sameness which unites all differentiations is the original, natural essence. It is supreme truth. It is the inner medicine. The differentiations which originated in the sameness are the [result of the] subtle function of the process of reversal. The return to supreme truth from the subtle function is the outer medicine" (Chu Yün-yang, *Commentary on the Book of Awakening Truth by Chang Tzu-yang*) . Here, inner medicine is the true energy; outer medicine refers to the cultivation of mind and body and the use of golden *tan*.

2) True energy

"If a man is able to embrace Oneness, *tan* will be completed. Oneness brought forth two; two brought forth three; three brought forth all things. The process of producing human beings and all created things is this Oneness. Three returns to two; two returns to Oneness; Oneness returns to non-being. To become a sage or an immortal by going in reverse also achieves this Oneness" (Chu Yung-yang, *Commentary on the Unity of the Trio by Wei Po-yang*) . Oneness refers to the Way of the *Lao Tzu* which, in the School of Immortality, was the original true energy, the *tan*.

3) Inner and outer methods of refining *tan*

(a) **Protecting the three treasures.** In Immortalism, the three treasures are essence (精, *ching*), energy, and spirit. Chu Yün-yang said, "Those who cultivate the Way have three inner treasures and three outer treasures. Original essence, original energy, and original spirit are the three inner treasures; ears, eyes, and mouth are the three outer treasures. If you want to make the three inner treasures return to truth, you must cause the three outer treasures to be completely without leaks" (Chu Yün−yang, *Commentary on the Unity of the Trio by Wei Po-yang*). The three outer treasures refers to the body's nine openings (two eyes, two ears, two nostrils, one mouth, and two excretory orifices) which must not be allowed to leak essence, energy, or spirit. Protecting the essence requires retention of the semen and turning it inward to nourish the brain. Protecting energy requires training respiration so as not to breathe through the mouth, which would permit the true energy to leak out. Protecting the spirit requires restraint of desires and keeping the mind unmoved.

(b) **Eating a great medicine.** "To become immortal, one must do the important things. These are protecting essence, practicing [control of] energy, and eating a great medicine" (Ko Hung, *Pao P'u Tzu*, Inner Book, Ch. 8). "Great medicine" refers to golden *tan* or returning *tan*, which is made through alchemy. The method of making golden *tan* is described in detail in two books, the *Pao P'u Tzu* by Ko Hung and the *Unity of the Trio* by Wei Po−yang. The former discusses the method of collecting and refining minerals and medicines; the latter deals with the principles of refining the *tan*, using the thought of the *Lao Tzu* and the *Book of Changes*. Although both books are detailed, the treatment is so esoteric and there are so many assumptions of prior knowledge on the reader's part, that both theory and practice are still surrounded by mystery.

4) The relationship between *tan* and Lao Tzu's Way

The principle of *tan* came from the reversal/ returning (*fan*) of Lao Tzu. Chu Yün-yang said, "Golden *tan* is beyond ordinary reason. What is the meaning of reversal? The ordinary way is the natural [way], but the way of *tan* is its reverse" (Chu Yün-yang, *Commentary on the Unity of the Trio*, Ch. 22) . All of the methods used by the Immortalists followed the principle of reversal; for example, the turning inward of semen, not breathing through the mouth, and refraining from eating. Although they appeared, on the surface, to be following the principles of Lao Tzu, actually they were acting contrary to his thought. The reversal/returning that Lao Tzu emphasized was the ordinary and natural way, to which the way of *tan* was opposed.

10. 玄 (*hsüan*) DARKNESS/MYSTERY

Originally, the character *hsüan* signified the color red–black. In the *Analects* and the *Mencius*, *hsüan* appears only as a color; there is no philosophical meaning attached to the word by pragmatic Confucianists. In the *Lao Tzu*, however, we find occurrences of *hsüan* used philosophically to suggest mystery or profundity. For example:

1) *Hsüan* as the profound source

"Therefore, constantly non–being, one can contemplate the subtlety of the Way. Constantly being, one can contemplate the outcome of the Way. These two flow from the same source, but after they are manifested they have different names. That source is called *hsüan*. To be *hsüan* and then *hsüan* again is the gateway to myriad subtleties" (*Lao Tzu*, Ch. 1) . Here, *hsüan* is used to describe the profound source which is beyond relativism, in which being and non–being are one.

2) *Hsüan* as insight

"In washing and clearing your *hsüan* (profound) vision, can you purify it of all dross?" (*Lao Tzu*, Ch. 10) Here, "*hsüan* vision" means the spiritual insight which symbolizes the true mind. It is called *hsüan* because it provides insight into the depths of the source.

After Lao Tzu, Chuang Tzu took *hsüan* to indicate the superlative degree, as *hsüan* heaven, *hsüan* palace, *hsüan* darkness, *hsüan* ancient times, *hsüan* sage, *hsüan* virtue, and *hsüan* pearl. But in Chuang Tzu's *thought* the word has no additional connotations.

3) *Hsüan* as the Way

Later Taoists used *hsüan* as the Way. "*Hsüan* is the Way of Heaven, the Way of earth, the Way of man" (Yang Hsiung, *The Supreme Hsüan*, The Map of *Hsüan*). Yang Hsiung was a Han Dynasty Confucianist, but his philosophy had Taoist aspects because of the way he used *hsüan* as a key term in his writings.

Following Yang Hsiung, there were many Neo-Taoists in the Wei and Chin Dynasties who made *hsüan* their central concept and called their studies "*Hsüan* Learning".

11. 名（*ming*）NAME/FAME

The character *ming* generally means the name of a person or thing. In Chinese philosophy, by extension, it can indicate the title of an official, a person's fame, or a family role. For example:

1）Family role

Confucius' disciple, Tzu Lu, said, "The ruler of the state of Wei is waiting for you to begin work as an administrator; what do you think is the first thing to be done?" Confucius replied, "What is necessary is to rectify *ming* (names)" (*Analects*, XIII, 3). *Ming* in this dialogue refers to the proper relationship between father and son, because Confucius thought that the ruler of Wei should be filial to his father. From the naming (and, therefore, relationship) of father and son to the naming of ruler and subject and husband and wife, Confucius established his ideal political system, known as the Rectification of Names. This usage of *ming* is emphasized in Confucianism.

2）Official titles

"When *ming* and actualities are in agreement, good government results. When *ming* and actualities are not in agreement, disorder results" (Kuan Tzu, *The Nine Keep-ings*) . Kuan Tzu was an early Legalist who preceded Confucius. Here, *ming* refers to the titles of officials and "actualities" to the functions they perform. From this, later Legalists developed a system of examining officials' actions to see if they conformed to their titles.

3) Fame

Using *ming* to indicate fame or reputation is common, but in Chinese philosophy there are two different connotations. In Confucianism, *ming* is a good thing; it expresses a person's honor. For example, Confucius said, "The superior man dislikes that his name will not be mentioned after his death" (*Analects*, XV, 19) . In Taoism and Buddhism, however, *ming* is a desire or craving that causes problems. Chuang Tzu wrote, "Virtue is destroyed by *ming*; knowledge emerges from struggle" (*Chuang Tzu*, Ch. 4) .

4) *Ming* as a term used by Logicians

"What is spoken is *ming*; what the speaking means is substance. When the *ming* and the substance are in agreement, there is accord" (*Mo Tzu*, Vol. 10, Mo Ching) . Here, *ming* means the name of a thing or the term used to label a reality. Scholars who studied and analyzed this aspect of *ming* formed the Ming Chia, the School of Ming, or Logicians.

12. 志（*chih*）WILL/PURPOSE

Chih, as the determination to become an ideal person, is a popular term in China. In philosophy, particularly in Confucianism, this commendable generalization is shown as having specific functional aspects:

1）In beginning the practice of humanity

Confucius said, "If you set your *chih* to humanity, there will be no wickedness" (*Analects*, IV, 4). To Confucius, when a man wanted to practice humanity, his first task was to will his mind to follow the principle of humanity in all aspects of his life.

2）As the guide of energy, spirit, vital force（*ch'i*）

"*Chih* is the leader of energy, and energy pervades the whole body. *Chih* is the highest principle; energy comes next" (*Mencius*, Bk. 2, Pt. 1, Ch. 2). *Chih*, as master of our spirits and bodies, can control all of our actions.

3) As basic philosophical training

Asked about Lu Hsiang-shan's teaching, Cheng Chi answered, "I have studied under him for one month. What he taught was only to understand the *chih*" (*Complete Works of Lu Hsiang-shan*) . Lu Hsiang-shan, Sung Dynasty Confucianist, took *chih* as the cornerstone for learning. Actually, all Neo-Confucianists emphasized *chih* both as an important concept and as part of the training in philosophy.

Taoism and Buddhism differ from Confucianism in regard to *chih*. Lao Tzu advocated "weakening people's *chih*" (*Lao Tzu*, Ch. 3) — *i.e.*, reducing the sense of ego or individualism, and all Ch'an masters emphasized "no attach-ment" or "no mind" — *i.e.*, no desires or willfulness. But actually, Taoists and Buddhists still made the effort to become perfect or true men. Even in the Ch'an School, trying to avoid attachment to the Buddha, they said, "The great man has the *chih* to pierce the heaven; let him not follow the footsteps of the Buddha" (*Five Lamps Returning to the Same Source*, Ts'ui-yen) . One should follow his own Buddha nature rather than imitate outward forms or follow texts. Therefore, even in the Ch'an School, there is *chih*.

Perhaps the most important function of *chih* in Chinese philosophy is to support the scholar's determination to practice the Way and, in doing so, to assume responsibility for finding ways to relieve the suffering of the people.[①] Before Wen Tien-hsiang, a Sung Dynasty Confucianist official, chose to was killed rather than surrender to the Mongol enemy, he wrote on his belt, "Confucius says to achieve humanity; Mencius says to perform the duty of righteousness. Only when righteousness is completed will humanity be achieved. What instructions do we learn from the sages and from worthy men's books! From now on, I will feel no regret" (*History of Sung*, Wen Tien-hsiang) . This is a classic and often quoted example of the establish-ment of a life-goal that is representative of *chih* in Confucianism.

---

① In traditional China, such a statement was not just a pious platitude. Scholars were the reservoir from which government officials were chosen by China's famous civil service examinations. A district magistrate was the "father-mother" official of a county, responsible for the people's economic well-being (to make sure that tax-collectors' assessments would be met, if for no other reason), social harmony, and political loyalty. His success depended on his ability to apply to any given situation the accumulated wisdom of classical philosophy.

13. 忘（*wang*）FORGETTING/ OVERLOOKING/BEYOND

Wang generally means forgetting or overlooking. Only in the *Chuang Tzu* does it have philosophical meaning and a significant role in Taoism. It refers to attaining the highest state of mind, beyond all relativity.

1) Three kinds of *wang* in the *Chuang Tzu*

(a) *Wang* **oneself.** To *wang* oneself does not mean that one gets lost or loses one's memory; it means that one gets rid of attachment to one's material body and ego. "I smash my limbs and body, give up my perception and intellect, renounce form, leave knowledge, and make myself unite with the great penetration. This is called Sitting in *wang*" (*Chuang Tzu*, Ch. 6) . Sitting in *wang* is like forgetting oneself in meditation.

(b) *Wang* **all things.** *Wang* all things and *wang* oneself are two aspects of the same process. Each is complemented by the other. Without *wang* oneself, one is unable to *wang* all things, and vice versa. "*Wang* all things" does not mean to negate the existence of all things. It means that one sees through externals and does not become attached to their physical forms. In the *Chuang Tzu*, there is a story about Ting, a cook who was famous for his skill as a butcher. It quotes him as saying, "What I care about is the Way, which goes beyond skill. When I first began to cut up oxen, all I saw was the ox. After three years, I no longer saw the whole ox. Now, I see it by spirit and do not look with my eyes. Sense perceptions are limited, but spirit moves freely. I go along with the Heavenly principle. I strike in the big hollows and guide my knife through the big openings, following what is natural" (*Chuang Tzu*, Ch. 3) . When one understands the truth, one is *naturally* beyond all material things.

(c) *Wang* **being carefree.** If one wants to *wang* oneself and all things but is attached to the comforts of this state, one cannot really *wang*. Chuang Tzu said, "*Wang* your feet when your shoes are comfortable. *Wang* your waist when your belt is comfortable. *Wang* knowing right and wrong when your mind is comfortable. Nothing is changed inside and nothing can distract you outside; whatever you encounter is comfortable. If, in the beginning, you are carefree and never experience what is uncomfortable, it is because you are carefree when you *wang* being comfortable" (*Chuang Tzu*, Ch. 19) . "*Wang* being carefree" is a warning not to become attached to what you desire; therefore, do not become attached to *wang*. If you want *wang*, you cannot attain it.

2) *Wang* and the Way

Wang is easily misunderstood because many people think it looks easy. But *wang* is not just forgetting. If a man takes only *wang* as his goal, he cannot really *wang*. The true meaning of *wang* is to live in the Way. "Fish abide in water; men abide in the Way. Those who abide in water swim in a pond and are nourished; those who abide in the Way do nothing and their minds are tranquil. So it is said that fish *wang* each other in the rivers and lakes (*i.e.*, are unaware of both self and water), and men *wang* each other in the Way" (*Chuang Tzu*, Ch 6) . "*Wang* in the Way" describes one who has awakened to his true self and recognizes the true self of all things and who can, therefore, really *wang* himself and all things. *Wang* is the state of one who has attained the Way — it is a combination of the Way and *wang*.

14. 孝（*hsiao*）FILIAL PIETY

The character *hsiao* has two parts; the upper means "old", and the lower means "son", signifying that the son must be dutiful to his parents. *Hsiao* is a major virtue in Chinese culture and philosophy. Particularly in Confucian−ism, *hsiao* is significant for its links with all other virtues.

1）*Hsiao* in relation to the other virtues

Yu Tzu said, "There are few among those who have *hsiao* and brotherly respect who will be fond of offending their superiors. There have been no cases of those who, not liking to offend their superiors, yet like to create disorder. A superior man applies himself to the fundamentals. When the root is established, the Way will appear. *Hsiao* and brotherly respect are the root of humanity" (*Analects*, I, 2). Yu Tzu was Confucius' leading disciple; what he said here was in accord with Confucius' thought. In this quotation we find that, in Confucianism, *hsiao* is the beginning and foundation for practicing humanity. Humanity encompasses all virtues; therefore, *hsiao* is also the beginning and foundation of practicing them.

2) The practice of *hsiao*

As with any virtue, the value of *hsiao* depends on how it is practiced. Confucius laid down specific conditions. *Hsiao* must be practiced:

(a) **Without disobedience.** Meng I Tzu asked about *hsiao*. Confucius said, "Never disobey... When parents are alive, serve them according to propriety; when they die, bury them according to propriety; and sacrifice to them according to propriety" (*Analects*, II, 5) . Obedience required that the son should serve his parents according to the rules recorded in the Classics as the *Record of Rites*.

(b) **As continuing the will of the father.** Confucius said, "When one's father is alive, one observes his will; when one's father is dead, one studies his actions. If for three years after his father's death one does not change the way of his father, one may be called *hsiao*'" (*Analects*, I, 11) . Although not all fathers' thoughts and actions are good, in Confucianism the way of the father symbolizes the accumulated wisdom and experience of the elders that can guide their sons.

(c) **Without confrontations.** Confucius said, "In serving his parents, a son may remonstrate gently with them. When he finds that they do not accept his advice, he still obeys them with respect and serves them without complaint" (*Analects*, IV, 18) . Confucius did not want sons to obey their fathers blindly. If a son thinks that his father is wrong, he should say so, but gently. If his father does not accept his advice, he still is respectful.

(d)**With reverence.** Confucius said, "The *hsiao* of today means [only] to support one's parents. But dogs and horses are supported by us. What is the difference between these two supports if without reverence [for one's parents] ?" (*Analects*, II, 7) Confucius was keenly aware of the danger that habitual performance of any act, however vital, can become empty ritual.

(e)**With a pleasant demeanor.** Confucius said, "The difficulty is to show a good countenance. The young ones should provide services to help elders who have troublesome problems. If, when a young one has wine and food, he offers it first to the elders, is this enough to be considered *hsiao*?" (*Analects*, II, 8) Again, observing the formalities is not enough, nor is the grudging performance of duties. The filial son is alert for opportunities to serve his parents with a smiling face. He will take care that his parents are not aware of his own problems lest it mar their happiness.

(f)**With recognition that it sets a sound standard of behavior.** For example, "Our body and hair and skin are given by our parents; therefore, we dare not let them get hurt. This is the beginning of *hsiao*. Establishing ourselves, practicing the Way, and causing our names to be known by coming generations, we repay our parents with these actions. This is the end of *hsiao*" (*Book of Filial Piety*, Book 1). This means that the great filial son sacrifices himself for the people and his country in order to make his parents respected by others.

3) The importance of *hsiao* to Confucianism

In Confucianist philosophy, *hsiao* is not only an ethical imperative, it is a function of universal order. "In the nature of Heaven and Earth, human beings are most valuable. In the actions of human beings, nothing is greater than *hsiao*. In practicing *hsiao*, nothing is greater than to make the way of the father respectable. In making the way of the father respectable, nothing is greater than to be in accord with Heaven" (*Book of Filial Piety*, Ch. 9) . This equates the way of the father with the way of Heaven. The virtue of Heaven is to give life to all things. *Hsiao* continues the function of Heaven, because to be filial to our parents is to be grateful for their giving life to us, and we should continue this life as repayment to them.

4) *Hsiao* in Chinese culture

Later Confucianists made *hsiao* the foundation of Chinese society; they established an inseparable relationship between *hsiao* and religion, politics, ethics, and all social relationships. Confucius said, "King Wu and Duke Chou were indeed illustriously *hsiao*. Men of *hsiao* are those who are good at carrying out the wishes of their forefathers and showing, [in their own lives, the values and] works of their ancestors. In spring and autumn they repaired their ancestral temples, displayed their ancestral vessels, set forth their ancestral clothes, and offered the food of the season. In the ritual of the ancestral temple, the kindred were placed on the left (higher) or the right (lower) according to their order of descent. Ranks were ordered to distinguish between the honorable and the humble. Services were ordered to distinguish the differences of ability. In pledging ceremonies, the inferiors presented the cup to their superiors; this gave the people of lower position something to do. In the concluding feast, places of honor were given to the people with white hair in order to distinguish the differences of age. They (King Wu and Duke Chou) occupied their forefathers' places, practiced their rites, and performed their music. They revered those whom their forefathers respected, loved those to whom their forefathers were dear. Thus, they served the dead as they would have served them if alive and served the departed as they would have served them if still present. This is perfect *hsiao*" (*Doctrine of the Mean*, Ch. 19) . This passage summarizes both the practices of ancient Chinese society and the principles on which they were based.

15. 命（*ming*）LIFE/FATE/DESTINY

Ming is a frequently used word in Chinese thought. Except for the meaning of "order", which is generally regarded as a verb, there are six ways in which it is used by Chinese philosophers:

1) Life

"Unfortunately, his *ming* was short and he died" (*Analects*, VI, 2) . Here, *ming* simply means "life" or "life span." There are no philosophical implications.

2) Fate

When Pai–niu was sick, Confucius went to ask for him, held his hand through the window, and said, "If he is going to die, it is because of *ming* (fate) . That such a man should have such a sickness!" (*Analects*, VI, 8) Here, *ming* means a fate that man cannot change. In Confucianism, this kind of *ming* is not discussed. But it is dealt with by Chuang Tzu. "Life, death, existence, loss, failure, success, poverty, riches, worthiness, unworthiness, slander, praise, hunger, thirst, cold, heat, which are the circumstances of ordinary life and which are the functions of *ming*? Knowing that we cannot change them, we regard them as *ming*. Only the man who has virtue can do this" (*Chuang Tzu*, Ch. 5) . According to Chuang Tzu, if we take all things that we cannot control as *ming*, they will not disturb us. Then our minds will be tranquil.

3) Heavenly mandate

To Confucius, *ming* had a deeper meaning; it was the Mandate of Heaven. "If my way is to advance, it is *ming*. If my way is destroyed, it is *ming*. What can Kung-po Liao do to my *ming*?" (*Analects*, XIV, 38) "Since the death of King Wen, has not the duty to spread the culture fallen to me? If Heaven lets our culture be destroyed, I cannot do anything about it. If Heaven does not want our culture to be destroyed, what can the people of Kung do to me?" (*Analects*, IX, 5) From these quotations, we conclude that what Confucius meant by *ming* was the Mandate of Heaven, which is equivalent to the Way of Heaven. In the *Analects*, *ming* most often has this meaning of a supreme power that arranges everything. This power is not an attribute of the Gods or of some mysterious Being; it is a reasonable principle that we can understand but cannot change. "Without understanding *ming*, one is unable to be a superior man" (*Analects*, XX, 3) . Thus, our duty is to follow and practice the Way of Heaven.

4) Nature

"To return to the root is called tranquility. It means to return to *ming*. To return to *ming* is called eternity" (*Lao Tzu*, Ch. 16) . Here, *ming* refers to the nature of all things or the nature of the universe. It is true nature or true life.

5) Principle

Developing Confucius' definition of *ming* as the Man–date or Way of Heaven, Sung Dynasty Neo–Confucianists regarded it as principle or the principle of Heaven. Ch'eng I said, "That which is in Heaven is called *ming*; that which is righteous is called principle; that which is human is called nature; that which masters the body is called oneness. Actually, all of these are one" (*Literary Remains of the Two Ch'engs*, 18) . Chu Hsi said, "What Heaven mandates is called *ming*; it also is principle" (*Classified Conversations of Chu Hsi*, 4) . Thus, Neo–Confucianists made *ming* easier to understand and practice by equating Mandate of Heaven, *ming*, and life with principle.

6) Spirit

"... establishing *ming* for all people" (*Records of the Dialogues of Chang Tsai*) . Here, *ming* means not only the life of the people but their spirit as well, which is much more important than physical existence. The spiritual life is the life of virtue or wisdom. So, Confucianists insisted that we should practice virtue instead of being attached to life and *ming*; we should do our duty, which comes from Heaven, and not be concerned about our lives and *ming*.

16. 和（*huo*）HARMONY/PEACE

The character *huo* originally meant two things responding harmoniously to each other; by extension, it meant 'peace'. Philosophers used it in several contexts and with several shades of meaning.

1）*Huo* in Heaven

An initial usage referred to the supreme harmony which preceded the production of dark（*yin*）and light（*yang*）. "The way of *ch'ien*（the Creative）is to change and transform, which causes everything to have its correct nature and life and preserves the supreme *huo*"（*Book of Changes*, Hexagram 1, *Ch'ien*）. "The supreme *huo* is called the Way（Chang Tsai, *Correct Discipline for Beginners*, Ch.1）. Here, the supreme *huo* is synonymous with the Supreme Ultimate.

A related usage referred to the *huo* between dark and light." All things carry the dark and embrace the light and *huo* them with desireless energy"（*Lao Tzu*, Ch. 42）.

2）*Huo* in mind

"Before the emotions of pleasure, anger, sorrow, and joy are aroused, there is equilibrium（中, *chung*）. When these emotions are aroused in their right way at their right time, there is *huo*"（*Doctrine of the Mean*, Ch.1）. Thus, our mind functions harmoniously in relation to outside things.

3）*Huo* in time

"Now a dragon, now a snake, he transforms according to what is timely and never becomes attached to one extreme. Now up, now down, he takes *huo* as the measure"（*Chuang Tzu*, Ch. 20）. This is a key statement of the well−known Chinese distrust of arbitrary, fixed positions. A reasonable person always considers the circumstances when making a decision or taking action. The question to be asked is, "What would an ethical person do in this situation?" rather than, "What actions are always good; which are always bad?" Past experience, history, and writings of the sages provide guides that must be consulted, but ultimately there is no fixed standard. By doing what is "timely", one acts in harmony with nature.

4）*Huo* that transcends relativity

"The sage *huo* with both right and wrong and rests in Heavenly equilibrium"（*Chuang Tzu*, Ch. 2）. Here, *huo* with both right and wrong means to be beyond right and wrong, which also means to transcend temporal relativities such as life and death, failure and success, poverty and riches. If we are beyond them, say the adherents of Taoism and the Ch'an School, they cannot disturb our minds; our minds will be *huo*.

6) *Huo* with morality

"To benefit means to be in *huo* with righteousness" (*Book of Changes*, Hexagram 1, *Ch'ien*) . The real benefit from anything comes from a proper practice of righteousness.

17. 直 (*chih*) UPRIGHT/STRAIGHT FORWARD

Chih is another of the popularly−invoked virtues in China with aspects of meaning that vary from school to school. Confucianists relate it particularly to justice, Taoists to true mind, and Buddhists to the desire−free mind.

1) Conduct of justice

The common meanings of *chih* include justice, uprightness, correctness, honesty, and related concepts. Duke Ai asked, "What should be done in order to cause people to submit?" Confucius replied, "Advance the *chih* instead of the crooked, then the people will submit; advance the crooked instead of the *chih*, then the people will not submit" (*Analects*, II, 9) . Here, *chih* refers particularly to honest and just officials.

2) True affection

The Duke of Sheh said to Confucius, "There is a man in my country who is *chih*. If his father stole a sheep, he would bear witness to the fact." Confucius replied, "In my community, the men of *chih* are different from yours. The father conceals the misconduct of the son, and the son conceals the misconduct of the father. *Chih* is to be found in this" (*Analects*, XIII, 18) . Here, *chih* is defined by the nature of the relationship between parents and children, which is without affectation.

3) True self

"Inwardly, *chih* means that I can be the companion of Heaven. Being inwardly *chih*, I know that the king and I are equally the sons of Heaven. Why should I worry about whether my opinions are praised by other people? A man such as I am is called 'The Child'" (*Chuang Tzu*, Ch. 4) . Here, *chih* means that one recognizes his true mind which, endowed by Heaven, is equal to everything.

4) Desire-free mind

"To practice *samadhi* (meditation) means to practice constantly the *chih* mind on all occasions — walking, standing, sitting, or reclining. The *Vimalakirti Nirdesa Sutra* says, 'The *chih* mind is the Pure Land'" (*Platform Scripture*, Ch. 4) . The *chih* mind is pure mind which is free from any desire.

18. 易（*i*）CHANGE/EASINESS

The original meaning for the character *i* was "change". "*I* depicts a lizard or gecko" (Hsü Shen, *Explanation*) . The lizard, it is said, changes color many times a day; so, the character *i* takes the lizard as its form and change as its meaning. *The Secret Book*, a Taoist text, says that "*i* is the sun and moon", meaning the alternation of sun and moon, which also means change.

Three philosophical meanings are derived from usages in the *Book of Changes*:

1) Change

"The *I Ching* is a book which is always with us. Its Way is one of continual change; it changes and moves constantly, never staying in any one place. It moves cyclically in the six lines [of the hexagram] . It ascends and descends without consistency. Its hard line (*yang*) and soft line (*yin*) alternate. Thus there is no certainty of principle. Only the change is its Way" (*Book of Changes*, Great Appendix, Sec. 2, Ch. 8) . Here, *i* refers to all changes in the universe and the changes in all lines of the sixty-four hexagrams.

2) Changelessness

This term is used in two ways. One relates to the position of lines in the hexagrams. "Heaven is lofty, Earth is low; thus *Ch'ien* and *K'un* are determined. Things low and high are displayed; thus noble and mean are assigned by their positions. Movement and rest have their regular way; thus, hard and soft lines are judged" (*Book of Changes*, Great Appendix, Sec. 1, Ch. 1) . Positions of lines, therefore, are fixed.

The other usage relates to the essence of *i*. "The way of Heaven and Earth is eternal, without ceasing. Wherever one goes, it will be advantageous (reference to use in divination) . When it comes to its end, it will begin again. The sun and moon, being in Heaven's course, are everlasting in their shining. The four seasons, by their changes and transformations, achieve constancy. The sages are constant in the Way and cause the whole world to be transformed completely. Contemplating the constancy of *i*, the reality of all things will be seen" (*Book of Changes*, Hexagram 32, *Heng*) . Constancy is the changeless substance of change. What is the essence of *i*? The best answer is the production or giving of life [to all things] . "The great virtue of Heaven and Earth is productivity" (*Book of Changes*, Great Appendix, Sec. 2, Ch. 1) . Only everlastingly producing or giving life can be constant; therefore, the changeless substance of *i* is the production of or giving of life to all things.

3) Easiness

Although the *changes* of the universe are very complex, the principle of the changes — the method of changes — is very simple. "The Creative's (*Ch'ien*) wisdom is based on *i* (the easy); The Receptive's (*K'un*) capacity is based on the simple. What is *i* is easy to know; what is simple is easy to follow. Those who are easy to know will have adherents, and those who are easy to follow will have merit. Those who have adherents can be everlasting; those who have merit will become great. To be everlasting is the virtue of the worthy man; to become great is the career of the worthy man. To be *i* and simple is to master the principle of the world. To comprehend the principle of the world is to achieve a good position in the world" (*Book of Changes*, Great Appendix, Sec.1, Ch.1) . Thus, according to the *Book of Changes*, if one handles well the hard and soft lines [of *yang* and *yin*], one can control all the changes of the world.

These three meanings are emphasized only in the *Book of Changes*, but they are influential throughout Chinese philosophy. All Chinese philosophers, for example, have followed the principle of easiness. They not only have expressed their ideas in ways that are easy to understand, they have lived simply and without selfish desires.

19. 物（*wu*）THING/MATTER

The character *wu* originally meant any material thing in the world. That is still its common meaning, but it has philosophical implications.

1) The companion of human beings

Chinese philosophers do not think of *wu* simply as inert matter to be controlled and used. They see things as having the same relationship to human beings as other people. "Heaven is my father and Earth is my mother. Even such a small creature as I live as one with them. Therefore, what fills the universe is my body, and what masters the universe is my nature. All people are my brothers and sisters, and all *wu* are my companions" (Chang Tsai, *The Western Inscription*) .

2) The same substance as human beings

"Heaven and Earth were born at the same time I was; all things are one with me" (*Chuang Tzu*, Ch. 2) . Chuang Tzu argued that the Way exists everywhere and in everything and that everything is shared reality. Therefore, since, in the Way, all things are involved in transformation (see *hua*, 2), man can transform himself together with all things.

3) Desire or environment

"*Wu*" has a negative meaning in Taoist and Buddhist thought that, sometimes, occurs also in Confucianism. "Once a man receives his material body, even if it does not die now, he is but waiting for its end. He clashes with and is destroyed by *wu* every day. He runs his course like a galloping horse and cannot stop. Is this not pathetic?" (*Chuang Tzu*, Ch. 2) "Bodhi originally is not a tree. The bright mirror (true mind) is not a stand−mirror. In Original Nature, there are no *wu*. On what can dust collect?" (*Platform Scripture*, Ch.1) Mencius said, "The senses of ear and eye do not think and are obscured by [external] *wu*. When this *wu* (sense) comes into contact with the other (external) *wu*, it just means that one thing leads to another thing" (*Mencius*, Bk. 6, Pt. 1, Ch. 15) . All uses of *wu* in these quotations refer to the desires that come from attachment to external, material things.

20. 忠（*chung*）LOYALTY/FAITHFULNESS

Chung is a virtue that, in China, dates from earliest times. Originally, it meant only that officials and the people were expected to be loyal to their rulers and their states. But, as philosophy developed, the term acquired new shades of meaning.

1) *Chung* to ruler and state

Confucius said, "The ruler employs his ministers according to propriety; the ministers should serve their ruler with *chung*" (*Analects*, III, 19) . This is the classic statement of the basic requirement for ministers and subjects.

2) *Chung* to friends and others

Tseng Tzu said, "I reflect on three points every day; the first is that whether, in counseling others, I have been *chung*" (*Analects*, IV, 1) . This meaning of *chung* is particularly emphasized by Confucianists.

3) *Chung* to the people

"The ruler who injures people lacks *chung*" (*Tso's Commentary*, Duke Hsian, 2). Mencius said, "To teach people what is good is called *chung*" (*Mencius*, Bk. 3, Pt. 1, Ch. 4). The use of *chung* in these quotations is uncommon; admonitions to govern well and teach people with kindness usually are expectations that rulers will treat their subjects with humanity that they will be humanitarian. Interestingly, Sun Yat−sen, father of the Republic of China, recalled the ancient usage of *chung*; to him, it was essential that all who were involved in governing should be dutiful and good to the community, the country, and the people.

4) The mind of *chung*/the Way of Heaven

Neo−Confucianists gave *chung* a new definition, deriving it from the *Doctrine of the Mean*, where it is associated with sincerity. They interpreted *chung* as the mind of sincerity or the Way of Heaven. For example, Chu Hsi said, "The mind of doing your best for others is *chung*" (*Commen-tary on the Doctrine of the Mean*, Ch.13). Ch'eng I said, "*Chung* is the Way of Heaven" (*Commentary on the Analects* by Chu Hsi, Ch. 4). In such comments, *chung* was given a philosophical depth that made Neo−Confucianists practice it in cultivating their minds.

21. 知 (*chih*) WISDOM/KNOWLEDGE

The characters 知 and 智 are used interchangeably in Chinese. Generally, 知 can be used as a verb or noun, but 智 can be used only as a noun. Hsün Tzu said, "That which a man knows in his mind is called 知; the 知 corresponding to external reality is called 智" (*Hsün Tzu*, On the Rectification of Terms) . This definition of as the ability to know and of 智 as the ability to gather knowledge from objective data applies only to Hsün Tzu's thought. In other usage, both common and philosophical, the terms remain interchangeable; it is unnecessary to differentiate between them when discussing knowledge. However, it is *very* important to distinguish between knowledge and wisdom, both of which are *chih*.

Chih has different meanings, some positive and some negative, in the different philosophical schools.

1) *Chih* in Confucianism

In Confucianism, *chih* is a basic virtue. "*Chih*, humanity, and courage are the universal virtues... To love to learn is near to *chih*; to practice with vigor is near to humanity; to know what is shameful is near to courage" (*Doctrine of the Mean*, Ch. 20). Feeling ourselves ignorant, we want to learn more in order to perfect ourselves. Here, *chih* has the connotations of both knowledge and wisdom — both are involved in becoming a superior man or sage.

2) *Chih* in Taoism

In Taoism, knowledge and wisdom are separated. Taoists value wisdom and renounce knowledge. Lao Tzu said, "One who is *chih* does not speak; one who speaks is not *chih*" (*Lao Tzu*, Ch. 56). Here, *chih* means wisdom. He also said, "He (the sage) always causes the people to be without *chih* and without desires, so that those who have *chih* dare not act" (*Lao Tzu*, Ch. 3). This *chih* refers to the knowledge or acumen that enables and encourages one to take advantage of others. Most of the occurrences of *chih* in the *Lao Tzu* are of the latter kind. In the *Chuang Tzu*, also, the two kinds of *chih* are differentiated. Chuang Tzu called them 'great *chih*' or 'true *chih*' (wisdom) and 'small *chih*' (know−ledge). For example, "There must be first a true man, then there can be true *chih*" (*Chuang Tzu*, Ch. 6), and "*Chih* (wisdom)penetrates to the spirit" (*Chuang Tzu*, Ch.12). He also said, "*Chih* is a weapon for struggle" (*Chuang Tzu*, Ch. 4) and "*Chih* is a troublemaker" (*Chuang Tzu*, Ch. 4). Here, *chih* means knowledge. In Taoism, the *chih* of knowledge, as shown in this quotation, also includes the desire to achieve fame through knowledge. The *chih* of wisdom, however, is to see through external things and understand the Way.

3) *Chih* in Chinese Buddhism

Buddhism, also, differentiated between the *chih* of knowledge and the *chih* of wisdom. Knowledge was defined as the state of making distinctions, which meant attachment to relativities like life and death, right and wrong. Wisdom was defined as the state of non-distinction, which is the highest state of mind. Some Chinese Buddhists still use the sound of the Sanskrit word *prajña* to mean wisdom, because *prajña*, in Buddhist thought, is near to Buddha-nature; others use both *prajña* and *chih*. For example, Seng Chao said, "However, *chih* has a vision which can see through darkness, but it is without *chih*" (Seng Chao, *Book of Chao*, Treatise on *Prajña* Without Knowledge) . Here, the first *chih* is wisdom and the second one is knowledge. The meaning is that wisdom is beyond knowledge.

22. 法（*fa*）LAW/METHOD/MODEL/DHARMA

The character 法, originally written as 灋, is a visual symbol for judging without favoritism. As defined by Hsü Shen, " 灋 means punishment. It symbolizes that [law] is as level as the surface of water; therefore, its left radical is water. The other part means to remove the crooked one" (Hsü Shen, *Explanation*) . From this basic concept developed the interpretations and extensions of the various philosophical schools.

1) Law

Most Confucianists did not emphasize *fa*, although they did not consider it trivial. To them, virtue in government was much more important than *fa*. In the *Analects*, *fa* appears only twice. In *Mencius* there are ten references to *fa*, but only three times concern the practice of law. "*Fa* alone," said Mencius, "cannot carry itself into practice" (*Mencius*, Bk. 4, Pt. 1, Ch. 1) .

Hsün Tzu, however, said, "*Fa* is the beginning of government" (*Hsün Tzu*, The Way of a Ruler) . His book has many references to *fa* and its importance, causing later philosophers to give it close attention. Hsün Tzu's student, Han Fei, the most influential Legalist, made *fa* the central concept of Legalism. "In a great king's state, there are no references to the Classics, only *fa* is taught; there are no speeches of former kings, only the officials are teachers" (*Han Fei Tzu*, Five Moths) .

2) Principle or natural law

"The superior people practice *fa* and wait for *ming* (the Mandate of Heaven)" (*Mencius*, Bk. 7, Pt. 2, Ch. 33) . Although this *fa* means law, it is not the law of government to which Mencius refers, but natural law or Heavenly principle. This concept of *fa* was shared by Chuang Tzu. "Heaven and Earth have their great beauty but do not speak of it; the four seasons have their bright *fa* but do not discuss it; all things have their principles of growth but do not talk about them" (*Chuang Tzu*, Ch. 22) .

3) Model, rule, or method

Although *fa* is generally used as meaning model, rule, or method in contexts unrelated to philosophy, it has a special use in Lao Tzu's thought. Lao Tzu said, "Man *fa* Earth; Earth *fa* Heaven; Heaven *fa* the Way; the Way *fa* Nature" (*Lao Tzu*, Ch. 25) . Here, *fa* means "follows" in the first three statements, but cannot mean "follow" in the fourth because the Way is on the same level as Nature. Therefore, this *fa* means "in accord with", which shows that man, following the principle or *fa* of Heaven, is in accord with Nature.

4) *Dharma*

When Indian Buddhism reached China, Chinese Buddhists translated the Sanskrit word *dharma* into *fa*. *Dharma* is "... used in the sense of all things, or anything small or great, visible or invisible, real or unreal, affairs, truth, principle, method, concrete things, abstract idea, etc." (W.E. Soothill, *A Dictionary of Chinese Buddhist Terms*) . So, *dharma* means anything from the highest statement of Buddhism to the lowest level of desire. To Chinese Buddhists, *fa* has the same inclusiveness. "Buddhist *fa* is not a dual *fa*" (*Platform Scripture*, Ch.1), and "If you see all *fa* and your mind does not attach to them, this is called thoughtlessness" (*ibid.*, Ch. 2) . Here, the *fa* in the first quo-tation means the true- suchness (reality or Sanskrit *bhutatathata*); the *fa* in the second refers to all relative things or ideas.

23. 性（*hsing*）NATURE

Hsing is a particularly significant term because Chinese philosophy could be characterized as learning the cultivation of mind and *hsing*. Speculations on the definition of *hsing* have led to the formation of various theories, ideological systems, and accepted practices in Chinese thought.

1) Life, livelihood

"Heaven produces people and selects a ruler for them. It makes officials govern the people and does not let them lose their *hsing*" (*Tso's Commentary on the Spring and Autumn Annals*, Duke Hsiang, 14). Originally, as here, *hsing* simply meant the people's lives or livelihood. It was when philosophers began to investigate the essence of life and used nature to name it that *hsing* became a philosophically significant term.

2) Human *hsing*

Lao Tzu did not use the term *hsing*. In the Confucian *Analects*, it appears only twice, when Tzu-Kung said, "We hear our Master on culture and its manifestation, but we do not hear him talking about *hsing* and the Way of Heaven" (*Analects*, V, 12), and when Confucius said, "*Hsing* are all alike, but through [habitual] practice they become far apart" (*Analects*, XVII, 2). In both passages, *hsing* means human *hsing*, but Confucius did not make it a topic for discussion.

After Lao Tzu and Confucius, in the Period of Warring States, most philosophers, including Mencius, Hsün Tzu, and Chuang Tzu, became interested in discussing *hsing* as human *hsing*. Mencius and Hsün Tzu differed almost diametrically in their theories regarding it. Mencius said, "The goodness of man's *hsing* is like the downward flow of water" (*Mencius*, Bk. 6, Pt. 1, Ch. 2). Hsün Tzu said, "Man's *hsing* is evil; his goodness comes from making an effort" (*Hsün Tzu*, Human Nature is Evil). The debate over inherent *vs.* acquired characteristics has been as much a topic of interest in China as in the West.

3) The essence of life

In the *Chuang Tzu*, *hsing* does not appear in the first seven chapters, the part regarded as having been written by Chuang Tzu himself. It occurs frequently in later chapters, always used to express the idea that "*Hsing* is the essence of life" (*Chuang Tzu*, Ch. 24). This meaning was emphasized by later Taoists and became an aspect of learning how to become immortal in religious Taoism.

4) Instinct

"That which at birth is original is called *hsing*. *Hsing* is produced by the harmony [of dark (*yin*) and light (*yang*)] . Their essence is in accord with the stimulus and reaction that naturally, without training, is called *hsing*" (*Hsün Tzu*, On the Rectification of Names) . Hsün Tzu thus defined *hsing* as instinct, which he identified as desire.

5) The *hsing* of all things

"If you are like a baby who has no desires, all things will be perfect and their *hsing* will be complete" (*Wang Pi's Commentary on the Lao Tzu*, Ch. 10) . Here, *hsing* means the *hsing* of all things.

6) Self-*hsing*, true self, or Buddha-nature

"If only you hold the *Diamond Sutra*, you can immediately see your *hsing* and directly become a Buddha" (*Platform Scripture*, Ch.1) . *Hsing* is a central term in the Chinese Ch'an School, where it means true mind, true self, original face, or Buddha-nature.

7) Principle, energy, and mind

Neo-Confucianists of the Sung Dynasty developed a theory of nature based on "What Heaven imparts is called *hsing*" (*Doctrine of the Mean*, Ch.1) . Ch'eng Hao and Ch'eng I defined *hsing* as principle (*li*) and as energy (*ch'i*): "*Hsing* is principle; it is what is referred to as principle–nature" (*Literary Remains of the Two Ch'engs*, 22A) . "Life is called *hsing. Hsing* is energy, energy is *hsing*, which means life" (*ibid.*, 1) . Wang Yang–ming said, "Mind is *hsing*; *hsing* is principle" (*Complete Works of Wang Yang-ming*, Record of Instructions, Sec.1) .

24. 勇（*yung*）COURAGE/BRAVERY

In common usage, *yung* is simply a descriptive term for human behavior. In Chinese philosophy, it acquires depth as a major virtue. In Confucianism, "Wisdom, humanity, and *yung* — these three are the universal virtues" (*Doctrine of the Mean*, Ch. 20). Confucius said, "The *yung* one is fearless" (*Analects*, IX, 28). That this is not simply a facile exchange of synonyms becomes clear when the definition is explored.

1) Having a feeling of shame

"To have a feeling of shame is near to *yung*" (*Doctrine of the Mean*, Ch. 20). This means that a man who knows what is wrong does not do it; if he has done wrong, he has the *yung* to make amends.

2) In accord with righteousness

Confucius said, "The superior man takes righteousness as the highest principle. A superior man who is *yung* without righteousness will create disorder; an ordinary man who is *yung* without righteousness will commit robbery" (*Analects*, XVII, 23). This refers to moral *yung*; the really *yung* must act righteously.

3) **Based on compassion**

"To be compassionate is to be able to be *yung*, to be thrifty is to be able to be expansive, not daring to be ahead of the world is to be able to be chief of all vassals (things) . Now, if one wishes to be *yung* without compassion, expansive without thriftiness, and ahead without retreat, this is the path to death" (*Lao Tzu*, Ch. 67) . Buddhism shares this idea of compassion as essential to courage; Buddha is called "the great compassionate one" and "the great *yung* one." Confu-cius said, "Men of humanity are sure to be *yung*; but those who are *yung* may not always be humane" (*Analects*, XIV, 5). Here, by humanity Confucius meant "to love"; so, it was equivalent to saying that the really *yung* one must be kind or compassionate to all people.

4) **Knowing fate**

"To know that hardship is a matter of fate, that success is a matter of the times, and to face great difficulties without fear, this is the *yung* of the sage" (*Chuang Tzu*, Ch. 17) . The really *yung* one, who takes everything he encounters as fate, is beyond the influence of things.

5) **Restraining oneself**

"When one is about to speak happily, one is able to cut it off, to have the patience to remain silent; when one's will and energy are rising, one is able to draw them back; when one's anger and desire are reaching the boiling point, one is able to make them disappear — only the person of great *yung* is able to do these" (*Complete Works of Wang Yang-ming*, Letter to Huang Tsung-hsien) . Here, *yung* refers to having a determination to cultivate one's mind.

25. 真（*chen*）TRUE/TRUTH

Chen is not found in the *Analects*, the *Mencius*, or the *Five Classics*; it appears first with a single occurrence in the *Lao Tzu* and then sixty-six times in the *Chuang Tzu*. Confucianists devoted attention to the distinction between right and wrong; Taoists discussed truth and falsity. These philosophical positions were not necessarily mutually exclusive for, in Confucianism, sincerity had the same meaning as truth. Confucianists were concerned primarily with ethics and politics, which were seen in terms of right and wrong. Taoists, however, with their interest in metaphysics and cultivation of the mind, were concerned with truth and falsity. Meanings of *chen* found in Taoism include 'truth', 'essence', and 'true self' or 'true nature'.

1) Truth

"The essence is very *chen*; within it there is sincerity" (*Lao Tzu*, Ch. 21) . Being *chen* and sincere, the essence has real existence.

2) Essence

"Whether you find his identity or not, it neither increases nor decreases his *chen*" (*Chuang Tzu*, Ch. 2) . Here, *chen* would mean essence, which is beyond knowing.

3) *Chen* self/*chen* nature

"He who does not depart from *chen* is called the perfect man" (*Chuang Tzu*, Ch. 33) . Note, by the way, that, in the *Chuang Tzu*, '*chen* mind', '*chen* self', or '*chen* nature' is referred to as True Master or True Lord; all of these are *chen*.

26. 神 (*shen*) SPIRIT/IMMORTALITY/ SOUL/ GODS

Originally, *shen* meant "gods" but acquired the meaning of "spirit" because Chinese philosophers taught that men can be in accord with Heaven.

1) Gods or spirits

In the *Analects*, *shen* appears six times, each referring to gods, ancestors, or spirits. For example, "While respecting *kueo* (鬼 spirits, ghosts) and *shen*, keep them at a distance" (*Analects*, VI, 20). In this context, *kueo* and *shen* always are used together as a compound word referring to gods or spirits.

2) Ancestors

Confucius said, "I cannot find any flaw in Emperor Yu! He was frugal in food and drink, but displayed filial piety to *kueo* and *shen*" (*Analects*, VIII, 21). Emperor Yu was noted for sacrifices to his ancestors; therefore, *shen* here must refer to them.

3) The spiritual brilliance of virtue and nature

In the *Mencius*, *shen* occurs three times. One refers to spirits; the other two are concerned with superlatives of virtue and nature. "Whenever the superior man passes through, transformation follows; whenever he abides, it is *shen*. He flows with the current of Heaven and Earth" (*Mencius*, Bk.7, Pt. 1, Ch. 13) . "When he is great and transformed, he is called a sage; when a sage is beyond knowing, he is called *shen*" (*Mencius*, Bk. 7, Pt. 2, Ch. 25) .

4) The spirit

In the *Lao Tzu*, *shen* appears four times; all refer to spirits. In the *Chuang Tzu*, *shen* occurs many times, usually referring to 'spirit' or the highest state of cultivation. For example, "By concentrating his *shen*, he will cause all things to be free from sickness" (*Chuang Tzu*, Ch. 2) .

5) Subtle essence/wisdom

Shen appears frequently in the *Book of Changes*, most often referring to spirits, gods, and spiritual brilliance. How−ever, there are two special uses; first, in reference to the subtle essence. "*Shen* means the subtle essence of all things" (*Book of Changes*, Treatise of Remarks on the Trigrams), and, "That which is unfathomable in the dark and light is called *shen*" (*ibid.*, The Great Appendix, Sec.1,

Ch. 5). The second usage indicates wisdom; for example, "By *shen*, he is able to know coming events; by knowledge, he is able to store up the past" (*ibid.*, The Great Appendix, Sec. 1, Ch. 11) .

6) Immortality

In religious Taoism, *shen* became 'immortality'. "Knowing whiteness (the outer) and keeping blackness (the inner), *shen* will come naturally" (*Unity of the Trio*, Ch. 7) .

27. 时（*shih*）TIME

Shih is a very common word, but Chinese philosophers used it in their theories to indicate timeliness — relating thought to the temporal practicalities of daily life.

1）*Shih* in the Book of Changes

Although there is only one *shih* in the sixty–four hexagrams, there are fifty–seven in the *Ten Wings*, the commentaries that explain how the Book of Changes functions. They have at least three meanings:

（a）**The four seasons.** "In its change and penetration, it corresponds to the four *shih*"（*Book of Changes*, Great Appendix, Sec.1, Ch. 6）. Depending on the context, "four seasons" also can be a metaphor for physical nature.

（b）**Chance/opportunity.** "The superior man who would advance his virtue and improve his work must catch *shih*"（*Book of Changes*, Hexagram 1, *Ch'ien*）. Opportunity must be grasped when the chance occurs. A Western equivalent would be the admonition to "seize Time by the forelock."

(c) Changes in the six lines of the hexagrams. "The [indications of the] six lines are achieved according to their *shih*. By *shih*, they drive through Heaven with the six dragons" (*Book of Changes*, Hexagram 1, *Ch'ien*) . Here, time refers to the sequence in which lines change.

2) *Shih* in Confucianism

Confucius was called the sage of time; his thought and action always was appropriate to the time or occasion. In relation to Confucius, *shih* has two meanings: First, everything he advocated or did showed awareness of its timing. Confucius said, "… people must be active in *shih* (*i.e.*, in seasons not devoted to planting, weeding, and harvesting, people must be engaged in public works ordered by the ruler)" (*Analects*, I, 5) . "My Master (Confucius) speaks when it is *shih* to speak; so, people do not tire of his speaking" (*Analects*, XIV, 14) . Second, his thinking always was current, but with due regard for the past. "Follow the calendar of the Hsia Dynasty; ride in the carriage of the Yin Dynasty; wear the ceremonial cap of the Chou Dynasty" (*Analects*, XV, 10) . Confucius was able to adopt and adapt from the systems of the different dynasties without becoming attached to any one of them.

3) *Shih* in Taoism

Meanings of *shih* in the *Lao Tzu* are the same as those in the *Analects*. The *Chuang Tzu*, however, adds two special meanings —

fate and duration. "If one lives at peace with *shih* and moves with it, neither grief nor joy has a way by which to enter one's mind" (*Chuang Tzu*, Ch. 3). "Accepting and flowing with the times one lives in is equivalent to accepting fate…" (*ibid.*, Ch. 17). Here, *shih* means that time is a continuum of duration; time is not subject to segmentation.

Later Taoists, especially in religious Taoism, hoped to control the universe by understanding *shih*. "We must know the method of 'crowding together'. It means to reduce a year to a month, a month to a day, and a day to an hour, — to differentiate movement (*yang*) and quietude (*yin*) in terms of minutes. All changes of the universe depend on the changes of fullness and emptiness of the trigrams of *K'an* and *Li*. This is called the way of *yin* and *yang* action" (Wei Po-yang, *Unity of the Trio*, Commentary on the Door of *Ch'ien* and *K'un* by Chu Yün-yang). They believed that, since every time interval is a dark-light cycle, one who can control a minute can control each larger cycle in turn until he controls the universe.

28. 气（*ch'i*）ENERGY/AIR/BREATH/ SPIRIT/MATERIAL FORCE

Ch'i is a complex word. It not only has many different meanings in the different schools of philosophy but is, itself, a combination of words that include both material and non-material aspects. Sometimes it is a metaphysical term; sometimes it refers to phenomena. *Ch'i* is invisible, but it is closely related to visible things. It plays an important role in both Taoism and later Confucianism.

1）Air, the energy of Heaven and Earth

'Air' is the original meaning of *ch'i*. Ancient Chinese defined *ch'i* as cloud−energy, meaning "the energy of the universe." This usage was common in Taoism and Neo−Confucianism. "Human beings are in *ch'i*; *ch'i* is in the bodies of human beings. From Heaven and Earth to the ten thousand things, none of them can exist without *ch'i*" (*Pao P'u Tzu*, The Perfect Principle). "The Great Clod (nature) belches out *ch'i* and its name is wind" (*Chuang Tzu*, Ch. 2). "These two *ch'i* respond to each other and thereby form a union" (*Book of Changes*, Hexagram 31, *Hsien*). Here, the two *ch'i* are the energies of *yin* and *yang*, the complementary factors of the cosmos.

2) Breath

In the human body, *ch'i* is breath. This breath, combining air and energy, was the focus of Taoist practices in meditation and attempts to become immortal. "Make your will one! Don't listen with your ears, listen with your mind. Don't listen with your mind, but with your *ch'i*" (*Chuang Tzu*, Ch. 4) . "In beginning to learn the moving of *ch'i*, inhale *ch'i* through your nose and hold it. After your mind counts to one hundred, breathe out slowly through your mouth. When you breathe, don't let your ears hear the sound of your breath" (*Pao P'u Tzu*, Release Standstill) .

3) Spirit

In the *Analects*, *ch'i* combines energy and spirit. "The superior man guards against three things: in youth, when his passionate *ch'i* is not yet settled, he guards against lust; when he is strong and his passionate *ch'i* is full of vigor, he guards against conflict; when he is old and his passionate ch'i is decaying, he guards against greed" (*Analects*, XVI, 7) . In Mencius' thought, the meaning of *ch'i* shifts from passion or energy to spirit. "The will is the leader of *ch'i*. *Ch'i* pervades and animates the entire body" (*Mencius*, Bk. 2, Pt. 1, Ch. 2) .

4) Essence of Heaven and Earth

In Chuang Tzu's thought, *ch'i* is the all−pervasive essence of the universe. "The ten thousand things really are one. What we think beautiful are spiritual and unearthly things. What we think ugly are the foul and rotten things. But the foul and rotten things may turn into spiritual and unearthly things; the spiritual and unearthly things may turn into foul and rotten things. So, it is said, all things in the world are pervaded by a single *ch'i*" (*Chuang Tzu*, Ch. 22) . Here, Chuang Tzu means a *ch'i* that is closely related to the energies of *yin* and *yang* as the motivational factors of the universe. Later Taoists and Confucianists, especially Neo−Confucianists, developed this thought and emphasized that *ch'i* was the essence of the universe. "The *ch'i* of Heaven and Earth was one. It was divided into dark (*yin*) and light (*yang*), then separated into the four seasons and displayed as the five movements (*wu hsing*, often translated as the five agents or, with less validity, as the five elements')" (Tung Chung−shu, *Luxuriant Dew of the Spring and Autumn Annals*, The Five Movements Producing Each Other) .

5) Matter/material force

Because later Taoists and Confucianists turned the energy of dark and light into the energy of the five movements, *ch'i* was divided into two kinds. The pure one became the principle of spirit; the turbid one became the matter of which all things were made. "*Ch'i* fills the supreme Emptiness (Heaven and Earth). It ascends and descends, flies and spreads without stopping... When it is pure, *ch'i* becomes pervasive; when it is turbid, it becomes obstructive... When the Supreme Emptiness is pure and without obstruction, then it becomes spiritual; otherwise, it is turbid and obstructive — then it has form" (Chang Tsai, *Correct Discipline for Beginners*, Ch.1).

29. 悟 (*wu*) ENLIGHTENMENT

"*Wu* means awakening" (Hsü Shen, *Explanation*). Awakening was both the original and the common meaning. In the *Analects*, *Mencius*, and *Lao Tzu*, there are no examples of awakening. Although there are four occurrences in the *Chuang Tzu*, none had any relationship with philosophical ideas. However, when Indian Buddhism began to influence Chinese thought, *wu* was used to conceptualize awakening to the Way or to the enlightenment which played such an important role in Chinese Buddhism. Especially in the Ch'an school, it became a key idea. Thus, in philosophy, enlightenment is a Buddhist term. It should be noted, however, that although *wu* in the *Chuang Tzu* has the common meaning of awakening, Chuang Tzu used another term, *chüeh* (觉), for the meaning that the Ch'an school gave to *wu*.

Wu, in Chinese Buddhism, has several levels:

1) General *wu*

"In order to cause all creatures to *wu* (awaken to) Buddha's wisdom and insight, he (Buddha) appears in this world" (*Dharma-*

Flower Sutra, Ch. 2) . Here, enlightenment simply refers to understanding truth through reading sutras and practicing the Buddha's teachings. Sometimes, it means to understand the principle of reality or truth—suchness (*Bhütatathata*) . Although it also means to understand the Way, in itself it has no special meaning or content.

2) Small sudden *wu*

"The small sudden *wu* is as Chih Tao—lin said, 'On the Seventh Ground (step or level), one begins to see the state of non—birth'" (Hui—ta, *Commentary on the Book of Chao*) . In Buddhism, there are various theories about the Ten Grounds — the ten stages by which a bodhisattva becomes a Buddha. The Seventh Ground indicates a bodhisattva who has understood the principle of non—birth, that Buddha—*dharma* is eternal, without birth or death. Because there are still three more stages before full *wu*, this level of understanding is called the small sudden *wu*.

3) Great sudden *wu*

"The monk Tao—sheng's description of great sudden *wu* is as follows: What 'sudden' refers to is that the principle cannot be analyzed, so that the state of *wu* is the ultimate insight. When the absolute *wu* corresponds to the unanalyzed principle and causes the principle and wisdom (insight) to be completely without obstruction, this is called the sudden *wu*" (Hui—ta, *Commentary on the Book of*

Chao). This quotation refers to Tao−sheng's sudden enlightenment which, having no grounds or stages, is called the great sudden *wu* in contrast with the small sudden *wu*. Since Tao−sheng himself left no written records, we cannot be sure of what he really meant.

4) Sudden *wu* in the Chinese Ch'an school

Wu is the term on which the whole system of the Ch'an school was established. In its literature, *wu* appears in many ways; some are general, some are small, and some are great. It is difficult for readers to differentiate among them. But the highest ideal and central thought is sudden *wu*, which was defined in a variety of ways by Sheng−hui, a disciple of Hui−neng: "To understand events with both intelligence and wisdom is called sudden *wu*. It is not attained through gradual steps; it is natural (spontaneous) . [To know that] the mind, originally, is empty and still; this is sudden *wu*. That this mind grasps at nothing is sudden *wu*. That the mind is awakened by *dharma* and does not seek for gain is sudden *wu*. Knowing all *dharmas* as themselves is sudden *wu*. When hearing someone speaking about emptiness, attaching neither to emptiness nor to non−emptiness is sudden *wu*. When hearing someone talking about self, grasping neither at self nor at non−self is sudden *wu*. Entering the state of Nirvana without departing from life and death is sudden *wu*" (*Record of the Conversations of Shen-hui*) . Although Shen−hui's explanation is pertinent to understanding the meaning of sudden *wu*, it has been criticized as unnecessarily complex. Out of all the varied definitions, three essential elements emerge:

(a) **Being beyond cultivation of externals.** "If a man *wu* by the teachings of the Sudden School, he is not attached to cultivation of externals. His real and correct view is illuminated, and he is free from all trouble and toil. This is to see self-nature." (*Platform Scripture*, Ch. 2) . Cultivation of externals refers to reading sutras, keeping precepts, meditation, and so forth.

(b) **Being awakened by a single thought.** "If a real contemplation of wisdom (*prajña*) arises in a man's mind, if only for one moment, all of his false thoughts disappear. If he recognizes his self-nature, he is able to attain Buddhahood in a single *wu*" (*Platform Scripture*, Ch. 2) . A single thought, being free of doubts and qualifications, is virtually instantaneous, hence is sudden enlightenment.

(c) **Enlightened self-nature.** "If your self-nature is *wu*, common nature becomes Buddha-nature. If your self-nature is confused, Buddha-nature becomes common nature" (*Platform Scripture*, Ch. 2) . In the Ch'an school, self-nature is equal to Buddha-nature, but is more personal. It is man's original mind or true self. Sudden *wu* has seeing the self-nature as its ultimate goal; without seeing one's self-nature, the experience is not sudden *wu*.

30. 恕 (*shu*) EMPATHY/RECIPROCITY

Shu is one of those simple words that, in philosophy, becomes difficult to explain. Although it appears only twice in the *Analects* and once in the *Mencius*, it is a very important virtue in Confucianism. It does not appear at all in Taoist and Buddhist texts, yet it is regarded as a significant characteristic of Chinese culture. It has been translated into English as 'compassion', 'forgiveness', and 'altruism', but none of these expresses its true meaning.

1) The meaning of *shu*

Confucius' disciple, Tzu-kung, asked, "Is there one word which can be used throughout one's entire life?" Confucius said, "It is *shu*. Do not do to others what you do not want them to do to you" (*Analects*, XV, 23) . This well-known definition is based on the reasoning that you do not treat others badly because you do not want others to treat you badly. It is the same as the *Great Learning*'s application of a measuring square (yardstick would be the American colloquial equivalent) to conduct: "The superior man has a way of using a measuring square. What a man dislikes in his superiors, he does not do to his inferiors; what he dislikes in his inferiors, he does not do to his superiors; what he dislikes in those in front of him, he does not do to those behind him; what he dislikes in those who are behind him, he does not do to those in front of him; what he dislikes in those on the right, he does not do to those on the left; what he dislikes in those on the left, he does not do to those on the right. This is the way of using the measuring square" (*Great Learning*, Ch. 10) .

2) *Shu* as a function of humanity

Confucius said, "Ts'an, my Way is to perform all actions in Oneness." Ts'an Tzu said, "Yes." After Confucius went out, the disciples asked him, "What did he say?" Ts'an Tzu replied, "The way of our master is nothing but loyalty and *shu*" (*Analects*, IV, 15) . Loyalty and *shu* are functions of humanity, which was Confucius' key virtue.

Some scholars regarded *shu* as synonymous with humanity. "*Shu* means humanity" (Hsü Shen, *Explanation*) . But *shu* is not humanity; it is a function of humanity. Its function is, taking oneself as an example, to turn inner feelings into outer actions. Confucius said, "The Way is not far from man. If a man pursues the Way but stays away from man, what he does is not in the Way. The *Book of Poetry* says, 'In hewing an ax handle, the pattern is not far off.' If a man grasps one ax handle to hew another ax handle and looks askance at the handle he is hewing, he may still think that it is far from the pattern. Therefore, the superior man governs men as men. When the people become good, he stops. Loyalty and *shu* are not far from the Way. What you do not want others to do to you, you do not do to them. There are four things in the Way of the superior people; I have not as yet done any of them. I have not yet served my father as I would want my son to serve me. I have not yet served my ruler as I would want my ministers to serve me. I have not yet served my elder brother as I would want my younger brother to serve me. I have not yet treated my friends first as I would want them to treat me" (*Doctrine of the Mean*, Ch. 13) . Pursuing the Way through human nature, governing people through their own nature, and using oneself as a guide in treating others — this is the way of humanity and is also *shu*. The meaning of *shu* is very close to that of humanity; it is in their relationship that they are differentiated. Humanity is the essence of *shu*; *shu* is the function of humanity.

Mencius was a notable exponent of *shu*, though he did not often use the term. "To respect the elders in your family and then to extend this respect to others' elders, to love the young in your family and then extend this love to others' youths — extending your kindness, you can protect all people within the four seas; otherwise, you cannot protect even your wife and children. The reason that the ancient sages were greater than ordinary people is that they were good at extending their actions" (*Mencius*, Bk. 1, Pt. 1, Ch. 7) . Extending oneself to others turns the mind of humanity into the action of humanity. This extending is *shu*; so, *shu* is the function of humanity. Because it is a function of humanity, human-ity can include it. When Confucius and Mencius discussed humanity, they also referred to the Way of humanity — *i.e.*, *shu*. Thus, without using the specific character, they made *shu* a very significant Confucian virtue.

3) The special relationship of *shu* with loyalty and sincerity

Shu, as the function of humanity is related to all virtues; among them, there are two with which the relation-ship is particularly close:

(a) **Loyalty** (*chung*) . Loyalty and *shu* are like twins. In Confucian books, loyalty and *shu* are linked (in English, they would be hyphenated) to form a term in which loyalty always refers to honesty of mind, which provides a foundation for *shu*; in other words, without loyalty, *shu* has nothing to carry out or extend. Only if one is honest in one's mind, can *shu* be practiced. "Someone said, 'That you do not do to others what you do not want others to do to you is *shu*. Why did Tzu Ssu (author of the *Doctrine of the Mean*) say that it is *shu* and loyalty?' Chu Hsi answered, 'loyalty and *shu* cannot be separated. When you are loyal you are unable to see *shu*; when you are *shu*, loyalty is with you. Without loyalty, one is unable to be in the state of not doing to others what you do not want others to do to you. Therefore, without loyalty, *shu* is incomplete'" (Chu

Hsi, *Classified Conversations*, Vol. 63 ）. When loyalty and *shu* are connected, they form a term that emphasizes *shu* but also symbolizes that it cannot be separated from loyalty.

（**b**）**Sincerity** （*ch'eng*）. Mencius said, "All things are already complete in oneself. There is no greater happiness than to examine oneself and find that one is sincere. If one makes the effort to practice *shu*, humanity is in one's hand" （*Mencius*, Bk.7, Pt. 1, Ch. 4）. In this passage, Mencius connected the three virtues of sincerity, *shu*, and humanity. Here, sincerity resembles loyalty, but is deeper. Sincerity refers to mind−without−falsehood. Sincerity, in the *Doctrine of the Mean*, is the Way of Heaven, which is perfect goodness. If a man were to say, "I do not want others to love me; therefore, I do not love others," this would not be sincere, and it would not express *shu*. There−fore, sincerity is the foundation that makes it possible for *shu* to be practiced properly.

In Neo−Confucian thought, loyalty was interpreted as the equivalent of sincerity. This is why some neo−Confucianists, such as Ch'eng I and Chu Hsi, regarded loyalty as the Way of Heaven; they understood loyalty as sincerity. For example, Ch'eng I said, "Loyalty is the Way of Heaven, and *shu* is the way of man" （*Analects*, *Commentary of Chu Hsi*, XV, 4）, and Chu Hsi said, "In the sage, loyalty is sincerity, and *shu* is humanity" （*Classified Conversations of Chu Hsi*, vol. 27）.

4) *Shu* as a characteristic of Chinese culture

Although Taoism and Chinese Buddhism do not stress *shu*, they use terms that, in general, are consonant with it. For example, Lao Tzu emphasized humility, Chuang Tzu emphasized the equality of all things, and the Ch'an school taught that common people are Buddha; all of these recognized the importance of other people. This is also a fundamental aspect of *shu*. Because of this, a characteristic of Chinese culture is that there is no effort to impose one's pattern on others or to force others to follow one's ideas. For example, Confucian filial piety emphasizes that you must be filial to your parents and allow your children to be filial to you. It does not require you to be filial to my parents. Confucianism is not a religion; there is no insistence that others worship "my" god. Correspondingly, Taoist non-action permits everyone to follow his own nature. Finally, the Ch'an school wants everyone to awaken to his own original face. Therefore, in the Chinese culture, anyone or everyone can become a sage or a god to the people who think he has great merit.

5) The difference between *shu* and compassion, forgiveness, and altruism.

In Indian Buddhism and the Western religions, compassion and forgiveness are familiar terms. They refer to sympathy for others who are suffering or evil. Therefore, when you express compassion or forgiveness for others, the implication is that you are right and they are wrong and thereby pitiable. Others are seen as lower than oneself. But *shu* requires thinking of others by extension of oneself, with all placed on the same level.

Altruism is a concept that emphasizes sacrifice of oneself for others, the eradication of self−centered desires in order to devote oneself to the welfare of others. Moism was typically altruistic. Moists were for others, selflessly. Their thought was not consistent with human nature; therefore, they were not *shu*.

Most of the world's literate cultures have produced examples of what has come to be known as the Golden Rule, commonly expressed as, "Do unto others as you would have others do unto you" (derived from *Matthew*, VII, 12) . Grounded in *shu*, however, the Confucian version is not merely a negatively worded mirror image of this injunction. Action according to "Do unto others" implies that we consider our ideas normative and that others should act as we see best. We become like salesmen who see value only in their own products. This is a particularly dangerous attitude in matters of faith, for the advocacy of religion has led to many of the world's bitterest wars. However, if we follow the principle of *shu*, we will not cause trouble, for we simply do not do to others what we do not want done to us. For example, in the relationship between husband and wife, "Do unto others" implies "I do to him/her as I want him/her to do to me." But with *shu*, the husband (for example) puts himself in the wife's place; he thinks, "If I were she, what would I want me to do?" The spirit of *shu* requires recognition of others' personalities and valuation of others' freedom.

31. 虚（*hsu*）EMPTINESS

The character *hsu* originally meant "big hill". Because of the spatial imagery of large hills, *hsu*, by extension, came to mean "vast" and "expansive" which, in turn, implied 'emptiness', its meaning in philosophical usage.

1）The meaning of *hsu*

Hsu occurs only twice in the *Analects* and twice in the *Mencius*; in each, it has the philosophical implication of emptiness. "The man who has not but thinks that he has is *hsu* but thinks that he is full, is tense but thinks that he is at ease, and has difficulty being constant" (*Analects*, VII, 25).

2）*Hsu* of heart or mind

In Taoism, *hsu* is a term that means the cultivation of mind, as in "*hsu* their hearts" (*Lao Tzu*, Ch. 3). Here, 'hearts' means desires or the emptying of desires from the heart. Hsün Tzu, the great Confucianist, said, "That which does not let what is already stored obstruct what is about to be received is called *hsu*" (*Hsün Tzu*, The Removal of Prejudices). Here, *hsu* is absence of prejudice.

3) *Hsu* of self

"If a man, as he rows across a river, has his boat touched by a *hsu* boat, he will not get angry no matter how hot–tempered he is. If there is a man in the other boat, he will shout to him to give way. If his first and second shouts are ignored, he will shout a third time and follow this with a scolding. In the first instance, he is not angry, for the boat is *hsu*; in the second he is angry, because the boat is occupied. If a man could *hsu* himself and wander in the world, who could do him harm?" (*Chuang Tzu*, Ch. 20) Here, emptying means renouncing or being beyond ego.

4) Without form or space

"The perfect man of ancient times took *jen* (human–ity) as his path, *i* (righteousness) as his shelter, and wandered in the *hsu* of freedom and ease" (*Chuang Tzu*, Ch. 14) . Here, *hsu* means space, which has no form.

5) Lines of the hexagrams in the *Book of Changes*

"Their changes and movements are unstayed; they flow into any of the six *hsu*" (*Book of Changes*, The Great Appendix, Sec. 2, Ch. 8) . Here, *hsu* refers to the lines of the hexagrams because these six lines represent the space between Heaven and Earth; each line is like an empty receptacle waiting to be occupied by things.

32. 理（*li*）REASON/PRINCIPLE

According to the *Explanation of Script and Elucidation of Characters*, *li* originally meant 'to work on jade'. Since jade is a gemstone with veins and clouds of varying color, the carver had to be adept at following the veining. Following a train of reasoning or pursuing the ramifications of a statement of principle in gems of philosophical thinking can require equivalent discipline; so, by extension, *li* gradually assumed the meaning of 'reason' or 'principle'. Before the Sung Dynasty, *li*, as reason, generally was understood by philosophers as meaning to follow the Way or to practice virtue. In the Sung Dynasty, however, Neo-Confucianists appropriated *li* to take the place of *fa*, which had acquired the Buddhist meaning of *dharma*. In its Buddhist definition, *fa* stood for all events, but was empty of substance. *Li*, in Neo-Confucianism, also stood for every-thing, but its essence was reality. In Neo-Confucian thought, *li* became a key term, used more frequently than 'the Way' or 'humanity' in its relationships with other ideas or virtues and its different uses in various schools.

1) *Li* with righteousness

Li does not appear in the *Analects* and occurs only seven times in the *Mencius*. Of the seven, five simply mean "orderly" or "reasonable"; the other two have philosophical meaning. In both cases, *li* is associated with righteousness. For example, "What is it of which our minds approve similarly? It is *li* and righteousness" (*Mencius*, Bk. 6, Pt.1, Ch. 7) . Although Mencius did not emphasize *li*, clearly he recognized it as equivalent to righteousness in importance. After Mencius, *li* was accepted as following righteousness; they were combined into *i-li*, meaning principle, reason, or philosophy.

2) *Li* with propriety

Propriety, in Chinese, also is *li*, but written with a different character (礼) . The virtue of propriety is the foundation of China's system of social rules. Hsün Tzu emphasized it and connected it with *li* (principle) . He said, "Propriety is unchangeable *li*" (*Hsün Tzu*, On Music) .

3) *Li* with *ming* (name/term)

Ming comes from the School of Names, where reason and logic were discussed, but not *li*. In the Wei and Chin Dynasties, some philosophers discussed the topics of the School of Names, associating *ming* with *li* to form the Ming–li Sect. Thus *ming-li* became a term which meant the study of the analysis of terms. For example, "He was erudite and versed in *ming-li*" (*History of the Three Kingdoms*, Chung Hui).

4) *Li* with the Way

In Taoism, the Way is the ideal, the standard which is the *li* of all things. *Li* does not appear in the *Lao Tzu*, but the Way, as Lao Tzu used it, meant the *li* of all things. It appears frequently in the *Chuang Tzu*, where it was used as a definition of the Way, "The Way is *li*" (*Chuang Tzu*, Ch. 16). "Those who know the Way are certain to understand *li*" (*ibid.*, Ch. 17). Here, the Way and *li* were given the common meaning of 'principle' or 'reason'.

5) *Li* with normal relationships

The relationships between parents and children, husband and wife, elder and younger brother, ruler and people, friend and friend express ethical norms. "In practice, there is the *li* of ethics which is in accord with Heaven and Earth" (Tung Chung–shu, *Luxuriant Dew of the Spring and Autumn Annals*, People Matching with Heaven).

6) *Li* with Heaven

"Man is changed by things; they destroy Heavenly *li* and exhaust him with desires" (*Records of Propriety*, Records of Music).

This was the first appearance of Heavenly *li* in the classics. Neo-Confucianists adopted this term as a key idea.

7) *Li* with human nature

Sung Dynasty Neo-Confucianists equated Heavenly *li* with human nature and human nature with Nature. For example, "Nature is just *li*; it is the generic name of the ten thousand *li*. This *li* is just all of the common *li* between Heaven and Earth. When I have received it from Heaven, it belongs to me" (*Chu Hsi*, *Classified Conversations*, Ch. 117) . Because the Neo-Confucianists united Nature with *li*, their theories were called 'the learning of Nature–*li*' .

8) *Li* with mind

In the Neo-Confucian School of Mind, philosophers identified mind as *li*. "Mind is single mind; *li* is single *li*. When they are perfect, they return to the One. Their central meaning is 'without duality'" (Lu Hsiang-shan, *Complete Works*, Letter to Tseng Chai-chih) .

9) *Li* with all things and all events

"The sage sees through the beauties of Heaven and Earth and penetrates the *li* of the ten thousand things" (*Chuang Tzu*, Ch.22) . In Chuang Tzu's thought, "*li* of all things" simply means that every thing has its particular *li*. In Neo-Confucianism, however, "*li* of all things" refers to the *li* of mind, nature, and Heaven; all *li* are the one *li.* "Including Heaven, Earth, and the ten thousand things is the single *li*" (*Classified Conversations of Chu Hsi*, Ch. 1) .

10) *Li* with the Supreme Ultimate (*T'ai chi*)

In Chu Hsi's thought, the perfect *li* is the Supreme Ultimate. "The Supreme Ultimate is just the *li* of Heaven, Earth, and the ten thousand things" (*Classified Conversa-tions of Chu Hsi*, Ch. 1) .

33. 情（*ch'ing*）EMOTION/SENTIMENT/ LOVE

Ch'ing has played a significant role in literature, philosophy, law, and politics with notably diverse interpretations of its ordinary meaning of emotion, ranging from reality to human psychology. It has been said that the characteristics of Chinese culture are based on *ch'ing*.

1）Sincerity

There are a few examples of *ch'ing* with the meaning of sincerity in the *Analects* and the *Mencius*. "If a superior loves faithfulness, the people will not dare to refrain from showing their *ch'ing*" (*Analects*, XIII, 4).

2）Reality

Ch'ing occurs frequently in the *Chuang Tzu*, usually with the meaning of reality. "It seems that there is a True Master, but I cannot find his trace. He can act and is trustworthy, but I cannot see his form. He has *ch'ing*, but without form" (*Chuang Tzu*, Ch. 2).

3) Desire

In the *Chuang Tzu*, although *ch'ing* most often means reality, there are two exceptions. "When I talk about having no *ch'ing*, I mean that one does not allow likes or dislikes to enter and hurt oneself" (*Chuang Tzu*, Ch. 5) . "To decrease their *ch'ing* and desires is their internal aim" (*ibid.*, Ch. 33) . Here, Chuang Tzu's association of *ch'ing* with emotions and desires led not only later Taoists but later Confucianists as well to define *ch'ing* as 'desire' . "*Ch'ing* in man is the energy of darkness (*yin*), which has desire." (Hsü Shen, *Explanation*) . "Human beings' desires are called *ch'ing*" (*History of the Han Dynasty*, Vol. 56, Tung Chung–shu) . The introduction of Indian Buddhism led to the coinage of terms such as '*ch'ing* dust' (the six objects of sensation by the six sensory organs), '*ch'ing* having' (feeling of attachment to the phenomenal world), '*ch'ing* view' (regarding with affection or passion) and 'having *ch'ing*' (being human) . All of these have negative connotations.

4) Human nature

Hsün Tzu and the Legalists regarded emotion as human nature or as derived from human instincts. "*Ch'ing* is the essence of human nature" (*Hsün Tzu*, On the Rectification of Terms) . Sung Dynasty Neo–Confucianists also thought that *ch'ing* was a function of human nature. To them, human nature was essentially good; so, *ch'ing* was a feeling of good mind. "Generally, humanity, righteousness, propriety, and wisdom are aspects of nature. All feelings of commiseration, shame, modesty, and of distinguishing right from wrong are *ch'ing*" (Chu Hsi, *Collected Writings*, Letter to Fang Pin—wang) .

5) **Reason or psychology**

Two more popular terms are '*ch'ing* reason' and 'human *ch'ing*'. *Ch'ing* reason means that reason comes from the "true" sentiments, such as the love between parents and children, husband and wife, and friends. "Reason (or principle) keeps your *ch'ing* from being wrong. It will be impossible for your *ch'ing* to be wrong if you act from reason" (Tai Chen, *General Survey of Meaning of the Mencius*) .

Human *ch'ing* means human psychology, which can signify either good relationships between people or, conversely, selfish thoughts. The Legalists emphasized the latter. "To govern the world, one must take advantage of human *ch'ing*. Human *ch'ing* has likes and dislikes; therefore, rewards and punishments are useful" (*Han Fei-tzu*, Vol. 18, Eight Rules) .

34. 常（*ch'ang*）CONSTANCY/ ORDINARY

Ch'ang is a commonly used word that, in Confu-cianism, retained its original meanings of "often", "regular", or "ordinary" . In Taoism, however, especially in the *Lao Tzu* and the *Chuang Tzu*, it took on philosophical meanings. Translations of Indian Buddhist texts used *ch'ang* with negative connotations, but in Chinese Buddhism, especially in the Taoist-influenced Ch'an School, it had a significant role as a positive value.

1) Constancy, eternity

The first philosophical use of *ch'ang* was in the *Lao Tzu*. "The Way that can be talked about is not the *ch'ang* Way" (*Lao Tzu*, Ch. 1). Here, *ch'ang* indicates that the Way is constant, beyond change and relativism.

2) True life

"To return to life is called *ch'ang*; to understand *ch'ang* is called enlightenment" (*Lao Tzu*, Ch. 16) . Here, life is understood to mean true life or Heavenly life (see *ming*, life/fate).

3) Harmony

"To know harmony is called *ch'ang*; to know *ch'ang* is called enlightenment" (*Lao Tzu*, Ch. 55). The harmony of dark (*yin*) and light (*yang*) is the constant way of Heaven and Earth; so, here, *ch'ang* means the harmony of dark and light.

4) Nature, natural

"Do not bring calamities upon yourself. This is called returning to *ch'ang*" (*Lao Tzu*, Ch. 52). In the *Lao Tzu*, returning to *ch'ang* means returning to the Way or to nature; therefore, here, *ch'ang* means the natural way.

5) Human nature, the nature of all things

In the *Chuang Tzu*, *ch'ang* usually has the same meaning as in the *Lao Tzu*, but Chuang Tzu used the term in more practical ways. Sometimes, it refers to the constancy of human nature, as "All people have the *ch'ang* nature" (*Chuang Tzu*, Ch. 9). Sometimes, it refers to the norms and regularities of nature that we need for survival. "… The perch (fish) answered angrily, 'I have lost my *ch'ang*. I have no place to stay. If you can get me a dipper of water, I will remain alive'" (*ibid.*, Ch. 26).

6) True substance

In traditional Buddhism, *ch'ang* has two meanings, 'common' and 'constant'. The former is negative; '*ch'ang* view', '*ch'ang* path', and '*ch'ang* way' refer to the common delusions of relativistic thinking. The latter is positive; '*ch'ang* stillness', '*ch'ang* wisdom', and 'true *ch'ang*' are the true substance or true suchness that is constant, beyond relative ideas.

7) The ordinary

In the Ch'an School, *ch'ang* as the ordinary was transformed into the Way. "The *p'ing ch'ang* mind is the Way" (*Records of the Transmission of the Lamp*, Vol. 28, Ma Tsu). Here, *p'ing* (平, level) and *ch'ang* together mean ordinary, but this use of ordinary is unusual; it means a mind that is pure and without discriminations.

35. 术（*shu*）METHOD/SKILL

Although *shu* ordinarily means skill or method, it sometimes has the negative meaning of craftiness. Neither Confucius nor Lao Tzu used *shu*. Mencius used it five time in a positive sense, but it was not important in his thought. It was Chuang Tzu who introduced a negative usage, giving *shu* the stigma of sophistry. Thereafter, in the general culture as well as in philosophy, people respected the Way and looked down on *shu*. It has been hypothesized that this is why, historically, few of the intelligentsia studied it; in philosophy, methodology and epistemology received little emphasis; and there was little attention given to science and the scientific method. Three usages show us the position of *shu* in Chinese philosophy:

1）*Shu* with the Way

"Fish forget themselves in river and lake; people forget themselves in *Tao shu*"（*Chuang Tzu*, Ch. 6）. In this quotation, Chuang Tzu connected the two characters, reinforcing the Way and making it less abstract. But, in Chapter 33, *shu* appears as a deviation from the Way. "The later scholars, unfortunately, could not see the purity of

Heaven and Earth, the great essence of the ancient sages. The *Tao shu* was divided and broken by them" (*Chuang Tzu*, Ch. 33). Here, the divided or broken method of the Way became what Chuang Tzu referred to as *fang shu* (方术).

2) *Shu* in divination

Fang shu, in Chuang Tzu's thought, is the part of the Way that emphasizes method while neglecting substance or, by going to extremes, becomes deviant. "There are many people in this world who study *fang shu*, and each thinks that he has something that cannot be improved upon" (*Chuang Tzu*, Ch. 33). After Chuang Tzu, *fang shu* was used to identify the study of occultism, divination, and medical practice.

3) *Shu* with number

Here, *shu* means the relationship of changes in the lines of the sixty-four hexagrams in the *Book of Changes*; so, *shu* number refers to one way of studying the *Book of Changes*. Users of this method explained the changes of the universe by the changes of lines. Chu Hsi said, "Since the Dynasties of Ch'in and Han, those who researched the images and numbers became attached to the *shu* numbers and could not use the great and simple method (*i.e.*, Confucian thought)" (*Cheng Yi the commentary on the I Ching*).

36. 弱（jo）WEAKNESS

In ordinary usage, *jo* has the negative meaning of weakness. Of all Chinese philosophers, only Lao Tzu saw it as having positive value. Even Chuang Tzu ignored it. *Jo* appears only five times in the *Chuang Tzu*; of these, four have the common meaning, and the exception is in a description of Lao Tzu's thought.

1) The meaning of *jo*

In the *Lao Tzu*, *jo* is not the weakness of a sick person. To understand Lao Tzu's *jo* we need to see it in contrast with its opposite, as when he says, "Hardness and strength are the path of death" (Ch. 76), "The man of strength and violence will not die well" (Ch. 42), and "To control the breath (*ch'i*) by mind is called strength, [but] everything that becomes strong will become old" (Ch. 55) . All of these examples of strength treat it as the blind expenditure of energy or ability, which is contrary to nature. On the other hand, the practice of *jo* preserves one's energy or ability, without waste. To Lao Tzu, *jo* meant softness or yielding. "To keep to softness is strength" (Ch. 52), and "Softness and *jo* win over hardness and strength" (Ch.

36). Though *jo* is superficially weak, it has inner strength.

2) *Jo* as a function of the Way

In Lao Tzu's thought, *jo* is not only a skill or a technique for protecting one's energy or ability, "*jo* is the function of the Way" (Ch. 40) . But in the same chapter, Lao Tzu also said, "reversal (*fan*) is the movement of the Way." Thus, *jo* is the use of reversal and return. "One who has an abundance of virtue is like a newborn baby. Wasps and serpents do not sting it, nor fierce beasts seize it, nor birds of prey pounce on it. Its bones are tender and its sinews are soft, but its grasp is firm. Not yet knowing the union of male and female, its spirit is whole. This is the perfection of essence. It can howl all day without getting hoarse. This is the perfection of harmony. To know harmony is to be constant. To know constancy is to have insight. To try to increase one's lifespan is ominous. To control the breath (*ch'i*) by mind is called strength. To become strong is to turn toward being old. This is not the Way. One not in the Way will die soon" (Ch. 55) . Thus, keeping to *jo* is a protection from going to extremes. The man of *jo* always assumes a position of apparent weakness; therefore, nobody competes with him and he is able to develop without interference. This is the natural way.

3) *Jo* as a virtue

In the *Lao Tzu*, *jo* also is a virtue by which one can attain the Way.

Its aspects are contentment and humility.

(a) **Being content.** "No calamity is greater than not knowing contentment. No fault is greater than longing for gain. Therefore, the contentment of knowing content is constant contentment" (Ch. 46) . By being content, one is desireless.

(b) **Being humble**. "The superior has the inferior as its root. The high regards the low as its foundation. Therefore, dukes and kings call themselves 'the orphan', 'the widow', and 'the unproductive'" (Ch. 39) . As humility, *jo* is a key virtue in the *Lao Tzu*.

37. 几 (*chi*) OMEN/SMALL/ALMOST

Chi's meanings of "very small", "nearly", or "omen" have no philosophical implications except in the *Book of Changes* and the *Chuang Tzu*. In the *Book of Changes*, *chi* means "very subtle", which is difficult to describe or translate.

1) The subtlety of movement

Confucius said, "Does not the one who knows *chi* possess spiritual power? The superior man, in his relationship with the high, is without flattery, and, in his relationship with the low, is not rude. Does not this show that he knows *chi*? The *chi* is the subtlety of movement and the earliest omen of good fortune [or bad]" (*Book of Changes*, Great Appendix, Sec. 11, Ch. 5) . This is the best definition of *chi*; actually, the only explicit one. Subtlety of movement refers to the tenuous beginnings of movements or changes in the universe, the world of men, and the lines of the hexagrams. All events, actions, and changes in universe, men, or hexagrams have causes and reasons, and the three domains interact. Thus, if one knows the *chi* of the hexagrams, one can act well in human relations;

if one can handle the *chi* of the world of men, one can act in accord with Heaven and Earth. Consequently, *chi* is a very important element in the Way of Changes.

2) The subtle substance

In the *Book of Changes*, *chi* refers to the subtlety of movement; to act according to it is correlated with virtue. In the *Chuang Tzu*, *chi* means the subtle substance of material nature. "The seeds of all things have *chi*" (*Chuang Tzu*, Ch. 18) . Here, *chi* is seen as a kind of protoplasm that can become all things. But in the *Chuang Tzu*, this *chi* is used as an equivalent to another *chi* (机) which has virtually the same meaning. Chuang Tzu continued, saying, "Men, in time, return again to the *chi*. All things come out of the *chi* and also return to the *chi*" (*ibid.*) . In this part of the quotation, *chi* (机) means the original source and common substance of all things. Chuang Tzu used this *chi* with other words to form terms such as 'the *chi* of breath', 'the *chi* of Heaven', 'the mind of *chi*', and 'the machine of *chi*' . The first two have positive meanings; the *chi* of breath means the energy of *ch'i* (*q.v.*), and the *chi* of Heaven means wisdom. The latter two have negative meanings; the mind of *chi* means a cunning mind, and the machine of *chi* indicates mechanical production, man-made rather than natural.

38. 无（wu）NON-BEING/NON-EXISTENCE

Wu (無), in the *Book of Changes*, was written as 无; it is the same word in different form. *Wu* is a common word, meaning "no" or "nothing". Only in Taoist books, especially the *Lao Tzu* and the *Chuang Tzu*, does *wu* become a philosophical term and a key idea.

1) Non-being

Wu was first given philosophical prominence in the *Lao Tzu*, where it appears in thirty-five chapters. Most significant is the initial discussion in the first chapter. "*Wu* is the name of the origin of Heaven and Earth; being is the name of the mother of all things. Therefore, constantly in *wu*, one wishes to contemplate its subtlety. Constantly in being, one wishes to contemplate its path. These two come from the same source, but are different in name" (*Lao Tzu*, Ch. 1) . Here, *wu* means non-being as contrasted to being, both are metaphysical terms having their source in the Way.

2) Non-existence

In the *Lao Tzu*, sometimes, *wu* means non−existence. "Existence and *wu* give birth to each other. Difficulty and ease complement each other. Long and short contrast with each other. Sound and voice harmonize with each other. Front and back follow each other" (*Lao Tzu*, Ch. 2) . As this is a discourse on relativity, so, here, *wu* is a term of relativity that should be translated as 'non−existence' rather than 'non−being' .

3) Virtues of Taoism

Wu is joined with other words to become various virtues such as *wu*−action, *wu*−desire, and *wu*−knowledge. Although *wu* alone has the negative meaning of "no" or "not", the compounds always have the positive meanings. For example, "Acting by *wu*−action, then everything will be in order" (*Lao Tzu*, Ch. 3) . Although the literal meaning is "not doing", the actual meaning is "to do effectively" or "to do effortlessly."

4) The name of the Way

In the *Lao Tzu*, *wu* is not referred to in the sense of the Way, but in the Taoism of the Wei (220−265 A.D.) and Chin (265−420 A.D.) Dynasties, where it was called "The Learning of Mystery", *wu* was regarded as synonymous with the Way. Ho Yen said, "The Way is only *wu*" (*Treatise on the Name-less*), and Wang Pi said, "The Way is the name of *wu*" (*Explanation of Doubts of the Analects*) . Most scholars after them regarded *wu* as the essence of the Way.

5) The nature of *dharma*

Most Wei and Chin Dynasty Buddhists, were influenced by "The Learning of Mystery", they regarded *wu* as the nature of *dharma*. "The original *wu* has a different name but the same reality as the nature of *dharma*" (Hui Ta, *Commentary on Chao's Treatises*) .

6) Special use in Ch'an dialogue

In the Ch'an School, *wu* played a central role in the use of dialogue to achieve sudden enlightenment. "A monk asked Chao Chou, 'Has a dog the Buddha nature?' Chao Chou answered, '*Wu*'" (Wu Men, *The Pass Without a Gate*, Case 1) . This dialogue is considered to be the first use of a Ch'an "case" (*kung-an*) as a means of bringing about a student's sudden enlightenment. "Concentrate on the word *wu*. Carry it continuously day and night. Do not think of it as emptiness or take it as the relativity of existence and non-existence" (*ibid.*) . *Wu*, in Ch'an cases, is used to indicate that which is beyond speaking (*i.e.*, beyond relativities) . The Ch'an School always used *wu* as a special means by which to concentrate the mind in meditation or to go beyond relativities.

39. 象（*hsiang*）IMAGE/FORM

Hsiang is a pictograph of an elephant; by extension, it means image or form. It became a philosophic term in the *Book of Changes*, where it had two meanings.

1）*Hsiang* in Heaven

"Heaven creates spiritual things, and the sage follows them. Heaven and Earth change and transform, and the sage imitates them. Heaven displays（literally, "hangs out"）the *hsiang* which can be interpreted as omens of good fortune or bad fortune, and the sage makes *hsiang* from them"（*Book of Changes*, Great Appendix, Sec. 1, Ch. 11）. In this quotation, the first *hsiang* refers to the images displayed by Heaven. These have been explained by diviners as spirit−produced objects such as the *Ho* Map（brought forth by the Yellow River）and the *Lo* Writing（a product of the Lo River）; both were used in divination. The images have been explained by academicians as the natural phenomena of change and transformation in the universe. The former explanation became a part of supernatural or religious thought, the latter developed into science or philosophy.

Images in the *Book of Changes* can be interpreted both ways. In divination, snow in June is *hsiang*; to scientists, an apple falling from a tree onto Newton's head also is *hsiang*.

2) *Hsiang*in the hexagrams

The second *hsiang* in the quotation above refers to the images that appear in the hexagrams. The sage–author of the *Book of Changes* followed the images of Heaven in drawing the lines of the hexagrams; therefore, the positions and relationships of the lines are images. This *hsiang* can be read as referring to the images of a hexagram's lines or as the images of good or bad fortune, the advance or retreat of sorrow and happiness in life. "The sage set forth the hexagrams in order to contemplate *hsiang* and appended explanations in order to show their good or bad fortune. The hard and the soft [lines] displace each other, producing the changes and transformations. Therefore, good or bad fortune is the *hsiang* of gain or loss. Regret or difficulty is the *hsiang* of sorrow or anxiety. Change or transformation is the *hsiang* of advance or retreat. Hardness or softness is the *hsiang* of day or night" (*Book of Changes*, Great Appendix, Sec. 1, Ch. 2) .

In the Confucian *Ten Wings*, the theory of *hsiang* is used to explain how ancient people invented vessels and tools and established civilization. "In ancient times, when Pao–hsi was a ruler of the world, he contemplated the *hsiang* in the sky and observed the patterns of the earth. He contemplated the ornamental appearances

of birds and beasts and the suitabilities of soils [for various crops] .
Near at hand, he took examples from his own body; at a distance,
he took examples from all things. Then he created the Eight Trigrams
to communicate the virtues of the spirits and to classify the qualities
of all things. He invented nets for hunting and fishing by tying cords.
This idea probably was taken from the *Li* hexagram (No. 30) . After
Pao−hsi's death, Shen−nung cut wood to make a plow share and bent
wood to make a plow handle. He taught the people of the world the
advantages of plowing and weeding. This idea probably was taken
from the *I* hexagram (No. 42) ... In early ancient times, people
knotted cords in order to make records. Later sages substituted written
documents. By means of these, officials conducted the government
and understood all people. This idea probably was taken from the *Kuai*
hexagram (No. 43)" (*Book of Changes*, Great Appendix, Sec. 2,
Ch. 2) . This passage illustrates the relationship between the *hsiang*
of the hexagrams and the origins of civilization. This was not a matter
of divination but of actual development of imagination and reason in a
culture.

Unfortunately, later scholars who studied the *Book of Changes*
confined their research to *hsiang* in the hexagrams; they ignored the
ancient sages' contemplation of *hsiang* as a means of understanding
the changes of Heaven and Earth and establishing civilization in the
actual world. The more these scholars studied the *Book of Changes*,
the less useful it became. Their approach to *hsiang* was like being

locked into the abstract symbols, cut off from their sources in Heaven, and unable to use them in the real world. Therefore, the *Book of Changes* became word play and a divination game.

40. 道（*tao*）WAY/ROAD

Tao, used as a verb, simply means "saying" or "leading"; used as a noun, it is the soul of Chinese philosophy. We might say that the intent or purpose of Chinese philosophy is to learn and practice the Way. Originally, *Tao* meant the way as in, "Tao is the way that we walk on. It includes 辵 and 首. So, the only thoroughfare is called *Tao*" (Hsü Shen, *Explanation*). 辵 means walking and 首 means head. Therefore, *Tao* means the chief way. Although *Tao* can be considered the only way of all things, it has different meanings and various paths.

1）*Tao* in the *Book of Changes*

It is worth noting that *Tao* occurs frequently in the *Book of Changes*. It appears not only in the *Ten Wings*, which is said to have been written by Confucius and his students, but also in the sixty-four hexagrams, which were written before Confucius. In the hexagrams, *Tao* simply means "the way of man", but in the *Ten Wings*, there are elaborations. "To establish the *tao* of Heaven is called dark (*yin*) and light (*yang*). To establish the *tao* of Earth is called softness and hardness. To establish the *tao* of man is called humanity and righteousness" (*Book of Changes*, Treatise of Remarks on the Trigrams, Ch 2) . Thus, in the *Ten Wings*, *Tao* is relevant to Heaven (metaphysics), Earth (material nature) and man (morality) .

2) *Tao* in pre-Ch'in Confucianism

Although *tao* has a transcendental meaning in the *Ten Wings*, it is still very simple in the *Analects*, where Confucius was concerned only with politics and ethics. No wonder his student, Tzu Kung, complained, "We never hear our master discussing human nature and the *Tao* of Heaven!" (*Analects*, V, 12) Confucius had thoughts on human nature and the *tao* of Heaven, but they were recorded in the *Doctrine of the Mean* and the *Ten Wings*. In the *Analects*, which recorded his dialogues with his students, he discussed aspects of the *tao* of man.

(a) **Morality.** Confucius said, "The *tao* of the superior man is threefold, but I am unable to attain it. The man of humanity is free from worry; the man of wisdom is free from perplexity; the man of courage is free from fear" (*Analects*, XIV, 30) .

(b) **Government of the people.** Yu Tzu said, "Among the functions of propriety, to be in harmony is the most valuable. This was the best element in the *tao* of the ancient kings" (*Analects*, I, 12) .

(c) **Truth.** Confucius said, "If, in the morning, one hears the *tao*, one will be without regrets even if he die in the evening"

(*Analects*, IV, 8) .

(d) **The proper way or method.** Confucius said, "Wealth and honor are what everybody desires; but, we do not take them if they do not come by the *Tao*. Poverty and humbleness are what everybody dislikes; but, we do not avoid them if we cannot get rid of them by the *Tao*" (*Analects*, IV, 5) .

In the *Mencius*, *Tao* has the same meanings as in the *Analects* except for an occasional usage as method or theory, with no moral or transcendental implications. "If the *Tao* of Yang and Mo are not stopped, the *Tao* of Confucius will not be manifested" (*Mencius*, Bk. III, Pt. 2, Ch. 9) . Here, *Tao* means theory.

3) *Tao* in Taoism

Obviously, *Tao* is the central term in Taoism. Lao Tzu used it to establish a system of the Way of Heaven. In the *Lao Tzu*, *Tao* has seven meanings:

(a) **Truth/eternity.** "The *Tao* that can be talked about is not the constant *Tao*" (*Lao Tzu*, Ch. 1) .

(b) **Creator.** "*Tao* brings them (all things) forth" (*Lao Tzu*, Ch. 51) .

(c) **Dynamism.** "Reversing [and returning] is the movement of *Tao*" (*Lao Tzu*, Ch. 40) .

(d) **Pervasiveness.** "It alone stands without change. It is all-pervasive without being exhausted. It may be the mother of the world.

I do not know its name; but name it *Tao*" (*Lao Tzu*, Ch. 25).

(e) Principle. "If we hold to the *Tao* of ancient times, we can manage things in the present. That we can know the source is called the rule of *Tao*" (*Lao Tzu*, Ch. 14). Here, 'rule' means 'principle'. Knowing the source implies understanding the development.

(f) The supreme standard. "The attitude of Great Virtue is to follow only the *Tao*" (*Lao Tzu*, Ch. 21).

(g) Nature. "*Tao* follows Nature." (*Lao Tzu*, Ch. 25; see *fa*).

In the *Chuang Tzu*, *Tao* is used essentially as in the *Lao Tzu*. However, Chuang Tzu's concern for life inevitably suffuses his definition of the term.

(a) The life of nature. "When the springs dry up and the fish lie together on the ground, they spew moisture on each other and keep each other wet with saliva, but it would be better if they could forget themselves in the rivers and lakes. Rather than praise [sage−king] Yao and condemn [tyrant] Chieh, it would be better to forget both of them and transform ourselves into *Tao*" (*Chuang Tzu*, Ch. 6). *Tao* is to man as rivers and lakes are to fish, the natural condition of life.

(b) The essence of life. "To practice the pure, simple *Tao* is just to protect your spirit. If you do not lose your spirit [to desires], you will merge the *Tao* and your spirit into one" (*Chuang Tzu*, Ch. 15). This *Tao*, understood as the essence of life, was cultivated by later Taoists who wanted to become immortal.

4) *Tao* in Chinese Buddhism

Because the characteristics of *Tao* in Taoism resembled Buddhist concepts, early translators used it to translate key Indian Buddhist terms.

(a) **Path.** "All human beings in the Six *Tao* are walking the paths of life and death" (*Dharma Flower Sutra*, Preface) . *Tao* was the path by which one arrived at a good or bad existence; the Six *Tao* were the paths of hell, hungry ghosts, animals, spirits, human beings, and Heaven.

(b) **Statement of the Supreme.** Early Chinese Buddhists always used *Tao* to refer to any statement of the Supreme, such as *nirvana*, because *Tao* was the way to it. "*Nirvana* is named *Tao*, which is still, empty, and vast" (Seng Chao, *Treatise on Nirvana without Name*) .

(c) **The real nature, original face, true self, or Buddha Nature.** The Ch'an School was influenced by the thought of Lao Tzu and Chuang Tzu; therefore, *Tao* played the same role in it as in Taoism. Hui-neng said, "The non-dual nature is the real nature. The real nature neither decreases nor increases, whether one is a common person or a sage—its form and nature are always in suchness. It is permanent and immutable. It is called *Tao*" (*Platform Scripture*, Ch. 9) . Here, the real nature is the same as the original face, true self, or Buddha Nature.

5）*Tao* in Neo-Confucianism

Sung Dynasty Neo–Confucianists, influenced by both Taoism and the Ch'an School, used 'principle' as a bridge between the Way of Heaven and the Way of man.

（a）**Principle.** "The principle is called *Tao*"（Ch'eng I, *Literary Remains of the Two Ch'engs*, Ch. 1）.

（b）**Human nature.** "*Tao* is human nature. It is wrong to look for *Tao* outside of human nature or for human nature outside of *Tao*"（Ch'eng Hao, *Literary Remains of the Two Ch'engs*, Ch. 1）.

（c）**All things.** "There are no things outside of *Tao*, and there is no *Tao* outside of things. Therefore, between Heaven and Earth, *Tao* exists everywhere"（*Literary Remains of the Two Ch'engs*, Ch. 4）.

（d）**The Supreme Ultimate.** "*Tao* is the Supreme Ultimate"（*Classified Conversations of Chu Hsi*, Ch. 94）.

（e）**Mind.** "The mind is *Tao*, the *Tao* is Heaven"（Wang Yang–ming, *Records of Instructions and Practices*, Sec. 1）.

（f）**Innate knowledge.** "Innate knowledge is *Tao*"（Wang Yang–ming, *Records of Instructions and Practices*, Sec. 2）.

In Neo–Confucian reasoning, all of these definitions include principle（*li*）; therefore, they are not separate from the Way.

41. 敬(*ching*) REVERENCE/RESPECT

In common usage, *ching* means to revere or to respect; in philosophy, it becomes one of the virtues, as shown in the *Book of History* and the *Book of Odes*. "[If the] King (King Ch'eng) *ching* his actions, he cannot but *ching* virtue" (*Book of History*, Announcement of Duke Shao) . "Each of you *ching* yourself." (*Book of Odes*, vol. 12, Yu Wu Ching) . Here, in referring to action, *ching* implies acting with caution. Confucianists gradually came to interpret *ching* as a virtue for the cultivation of mind.

1) *Ching* in Confucius' thought

Ching appears twenty−one times in the *Analects*, with three spheres of application:

(a) **To one's work.** Confucius said, "To rule a country of a thousand chariots, one must be *ching* to one's work and trustworthy" (*Analects*, I, 5) . Whatever you do must be done sincerely and with *ching*.

(b) **To superiors or to gods and spirits.** "Confucius said of Tsu Ch'an that he had four characteristics of the superior man. In his conduct, he was humble; in serving a superior, he was *ching*; in taking care of the people, he was kind; in ordering the people, he was righteous" (*Analects*, V, 15) . Here, to serve a superior with *ching* refers to the king or high officials; but, in other chapters, it means to be filial to parents or elders. Confucius thought that filial piety should be expressed with an attitude of *ching* (see *hsiao*) . Sometimes, superiors are gods and spirits, as when Confucius said, "[Give] *ching* to the spirits and gods, and keep yourself far from them" (*Analects*, VI, 20) . Here, the reference is to popularly worshipped spirits and gods. Tzu Chang, Confucius' disciple, said, "... In sacrificing, his thought is *ching*" (*Analects*, XIX, 1) . Here, the objects of *ching* are the ancestors as well as the gods.

(c) **To self-cultivation.** When Confucius' disciple Tzu Lu asked about the Superior, Confucius said, "The cultivation of oneself is *ching*" (*Analects*, XIV, 45) . Here, *ching* indicates that self-cultivation results in acquiring the virtue of reverence.

2) *Ching* in Mencius' thought

In the *Mencius*, *ching* usually had the same meaning as in the *Analects*. Once, however, Mencius said, "To show that which is good and to stop that which is evil is called *ching*" (*Mencius*, bk. 4, pt. 1, ch. 1) . Although Mencius was referring to the evil thoughts of kings, Neo-Confucianists generalized the reference and ascribed to *ching* the function of stopping evil thoughts.

3) *Ching* in the Book of Changes

"The superior man, by *ching*, makes his inner [mind] straight; by righteousness, makes his outer [conduct] square" (*Book of Changes*, Hexagram 2, *K'un Wen-yen*). Here, the straight indicates sincerity; the square symbolizes being upright. Note that to make the "inner" straight is a way of cultivating mind that influenced Neo-Confucianism.

4) *Ching* in Neo-Confucianism

Sung Dynasty Neo-Confucianists, influenced by the special uses of *ching* in the *Book of Changes* and the *Mencius*, turned it into the cultivation of mind. *Ching* as a method was particularly emphasized by the School of Ch'eng Chu (Ch'eng Tzu and Chu Hsi and their students) because they wanted to avoid appearing to practice Taoist tranquility or Buddhist stillness. To them, the basic function of *ching* was to assist concentration on Oneness. Ch'eng I said, "In concentrating on Oneness, one will not lean neither to the east nor to the west, but remain centered; one will not attach himself to this or that but hold to the inside. Keeping this [concentration on Oneness], one will understand Heavenly principles naturally. Those who learn this should use *ching* to cultivate mind by making straight their inner being" (Chu Hsi, *Reflections on Things at Hand*, Vol. 4) . Because of Neo-Confucian study and practice, *ching* assumed two significant roles in Chinese philosophy:

(a) *Ching* **as an inner virtue.** In pre−Ch'in Dynasty philosophy, as illustrated by the thought of Confucius and Mencius, *ching* was only an element of common morality, referring to respectful or reverent behavior. In Neo−Confucianism, however, it became the cultivation of mind. We *ching* someone or show him *ching*, not only because he is worthy of respect, but in order to practice the virtue of *ching*.

(b) *Ching* **in meditation.** By their emphasis on meditation, the Neo−Confucianists differed substantially from Confucius and Mencius. However, their meditation, by focusing on *ching*, was distinct from Taoist and Buddhist practices.

42. 义（*i*）RIGHTEOUSNESS/ RIGHTNESS/JUSTICE

I originally meant expression of personal or individual attitude, because the character has the radical for "self", meaning self as a model. "*I* is self's majesty" (Hsü Shen, *Explanation*). In the thought of Confucius and Mencius, *i* became an important virtue.

1) Two significant aspects of *i*

Because of the relationship of *i* with self, it is all too easy to judge others by one's individual opinions. As Mo Tzu said, "Each person has an *i*; ten people have ten *i*; a hundred people have a hundred *i*; a thousand people have a thousand *i*. There are numberless people; so, there will be numberless *i*. Each person emphasizes his own *i* and criticizes others" (Mo Tzu, *Agreement with the Superior*, Sec. 3). Two qualifications help in avoiding this situation and understanding the true meaning of *i*.

(a) **Benefit.** "Benefit is the harmonizer of all *i*" (*Book of Changes*, Hexagram 1, *Ch'ien Wen-yen*). "*I* is the foundation of benefits" (*Tso's Commentary on the Spring and Autumn Annals*,

Duke Chao, 10th year). "*I* is benefit" (*Mo Tzu*, Vol. 10, *Ching*, Sec. 1) . All of these agree that righteousness must be beneficial to all people.

(**b**) **Appropriateness.** "*I* means appropriateness" (*Doc-trine of the Mean*, Ch. 20). "*I* means that one does everything suitably" (Kuan Tzu, *The Method of Mind*) . Here, *i* means rightness — that one should do everything at the right time, in the right place, and with the right relationships.

2) *I* in the thought of Confucius

In the *Analects*, *i* is a standard of behavior. Confucius said, "The superior man considers *i* to be essential [in everything]" (*Analects*, XV, 17) . "The superior people in the world, are not for or against anything; they follow only *i*" (*Analects*, IV, 10) . So, *i* is the standard of a superior people. Confucius did not tell us what the standard is, but he did say, "The superior people understand *i*; the inferior people understand profit" (*Analects*, IV, 16) . Here, *i* is the opposite of profit, but at the same time it is the foundation of benefits. Therefore, *i* is a 'great benefit', by which one does things for others, not for oneself. The superior people interpret this great benefit as *i*, but never as self-righteousness.

3) *I* in the thought of Mencius

It was Mencius who made *i* a key term in Chinese philosophy by developing three critical interpretations:

(a) **Union of** *i* **with humanity.** Mencius coined the term *jen-i*, which has become recognized as the essence of Confucianism. He did so to use *i* as a bridge between the inside and outside of mind, between humanity and propriety. "Humanity is the mind of man; *i* is the path of man" (*Mencius*, Bk. VI, Part 1, Ch. 11) . "*I* is the path; propriety is the door" (*Mencius*, Bk. V, Pt. 2, Ch. 7) . Here, Mencius saw *i* as the path which brings the humanity of mind to the door of propriety, through which it passes into action. To Mencius, *i* was the way to practice humanity.

At the time, many rulers of states cared little about propriety, and Confucius' humanity was too weak to restrict them (Mencius characterized it as just a feeling of commiseration) . Mencius stressed *i* because it was more powerful than humanity. *I* is the human way; if one does not follow it, one ceases to be human. The transformation of *i* from an outer standard of conduct to an inner virtue was completed when Mencius said, "Humanity, *i*, propriety, and wisdom are rooted in mind" (*Mencius*, Bk. VII, Pt. 1, Ch. 21) .

(b) **Discrimination between** *i* **and profit.** Although Confucius said, "The superior man understands *i*; the inferior man understands profit" (*Analects*, IV, 26), he did not consider profit as bad categorically. He wanted people to avoid single-minded pursuit of profit and advised thinking about *i* when opportunities for profit appeared. But to Mencius, *i* and profit were wholly incompatible. In his book, all references to profit have negative meanings. "One who gets up at cockcrow and is earnest in practicing goodness is a disciple of [sage-king] Shun; one who gets up at cockcrow and is earnest in seeking profit is a disciple of [big robber] Chih. If you want to know the difference between Shun and Chih, it is simply this — the difference between goodness and profit" (*Mencius*, Bk. VII, Pt. 1, Ch. 25) . Thus, for Mencius, *i* replaced profit as a motive for action.

(c) **Cultivation of *i* with energy.** By turning *i* inward, Mencius connected it with energy. "This energy is in accord with *i* and the Way. Without them, it will become starved" (*Mencius*, Bk. 2, Pt. 1, Ch. 2) . Thus, Mencius involves the practice of *i* with the cultivation of mind.

43. 诚 (*ch'eng*) SINCERITY

Before Mencius, *ch'eng* was not a philosophical term. In its few occurrences in the *Book of History*, *Book of Odes*, and *Analects*, it is used as a helping verb. After Mencius, *ch'eng* became important. Especially in Neo–Confucianism, it is the soul of cultivation of mind.

1) *Ch'eng* in pre-Ch'in Confucianism

In the Period of Warring States (403–222 B.C.), *ch'eng* acquired philosophical depth in the *Doctrine of the Mean*, the only major classic that devotes substantial attention to it. *Ch'eng* generally means truth, honesty, faith, and trust. All of these are extensions or implications of the cryptic state–ment, "*Ch'eng* is the Way of Heaven; to become *ch'eng* is the Way of man" (*Doctrine of the Mean*, Ch. 20) .

(a) **The Way of Heaven.** The first half of the above quotation means that *ch'eng* is equal to the Way of Heaven; in other words, it is the natural way that is the way of a sage. "*Ch'eng* is the way of Heaven. The man of *ch'eng* is one who, without effort, hits upon what is right and, without thinking, apprehends it. One who is naturally and easily in harmony with the Way is a sage" (*Doctrine of the Mean*, Ch. 20) . This Way is godlike and ceaseless.

(1) **Perfect** *ch'eng* **is godlike.** "The Way of perfect *ch'eng* is being able to foreknow. When a country is about to flourish, there are surely some fortunate omens; when it is about to perish, there are surely some omens of weird and monstrous things. These omens appear in divinations made with milfoil and tortoise [shells] and in the movements of our four limbs. Whether calamity or blessing is imminent, the good and the bad can be foreknown. Therefore, perfect *ch'eng* is like a spiritual power" (*Doc-trine of the Mean*, Ch. 24) . In this quotation, the reference to divination does not place *ch'eng* in a context of superstition but indicates its being in accord with Heaven so that it can intercommunicate with all events in the universe.

(2) **Perfect** *ch'eng* **is ceaseless.** "Perfect *ch'eng* is without cease. Being ceaseless, it is lasting. Being lasting, it is verifiable. Being verifiable, it is infinite. Being infinite, it is great and deep. Being great and deep, it is supreme and brilliant. Because it is great and deep, it can carry all things [like Earth] . Because it is supreme and brilliant, it can cover all things [like Heaven] . Because it is lasting and infinite, it can complete all things" (*Doctrine of the Mean*, Ch.26) . Thus, the function of *ch'eng* is the same as that of Heaven and Earth, which give life to all things without cease.

(b) **The Way of man.** The second half of the quotation is a declaration of virtue. "To become *ch'eng* is the Way of man... The one who wants to become *ch'eng* is to choose what is good and firmly hold it fast" (*Doctrine of the Mean*, Ch. 20) . There are two ways of practicing this virtue:

(1) **Self-completion.** "*Ch'eng* is self-completion, and its way is the way of self. *Ch'eng* is the beginning and end of all things. Without *ch'eng* there would be nothing. Therefore, the superior people value *ch'eng*" (*Doctrine of the Mean*, Ch. 25) . One practices virtue and improves knowledge and wisdom with *ch'eng* in order to complete oneself.

(2) **Completion of all things.** "*Ch'eng* means not only to complete oneself but also to complete things. To complete oneself is humanity; to complete things is wisdom. Both are the virtue of nature. This is the Way which is a union of the external and internal" (*Doctrine of the Mean*, Ch. 25) . To "complete things" is to let other people and things develop — to cause all people and all things to live in harmony and to develop according to their own natures.

2) *Ch'eng* in Taoism

Ch'eng is not a term emphasized in Taoism. It appears only once, as a helping verb, in the *Lao Tzu*. It appears sixteen times in the *Chuang Tzu*, but only eight have philosophical meaning — and none of these occurs in the first seven chapters, Chuang Tzu's basic text. These eight might have been inserted by later Taoists who had been influenced by the *Doctrine of the Mean*. Superficially, they resemble usages in the *Doctrine of the Mean*. The only major difference is that *ch'eng* in Confucianism is based on humanity and righteousness; but in the *Chuang Tzu*, it is a true essence of mind that is beyond humanity and righteousness. "The action of humanity and righteousness is really not *ch'eng*... Cultivate the *ch'eng* in your breast and use it to respond without grasping to the reality of Heaven and Earth" (*Chuang Tzu*, Ch. 24) . Here, *ch'eng* refers to a special Taoist form of cultivation of mind that has no relationship with Confucian morality.

3) Ch'eng in Neo-Confucianism

Generally speaking, *ch'eng* in Neo–Confucianism was influenced by the *Doctrine of the Mean*. Most Confucianists merely praised it, but Neo–Confucianists added three new ideas:

(a) *Ch'eng* **as the essence of all virtues.** Chou Tun–I (Chou Lien–hsi) made *ch'eng* the source of all virtues. "*Ch'eng* is the foundation of the sage" (Chou Tun–I, *Book of Penetration*, Ch. 1) . "*Ch'eng* is the foundation of the Five Constant Virtues (humanity, righteousness, propriety, wisdom, and faithfulness) and the source of all conduct" (*ibid.*, Ch.2) . Here, *ch'eng* is regarded as the foundation of humanity; in Chou's eyes, *ch'eng* was more important than humanity.

(b) *Ch'eng* **as a special cultivation of mind.** Having been influenced by Taoism and the Ch'an School, Ch'eng Hao (Ch'eng

Ming-tao) practiced *ch'eng* as a cultivation of mind. "When one understands the principle [of humanity], one preserves it with *ch'eng* and reverence; that is all. There is no need for caution or control nor for exhaustive search" (Huang Tsung-hsi, ed., *Writings of Sung and Yuan Philosophers*, Ch'eng Hao, On Understanding Humanity) . This method is like the meditation of Taoism and the Ch'an School; the only difference is that Ch'eng Hao concentrates *ch'eng* in his mind.

(c) *Ch'eng* **as a reality without falseness.** The explanation of *ch'eng* as a reality without falseness was created by Ch'eng I (Ch'eng I-ch'uan) and emphasized by Chu Hsi. "*Ch'eng* means that true reality is without false-ness. It is the natural or Heavenly principle" (Chu Hsi, *Commentary on the Doctrine of the Mean*, Ch. 20) . Although this thought came from "*Ch'eng* is the way of Heaven" (*Doctrine of the Mean*, Ch. 20), its definition of a reality without falseness took *ch'eng* into the realm of metaphysics. In Neo-Confucianist ideology, it took the place of Buddhist 'truth suchness'. Neo-Confucian eagerness to be free of Buddhism ensured the viability of this definition.

44. 数（*shu*）NUMBER

Originally, *shu* meant "number" or "to count". It became a philosophical term that eventually was associated with a school that concentrated on numerology.

1）*Shu* in ancient education

In the Chou Dynasty（1111−249 B.C.）, education consisted of the Six Arts: rites, music, archery, chariot driving, learning(reading and writing), and mathematics（*shu*）. Chu Hsi said, "All youth, from both royal and common families, had to attend the Small School at the age of eight. They were taught the proper way to clean a room, talk with superiors, visit and take leave of superiors, and to study rites, music, archery, chariot driving, learning, and *shu*"（Chu Hsi, *Com-mentary on Sentences and Chapters of the Great Learning*）.

2）*Shu* in Taoism

Lao Tzu seemed to be the first to use numbers to explain the cosmology in "Tao brings forth one, one brings forth two, two bring forth three, three bring forth all things"（*Lao Tzu*, Ch. 42）. But

Lao Tzu simply emphasized Oneness; he was not really interested in *shu*. Chuang Tzu used *shu* frequently, but just with the meaning of "many times." Only in his last chapter did philosophical meaning appear in "… They understood the basic *shu* and paid attention even to petty regulations" (*Chuang Tzu*, Ch. 33) . It was the later Taoists who were influenced by the *Book of Changes* and became interested in developing a relationship between *shu* and material nature.

3) *Shu* in later Confucianism and Legalism

In the *Analects* and the *Mencius*, *shu* merely meant "many times", which had no relationship with mathematics or the idea of number. In the thought of later Confucianists, such as Hsün Tzu, and the Legalists, *shu* became a kind of practical mathematics for accounting, economics, and statistics, all of which were related to law. "All people must be governed by the law and *shu*. Measure the land for establishing the country; count the profits for raising the people; examine people's abilities for giving them work. This will cause the people to be fitted to their jobs and all businesses to produce profits. The profits will be enough to support the people. All goods, such as clothes, food, and daily necessities, will not only be in balance; there will be a surplus. This is called accordance with *shu*" (*Hsün Tzu*, A Rich Country) . Here, Hsün Tzu related *shu* to law, resulting in its becoming a Legalist term. Chuang Tzu's definition was the same, but with a negative attitude, "Rites, laws, measures, *shu*, and the careful comparison of forms and names, — these are the trivia of good government" (*Chuang Tzu*, Ch. 13) .

4) *Shu* in the *Book of Changes*

In the *Book of Changes*, *shu* was an important term with two meanings:

(a) **The *shu* of Heaven and Earth.** "Heaven is one, Earth two; Heaven is three, Earth four; Heaven is five, Earth six; Heaven is seven, Earth eight; Heaven is nine, Earth ten. There are five Heavenly *shu* and five Earthly *shu*. They are in five places and each finds its complement. The sum of the Heavenly *shu* is twenty-five, that of the Earthly *shu* is thirty. The*shu* of Heaven and Earth together amount to fifty-five. It is by these that the changes and transformations are effected and the spirits and gods are caused to move" (*Book of Changes*, Great Appendix, Sec.1, Ch. 9) . In this paragraph, the author of the *Ten Wings* used *shu* to explain the images and the changes of Heaven and Earth. Although we do not know precisely what this series of numbers stands for, it influenced later scholars to form the School of Learning of Hsiang—Shu (image and number) . Some Sung Dynasty philosophers drew many diagrams in attempts to explain and develop the series.

(b) **The *shu* of lines in divination.** "The *shu* of the Great Expansion is fifty [stalks of the yarrow plant], of which forty-nine are used. They are divided into two heaps to represent the Two (Heaven and Earth or dark and light). One stalk is set apart (taken from the heap on the right and placed between the little and ring fingers of the left hand) to represent the Three (Heaven, Earth, and man). They (the heaps on both sides) are counted through by fours to represent the four seasons. The remainder is put aside (placed between the middle fingers of the left hand) to represent the intercalary month. Because there are two intercalations in five years, this operation is repeated... By means of the four operations, the changes are completed. Through eighteen changes, a hexagram is formed" (*Book of Changes*, Great Appendix, Sec. 1, Ch. 9). Here, the author of the *Ten Wings* used *shu* to create a method of divination.

5) *Shu* in Han Dynasty philosophy

In the Han Dynasty (206 B.C.−220 A.D.), even philosophers outside the School of Hsiang−Shu were influenced by the idea of *shu*, from which rose the Learning of Heaven and Man. Scholars thought that there were some mysterious spiritual relationships between Heaven and man through which they could respond to each other. One of these relationships was that of *shu*. Tung Chung−shu, the most famous investigator of *shu*, said, "The signs of Heaven and Earth and the correspondence of dark (*yin*) and light (*yang*) are set up in man's body. Man's body is like Heaven. The *shu* of both correspond to each other; thus, life and fate are connected with each other. Heaven uses the *shu* of days in a year to form man's body; so, it has three hundred and thirty-six small bones. There are twelve large bones in man's body; these correspond to the *shu* of months. The five viscerae correspond to the Five Movements. The four limbs correspond to the *shu* of the four seasons" (Tung Chung-shu, *Luxuriant Dew of the Spring and Autumn Annals*, Man Corresponding to the *Shu* of Heaven) .

6) *Shu* in Neo-Confucianism

Sung Dynasty Neo-Confucianists were influenced by *shu* in two ways:

(a) *Shu* in the Cosmological Chronology. Shao Yung (Shao K'ang-chieh), in the *Cosmological Chronology*, combined the learning of *hsiang* and *shu* with chron-ology to explain the relationship between Heaven's *shu* and the events of human history: "The course of the sun forms Heaven's cycle (*yuan*); the course of the moon forms Heaven's epoch (*hui*); the course of the stars forms Heaven's revolution (*yun*); the course of zodaical spaces forms Heaven's generation (*shih*)" (*Cosmological Chronology*, Treatise on the Observa-tion of Things) . The time scale is boldly conceived — a cycle is equal to thirty epochs; an epoch is equal to thirty revolutions; a revolution is equal to thirty generations; a generation is equal to thirty years. Shao Yung's theory is very complicated; this brief passage only suggests his use of *shu*.

(b) *Shu* as the expression of energy (*ch'i*) . "Energy is also *shu*. There is such a principle, there will be such an energy; there is such an energy, there will be such a *shu*" (*Classified Conversations of Chu Hsi*, 65) . Here, *shu* refers to the energy (*ch'i*) that is in different individuals.

45. 德（*te*）VIRTUE/MORALITY

Originally, *te* had the specific meaning of ascending or gaining. "*Te* means to ascend" (Hsü Shen, *Explanation*). "Gaining is *te*" (Hsü Shen, *Explanation*, Tuan's Commen-tary). Later, from this original definition, the term developed into 'virtue' or 'morality' in both philosophy and common usage. Various schools have filled the otherwise empty term with their own interpretations of morality.

1）*Te* in Confucianism

In Confucianism, *te* refers only to morality. It has the same meaning and functions in the *Analects*, the *Mencius*, and the *Hsün Tzu* — to cultivate oneself by *te* and to govern a country by *te*. Confucius said, "Set your will on the Way, depend on *te*, rely on humanity, and roam in the arts" (*Analects*, VII, 6). In this quotation, we note not only that man's action must be in accord with *te* or good conduct, but that Confucius separated humanity and *te*. Although humanity is a virtue, here it is interpreted as the mind or ideal of humanity; *te* is good social behavior, including righteous-ness, reverence, propriety, filial piety, and so on.

If we analyse *te* in the *Analects* and the *Mencius*, we find that in all instances it is used in reference to government. "Governing a country by *te*" (*Analects* II, 1) and "Leading people with *te*" (*Analects*, II, 3). "What *te* enables one to be a sage–king?" (*Mencius*, Bk. 1, Pt. 1, Ch. 7) and "One subdues men by *te*; they will be pleased in mind and submit sincerely" (*Mencius*, Bk. 2, Pt. 1, Ch. 3). This use of *te* in reference to government has three aspects: first, that a ruler practice virtue; second, that the ruler treat the people kindly; third, that the ruler pay attention to the conduct of the people. Here, for pre–Ch'in Dynasty Confucianism, *te* appears both as a precept of government and as propriety in social behavior.

2) *Te* in Taoism

In the *Lao Tzu*, *te* is shown as functioning on two levels: high, supreme, or absolute (virtue), and low, inferior, or relative (morality). "The man of supreme *te* is not attached to *te*; therefore, he has *te*. The man of low *te* fears the loss of *te*; therefore, he has no *te*" (*Lao Tzu*, Ch. 38). In other chapters, supreme virtue is spoken of as "mysterious *te*" (Ch. 10), "great *te*" (Ch. 21), "constant *te*" (Ch. 28), "abundant *te*" (Ch. 41), and "established *te*" (Ch. 41); all share the charac–teristics of not possessing, not taking credit, and not competing. Low *te* refers to general morality and the social virtues of humanity, righteousness, propriety, and so forth. Lao Tzu's *te* was the supreme virtue, a cultivation of mind through non–action and desirelessness, rather than the relative morality of low *te*. Wang Pi's *Commentary* explains Lao Tzu's 'virtue' by "*Te* means gain. It is constant gain without loss and benefit without harm. Therefore, it is named *te*. How is *te* gained? Through the Way. How is *te* fully completed? Through non-being" (Wang Pi, *Com-mentary on Lao Tzu*, Ch. 38) . Here, "gain" means achievement of mind; *te* in Taoism is an inner virtue.

In general, *te*, in Chuang Tzu's thought, is the same as in Lao Tzu's. However, Chuang Tzu described its charac-teristics and functions in greater detail as:

(a) **Beyond fame**: "*Te* is destroyed by fame" (*Chuang Tzu*, Ch. 4);

(b) **Harmony**: "The mind roams in the harmony of *te*" (*ibid.*, Ch. 5);

(c) **Non-action**: "Non-action is the *te* of Heaven" (*ibid.*, Ch. 12);

(d) **Tranquility**: "Tranquility has the same *te* as darkness(*yin*)" (*ibid.*, Ch. 13);

(e) **Beyond morality**: "All of these moralities, filial piety, brotherly love, humanity, righteousness, loyalty, trust, chastity, and integrity, merely drive one and make one a slave of *te*" (*ibid.*, Ch. 14);

(f) **Beyond emotion**: "Dislikes, desires, pleasure, anger, sadness, and happiness are the burden of *te*" (*ibid.*, Ch. 23);

(g) **Wisdom**: "Understanding completely is *te*" (*ibid.*, Ch. 26);

(h) **Without mind**: "There is no greater evil than that *te* has mind (i.e., desires)" (*ibid.*, Ch. 32) .

Thus, Chuang Tzu's *te* was a cultivation of mind, a tranquility unmoved by outside desires.

3) *Te* in the Ch'an School

In Buddhism, *te* is merely a general term for goodness or good conduct. It is supported by precepts called *chieh* (*sila* in Sanskrit) which are specific guides to behavior. The Chinese Ch'an School, influenced by Taoism, gave *te* a more detailed treatment. Hui−neng said, "To see nature is meritorious, to have equanimity is *te*; to be humble in mind is meritorious, to practice propriety is *te*; to establish our *dharma* by self−nature is meritorious; the essence of mind free from thoughts is *te*; non−separation of self−nature is meritorious, using without attachment is *te*; thinking without interruptions is meritorious, being straightforward in mind is *te*; to cultivate one's nature is meritorious, to cultivate one's body is *te*. Learned audience, merit, and *te* should be sought within one's self−nature; they cannot be acquired by almsgiving and supporting the monks" (*Platform Scrip-ture*, Ch. 3) . In this quotation, *te* is ascribed connotations of non−differentiation, accordance with propriety, non−ideation, non−attachment, straightforward mind, and cultivation of the body.

None of these differs appreciably from *te* in Chuang Tzu's thought. But it is noteworthy that the distinction between *te* and almsgiving and support of monks was a revolutionary idea that caused Ch'an monks to concentrate on the cultivation of mind and to seek sudden enlightenment through understanding mind and seeing nature.

Later Ch'an masters, especially in the Sung Dynasty, found that the method of sudden enlightenment had gone to extremes and that *te* had become an idle word. They tried to salvage the term by applying Confucian interpretations to its use in everyday life. For example, "The [ancient] sages and worthies guarded against [seeking] profit and respected humanity and righteousness, but the people of later generations cheated each other for advantage" (Miao−hsi and Chu−an, *Valuable Instructions of the Ch'an Community*, Ch. 3), and "He (Huang Lung) loves those who are reverential and filial to their parents" (*ibid.*, Ch. 14) . Here, Ch'an masters are seen publicly using Confucian moral teachings of humanity, righteousness, reverence, and filial piety in their lectures and writing.

46. 静（*ching*）TRANQUILITY/ STILLNESS

Ching is a description of the motionless. In Chinese philosophy, it was used to indicate the state of the universe and man's mind and became a method for the cultivation of mind. It had various connotations in the different schools and played an active role in the history of Chinese thought.

1）*Ching* as relative to movement（*tung*）

Ching does not appear in the *Analects* or the *Mencius*. The reason may be that these two books, concerned with ethics and politics, do not deal with cosmological or metaphysical ideas. Nor does *ching* occur in the sixty-four hexagrams of the *Book of Changes*. Also, its opposite, movement, occurs only once, although words such as staying, coming, and going are used frequently. However, both *ching* and movement appear often in the *Ten Wings* commentaries on the *Book of Changes*; for example, "If one's *tung* and *ching* are in the proper times, his way will be brilliant"（*Book of Changes*, Hexagram 52, *Ken*; *Ten Wings*, *Thwan* Commentary）. A reasonable explanation is that the hexagrams were used in divination, for which concrete terms were appropriate, while the *Ten Wings*, a philosophical study of the *Book of Changes*, required abstractions such as '*ching*' and 'movement'.

2) *Ching* as the foundation of movement

In the *Ten Wings*, *ching* is used six times, but there are sixty references to movement. The relationship between the two is not examined. It was the Taoists who saw the sig-nificance of *ching* as more basic than movement. "[Every-thing] returns to its root. To return to the root is to go to *ching*. It means to return to its true life… Heaven is the root of lightness; *ching* is the master of restlessness" (*Lao Tzu*, Ch. 26). Wang Pi, author of commentaries on the *Book of Changes* and the *Lao Tzu*, said, "When movement rests, then *ching*. *Ching* is not relative to movement" (Wang Pi, *Commentary on the Book of Changes*, Hexagram 24, *Fu*). Wang Pi did not consider *ching* to be simply an antonym of movement; they are not on the same level. *Ching* is the foundation of all things. *Ching* is permanent; movement is temporary.

3) *Ching* as desirelessness or the essence of mind

Chuang Tzu made *ching* a state of mind. He said, "The sage is *ching* naturally, not because he thinks *ching* to be good; therefore, he practices *ching*. His *ching* is because his mind is not moved by things"

(*Chuang Tzu*, Ch. 13) . Here, *ching* means desirelessness.

After Confucius and Mencius, later Confucianists gave attention to *ching* and regarded it as the nature of mind. Hsün Tzu said, "How can a man know the *Tao*? By the mind. How can the mind know? By its emptiness, oneness, and *ching*" (*Hsün Tzu*, Removal of Prejudices), and "Man was born with *ching*, this is the nature of Heaven; he is moved by external things, this is the desire of nature" (*Record of Rites*, Record of Music) . In both passages, *ching* was regarded as the essence of mind or nature, and the move−ment of mind was caused by desire. It is difficult to say whether they were influenced by Chuang Tzu.

Sung Dynasty Confucianists turned *ching* into a cultivation of mind. Chou Tun−i (Chou Lien−hsi) said, "The sage settles these affairs by the middle way of correctness, human−ity, and righteousness. He regards *ching* as fundamental, establishing the ultimate standard for human beings" (Chou Tun−i, *Explanation of the Diagram of the Great Ultimate*) . This kind of *ching* also is found in the *Hsün Tzu* and the *Great Learning*. "The Way of the Great Learning is to manifest bright virtue, love the people, and abide in the supreme goodness. Only by knowing what to abide in can one be settled; only by being settled can one be *ching*; only by being *ching* can one be peaceful; only by being peaceful can one deliberate well; only by deliberating well can one attain what one wants" (*Great Learning*, Ch. 1) . This *ching* was an attitude of mind or one step of progress in mind. The difference between the Confucianists and the Neo-Confucianists was that the latter interpreted *ching* as the method for the *practice* of virtue. Above all, they emphasized "sitting in *ching*", which was like — and may have been influenced by — the meditation practices of Taoism and Buddhism.

4) The relationship of *ching* with Buddhism

Two essential terms in Indian Buddhism are *nirvana* and *dhyana*. *Nirvana* is the essence of all events (*dharmas*); *dhyana* is the method of cultivation of mind. They are related in that the characteristic of *nirvana* is tranquil extinction and that of *dhyana* is tranquil thought or meditation. Both characteristics are applicable to *ching*.

47. 朴 (*p'u*) SIMPLICITY

The original meaning of *p'u* was "uncarved block" as in, "*P'u* is the plainness of wood" (Hsü Shen, *Explanation*) . Common usage denotes simplicity, purity, or plainness. Lao Tzu made simplicity a philosophical term and used it in various ways.

1) The pure mind

"Sincerely, as if *p'u*" (*Lao Tzu*, Ch. 15), "Display plainness and embrace *p'u*, reduce selfishness and restrain desires" (*ibid.*, Ch. 19), and "I have no desires, so the people return to *p'u* naturally" (*ibid.*, Ch. 57) . In each, *p'u* refers to the state of pure mind which is without desires. By extension, *p'u* also means that the people's nature is sincere and the society is customarily honest.

2) The *p'u* system in government

"Knowing the honor and keeping to the mean, one will be the valley of the world. Being the valley of the world, one's constant virtue is complete; one returns to *p'u*. When *p'u* is divided, it becomes vessels (all things or all political systems) . The sage uses it（ *p'u* ）to become a leader. There-fore, the great system is not cut" （ *Lao Tzu*, Ch. 28 ）. "Keeping to the mean" means that a ruler who is humble and does not display his acumen can govern with *p'u*. Here, it indicates the "simple system" of government by non-action. Non-action, in politics, is to follow the nature of the people and refrain from establishing a system of regulations that would interfere in people's lives. Hence, "the great system is not cut" could also be read as "the great system does not cut." The whole, integrated political structure is not cut up, nor is human nature fragmented.

3) *P'u* as Oneness or the Way

"The Way is constantly nameless. Although its *p'u* is small, no one in the world can subjugate it. If kings can keep to it, all things will return to them as guests. Heaven and Earth will be harmonized and sweet dew will fall. People, without being ordered, are equal to one another" （ *Lao Tzu*, Ch. 32 ）. As Oneness（ see *i*, One ）, *p'u* is small, but as an incarnation of the Way it cannot be subjugated. The function of *p'u*, like that of the Way, is to cause all things to develop naturally.

4) *P'u* as a method to reduce desires or solve problems

"The Way is constantly in [a state of] non-action, but it leaves nothing undone. If a king can keep to it, all things will transform themselves. If, in transforming, desires arise, I (the king) will put them to rest with the nameless *p'u*. Being desireless, it will create no desires. Being tranquil, the world will be kept in order" (*Lao Tzu*, Ch. 37) . This chapter raises an interesting question. If non−action means non−interference, letting people go their own way, people's desires will arise naturally. What can be done about them? Ordinarily, laws will be enacted or morality and propriety invoked to restrain desires.

To Lao Tzu, however, law, morality, and propriety were superficial or temporary solutions that would generate more and larger desires. Ambitious people would use laws for selfish ends. "The more taboos and prohibitions there are in the world, the poorer people are. The more sharp weapons they possess, the more chaotic the nations. The more crafty and skillful men are, the more strange things happen. The more laws and orders a nation has, the more robbers and thieves there are" (*Lao Tzu*, Ch. 57) . Empha−sizing propriety and morality would cause people to become hypocritical and generate more complicated problems. "When the great Way was abandoned, there appeared the morality of humanity and righteousness. When benevo− lence and knowledge arose, great hypocrisy appeared" (*Lao Tzu*, Ch. 18) . "Propriety is the thinness (lack) of loyalty and honesty and the beginning of disorder" (*Lao Tzu*, Ch. 38) . Therefore, Lao Tzu emphasized *p'u* instead of law, morality, and propriety to reduce desires, interpreting it as the natural way of the sage in causing people to live simply. "Not exalting ability, people will not compete. Not valuing rare goods, people will not steal. Not displaying desirable objects, people's hearts will not be disturbed. Therefore, the sage's [way of] governing is to empty their hearts, fill their bellies, weaken their willfulness, and strengthen their bones. He always causes the people to return to the state that is without knowledge (acumen) and without desires, so that those who have acumen will not dare to act selfishly. Acting by non-action, everything will be in order" (*Lao Tzu*, Ch. 3) . Using *p'u* to reduce people's desires is to emphasize the simple life and let people follow the natural way. Note that the state of being without knowledge does not imply reversion to animal-like existence; it means a life unencumbered by material or mental accumulations that interfere with the *p'u* that enables one to participate in the Way.

48. 儒 (*ju*) SCHOLAR/CONFUCIANIST

Ju is a general name for a scholar and a special name for a Confucianist. As a general term, it has deeper meaning than the word "scholar" in English. As a special term, it is defined by particular ideals and principles of conduct.

1) The gentle *ju*

"*Ju* means softness." (Hsü Shen, *Explanation*) . Here, softness means gentleness. "Scholar" was used to describe those who were erudite and gentle in action. "To be genial and gentle in teaching others and not to avenge unreasonable conduct, This is the strength of the people of the south. The superior people abide by it" (*Doctrine of the Mean*, Ch.10) .

2) The *ju* of the Six Arts

"*Ju* means softness. It is the name of those who have special skills" (Hsü Shen, *Explanation*) . *Ju* was the name given to scholars who had special skills in and were teachers of the Six Arts (rites, music, archery, chariot driving, literacy, and mathematics) that comprised education in the Chou Dynasty before Confucius. "*Ju* win the favor of the people by the Way. 'They use the Six Arts to teach the people'" (*Rites of Chou/Commentary*, Vol. 2) .

3) The *ju* as the superior man

Although *ju* appears only twice in the *Analects* and in the *Mencius*, it acquired new meanings thereby. In the *Analects*, the scholar was linked with morality. Confucius said to Tzu Hsia, "You should be a *ju* as a superior people and not be a *ju* as an inferior people" (*Analects*, VI, 11) . Although, originally, the difference between superior and inferior was one of rank, Confucius made the difference one of morality. This added a dimension of ethical responsibility to the task of the scholar-educator. Mencius saw enough similarity in scholars to think of them as a school. "Those who want to get rid of Mo naturally turn to Yang; those who want to be free from Yang naturally return to *ju*" (*Mencius*, Bk. 7, Pt. 2, Ch. 26) .

4) *Ju* as a name of Confucianists

At the time of Mencius, many philosophers and their disciples appeared and formed schools to advance their particular views. Mencius, to have a ground from which to criticize and argue with them, established a Confucian theory and school, choosing *Ju* as its name. In it, the *Six Classics* were used as texts, replacing the *Six Arts*.

49. 禅（*shan/ch'an*）SACRIFICE/ ABDICATION/MEDITATION

The character 禅 has two pronunciations, *shan* and *ch'an*. The former is used with the original meanings of sacrificing to Heaven and abdicating the throne. When Indian Buddhism was introduced, the term was adopted, because of its sound, as the translation for the Sanskrit *dhyana*（medita−tion）and pronounced *ch'an*. Thus, *shan* is an original Chinese term, but *ch'an* is a foreign one, and they were used in different contexts.

1）*Shan*（sacrifice）to Heaven

"*Shan* means to sacrifice to Heaven"（Hsü Shen, *Explanation*）. In ancient times, when a king ascended the throne, he went to Mount Tai in Shantung, one of the five holy peaks, to sacrifice to Heaven. This ritual was an acknowledgment that he had been given the kingdom by Heaven, a request for Heaven's blessing, and a verification of his right to rule. The ceremony was based on the Chinese theory of the interaction of man and Heaven.

2) *Shan* (abdication)

"Confucius said, 'T'ang (Emperor Yao) and Yu (Em-peror Shun) did *shan*; the sovereigns of Hsia, Yin (Shang), and Chou transmitted it to their sons. Their principle of righteousness was the same'" (*Mencius*, Bk. 5, Pt. 1, Ch. 6). It was said that from Emperor Yao to Emperor Yu there was a custom of *shan* whereby each abdicated his throne to a worthy successor. Many modern scholars doubt that this existed as a system; they suggest that it was an idealization created by Confucius. However, it also appears in the *Mo Tzu* and the *Chuang Tzu*. The possibility of *shan* as a system also is given credibility by the high regard of Chinese for the virtue of humility, a key element in their philosophy and culture.

3) *Ch'an* (meditation)in Indian Buddhism in China

The Sanskrit *dhyana* was originally translated into Chinese as *ch'an-na*, which was abbreviated to *ch'an*. *Dhyana*, meaning 'meditation' or 'tranquil thought', is a common method in all schools of Buddhism. Through it, one can attain the state of *samadhi*, which in Chinese is *shan-mei* or *ting* (定). In use, *ch'an* always is linked with *ting* to form a compound term that means meditation.

Hinayana (Theravada)Indian Buddhists entered China at the end of the Han Dynasty, bringing *sutras* concerned with contemplation; these *sutras* generally involved control of breathing. "There are four kinds of *anapana* (Sanskrit, breath–control): (1) counting [inhalations–exhalations], (2) following [the breath] (*i.e.*, allowing thoughts to flow out with the breath, without attention), (3) resting [attention on a single object, such as a Buddha image or mantra, without being disturbed by desires], (4) seeing with wisdom (the highest form of contemplation, completely internalized, with no external aids)" (*Great Anapana Concentrating Thought Sutra*, Vol. 1) .

Mahayana Buddhists, coming in the Wei (220–265 A.D.) and Chin (265–420 A.D.) Dynasties, brought *sutras* that emphasized *prajña* (wisdom) . They taught the attainment of wisdom through meditation, as in (4) above.

4) *Ch'an* (meditation) in Chinese Buddhism (the Ch'an School)

Few Chinese Buddhist schools emerged from the meeting of Indian with Chinese philosophy. However, Bodhidharma brought an esoteric form of *dhyana* to China in the Liang Dynasty (502–577 A.D.) to become the founder and first patriarch of the school that took *ch'an* as both name and central theme and developed a number of distinctive concepts. With two claimants to the title of Sixth Patriarch, the school broke into two sects, a northern under Shen–hsiu and a southern under Hui–neng. The northern school continued to teach a basically Indian form of meditation and, after a few generations, lapsed into obscurity. The southern school planted the seeds of Indian meditation in the rich soil of Chinese thought and developed what is generally recognized as an indigenous Buddhism, the Ch'an system, better known in the West by its Japanese pronunciation — Zen.

5) The different kinds of *ch'an*

Kuei−feng said, "About *ch'an*, there are depths and shallows. It has different levels. Those who have minds that make distinctions, who cultivate the high position and dislike the low position, are of deviate *ch'an* (*i.e.*, deviate from the school's fundamental concepts) . Those who believe in the principle of cause−and−effect and still make mental distinctions have the *ch'an* of common people. Those who are imperfectly awakened to the principle of the Void of self and cultivate self according to it are of Hinayana *ch'an*. Those who are awakened to the truth that both self and dharma are void and cultivate self according to it are of Mahayana *ch'an*. Those who are suddenly enlightened with the realization that their minds are originally pure and untroubled and have original non−leaking (passionless) wisdom and nature, and that their minds are Buddha−mind without differentiation, to be cultivated according to it, are of the supreme *ch'an*. It is also called Tathagata Pure Ch'an, or One Act Samadhi, or Truth−Suchness (*Bhutatathata*) Samadhi. This is the foundation of all *samadhi*. If one cultivates and practices it in every thought, one will naturally get hundreds and thousands of *samadhis*.

In Bodhidharma's school, this *ch'an* was passed on from one master to another" (Kuei−feng, *Comment on the Source of Ch'an*, Vol. 1) . Here, the highest form of meditation was, of course, that of the Chinese Ch'an School.

6) The standard definition of *ch'an*

Hui−neng established the standard definition of *ch'an*. "In our School, we sit in *ch'an*, dwelling neither on the mind, nor on purity, nor on non−motion. In our School, sitting means that thoughts do not arise and that your mind is free from all barriers and obstructions and beyond all states of good and evil. *Ch'an* means to see inwardly the self−nature that is not moved" (*Platform Scripture*, Ch. 5) . Here, *ch'an* requires non−attachment to either inward states of thought or outward states of things. In Hui−neng's thought, *ch'an* is not merely sitting in meditation but seeing self−nature (true nature, one's original face) . This led later Ch'an masters to criticize *dhyana* or *ch'an* if taken as a goal. In the Chinese Ch'an School, *ch'an* is merely a helpful device for achieving tranquility; it is not the essential objective. The essential purpose is enlightenment — through *ch'an* to see one's true nature or original face, which is Buddha−nature.

50. 礼 (*li*) PROPRIETY/RITE

Li, as propriety or rite, has had a central role in Chinese culture, philosophy, and history. Chinese people refer to China as the country of *li*. *The Record of Rites*, a Confucian classic that recorded rites and proprieties in precise detail, was the standard of social behavior in ancient China. *Li* can be examined in relation to culture, to philosophy, and to its functions.

1) *Li* in Chinese culture

(a) *In religion.* "*Li* means treading (practice) — serving gods or spirits in order to obtain blessings. The character includes 示 (showing) and 丰 (the vessels used in sacrifice) ." (Hsü Shen, *Explanation*) . Ori-ginally, *li* referred to sacrifice to ancestors or gods. For example, "*li* has five parts. The most important is the sacrifice." (*Record of Rites*, The Tradition of Rites) . The *li* of sacrifice shows man's sincerity toward the gods and ancestors through the systematized activities of *li*.

(b) *In society.* "*Li* places with certainty the foundation of Heaven, follows the principle of Earth, and functions between mankind and the spirits and gods. It extends to [correct] practice in funerals, sacrifices, archery, ceremonial drinking, capping ceremonies, marriage, and exchange of credentials. Therefore, the sage teaches people *li*, by which all circumstances can be governed in the proper way" (*Record of Rites*, The Movement of Rites) . Here, *li* is expanded to influence people's daily lives and mold the social system.

(c) *In* **education.** As one of the Six Arts, *li* was an integral part of ancient education. Confucius said, "Without learning *li*, one's character cannot be established" (*Analects*, XVI, 13) . Because *li* governed all social behavior, if one did not know it, one could not survive as a member of the society. "Without *li*, humanity, righteousness, and morality cannot be achieved; without *li*, correct customs and good instructions will not be complete; without *li*, arguments and suits cannot be judged; without *li*, [correct relationships of] rulers and ministers, superiors and inferiors, fathers and sons, and elder brothers and younger brothers cannot be established" (*Record of Rites*, Small Rites) .

2) *Li* in Chinese philosophy

(a) *In* **Confucianism.** Here, *li* is a key to the doors of ethics, politics, and religion; it is a medium that integrates social system, moral behavior, and mind.

In the *Analects*, *li* always is associated with music; this indicates origination in the Chou Dynasty（1111-249 B.C.）, where *li* and music were the two most important subjects of education.

Confucius thought it essential to follow Duke Chou's great work of systematizing *li* and music. In Confucius' thought, *li* had two major functions: First, it established the standard of all conduct. When his disciple, Yen Yuan, asked about humanity, Confucius answered, "To restrain oneself and return to *li* is humanity. If one does it for a single day, all the world will return to humanity. Practice of humanity depends on oneself. Does it depend on others?" Yen Yuan said, "Please show me the details." Confucius replied, "Do not look when your action would be contrary to *li*; do not listen when your action would be contrary to *li*; do not speak when your action would be contrary to *li*; do not touch when your action would be contrary to li" （*Analects*, XII, 1）. Second, rite and propriety were the foundation of government. "Lead the people by governmental orders and govern them by punishment; they will avoid wrong-doing but have no sense of shame. Lead the people by virtue and govern them by *li*; they will have a sense of shame and, more-over, will become upright" （*Analects*, II, 3）.

There is little difference between *li* in the *Mencius* and in the *Analects*. In the *Mencius*, however, *li* always is joined with righteousness as a compound term to indicate a virtue which has its root in mind. "The superior man has humanity, righteousness, *li*, and wisdom as his nature. All of these are rooted in his mind" （*Mencius*,

7A, 21 ） .

In Hsün Tzu's thought, *li* is the key idea, as important as humanity to Confucius and righteousness to Mencius. To Hsün Tzu, *li* was:

（1）**Perfect virtue**: "*Li* is the perfection of the way of man" （ *Hsün Tzu*, On Propriety ）;

（2）**The way of cultivation of mind**: "All methods of mastering your energy （ *ch'i*) and nourishing （ cultivating) your mind should depend on *li*" （ *Hsün Tzu*, Cultivating Oneself);

（3）**The foundation of law**: "*Li* is the great distinction of law" （ *Hsün Tzu*, An Encouragement to Study ） . Note that, in this, Hsün Tzu differed from Confucius who emphasized *li* instead of law.

（b）*In* **Moism.** Mo Tzu criticized the Confucian interpretations of *li*. "Confucianists, regarding this as the way to teach the people, hurt the people. They compli‑cated and trivialized the systems of *li* and music, causing people to enjoy them （ become addicted to their superficial forms ） . They emphasized lengthy funeral rituals and hypocritical mourning, causing people to deceive their relatives" （ *Mo Tzu*, Criticizing Confu‑cianism ） . As a pragmatist, Mo Tzu thought elaborate ceremonies were impractical.

（c）*In* **Taoism.** "Therefore, when the Way is lost, people resort to virtue. When virtue is lost, people resort to humanity. When humanity is lost, people resort to righteousness. When righteousness is lost, people resort to *li*. *Li* is the thinness （ lack) of loyalty and honesty and the beginning of disorder." (*Lao Tzu*, Ch.38) . This severe criticism of *li* seems to be at odds with the record that Lao Tzu was an historian well versed in its principles, — so much so that Confucius went to Chou to learn from him about it. Assuming the truth of the story, a reasonable explanation might be that Lao Tzu understood *li* as a principle of mind that became rigid and lifeless if people gave attention only to the formalities of *li* and ceremonies.

3) The functions of *li.*

(a) **Practice.** "*Li* means treading" (Hsü Shen, *Explana-tion*) . Treading is understood as practicing or putting into practice. Without being practiced, *li* is an empty term.

(b) **Harmony.** Confucius' disciple, Yu Tzu, said, "Of the functions of *li*, the most valuable is to maintain harmony" (*Analects*, I, 12) . The harmony to be maintained is that between man and man.

(c) **Humility.** "The mind of modesty and compliance is the beginning of *li*" (*Mencius*, Bk. 2, Pt. 1, Ch. 6) .

(d) **Differentiation.** "The characteristic of a true man is not that he has two feet and no feathers, but that he is aware of distinctions. Animals have fathers and sons, but there is no affection between them; they have males and females, but they are not properly separated. Therefore, the way of man cannot be without its distinctions. No differentiation is greater than division (ethics); no division is greater than *li*" (*Hsün Tzu*, Against Physiognomy) .

Here, distinction and difference refer to differentiation of roles between parents and children, husbands and wives, and other relationships.

(e) **Nourishment.** "The former kings hated confusion. They established *li* and righteousness to make distinc-tions (determine rights and duties) in order to nourish the people's desires and satisfy their needs. This caused [an equilibrium in which] desires should never be exhausted by things nor should things be used up by desires; each should support the other and develop well. That is the reason that *li* arises. Therefore, *li* means nourishment" (*Hsün Tzu*, On Propriety) . Here, Hsün Tzu resembles a modern sociologist in defining *li* as a reasonable balance that will nourish people's desires and needs without harming others or misusing things.

BIBLIOGRAPHY

CHINESE REFERENCES（cited）

Ch'an Lin Pao Hsün 禅林宝训, *Valuable Instructions of the Ch'an Community*, by Miao-hsi P'u-chüeh 妙喜普觉 and Chu-an Shih-kuei 竹庵士圭

Ch'an Yuan Chu Ch'uan Chi 禅源诸诠集, *Comment on the Source of Ch'an*, by Kuei-feng Tzung-mi 圭峰宗密

Chao Lun 肇论, *Book of Chao*, by Seng-chao 僧肇

Cheng Meng 正蒙, *Correct Discipline for Beginners*, by Chang Tsai 张载

Chin Ssu Lu 近思录, *Reflections on Things at Hand*, by Chu Hsi 朱熹

Chu Tzu Yü Lei 朱子语类, *Classified Conversations of Chu Hsi* 朱熹

Chu Wen Kung Wen Chi 朱文公文集, *Collected Writings of Chu Hsi* 朱熹

Ch'uan Hsi Lu 传习录, *Record of Instructions and Prac-tice*, by Wang Yang-ming 王阳明

Ch'uan Teng Lu 传灯录, *Record of the Transmission of the Lamp*, by Tao-yuan 道原

413

Chuang Tzu 庄子 or Nan Hua Ching 南华经, by Chuang Chou 庄周

Ch'un Ch'iu Fan Lu 春秋繁露, *Luxuriant Dew of the Spring and Autumn Annals*, by Tung Chung-shu 董仲舒

Ch'un Ch'iu Tso Chuan 春秋左传, *Commentary on the Spring and Autumn Annals*, by Tso Ch'iu-ming 左丘明

Chung Yung 中庸, *Doctrine of the Mean*, by Tsu Ssu 子思, (originally a chapter of the *Book of Rites*, edited into the *Four Books* by Chu Hsi)

Erh Ch'eng Yi Shu 二程遗书, *Literary Remains of the Two Ch'engs*, by Ch'eng Hao 程颢 and Ch'eng I 程颐

Fa Hua Ching 法华经, *Dharma-flower Sutra* (*Saddharmapundarika*)

Han Shu 汉书, *History of the Han Dynasty*, by Pan Ku 班固

Hsiao Ching 孝经, *Book of Filial Piety*, edited by Ch'in and Han Dynasty Confucianists

Hsün Tzu 荀子, *Book of Hsün Tzu*, by Hsün Tzu

I Ching 易经, *Book of Changes*, or Chou I 周易 *Chou Changes*

Kuan Tzu 管子, *Eclectic Work Attributed to Kuan Chung*

Kuan Wu P'ien 观物篇, *Treatise on the Contemplation of Things*, by Shao Yung, in Shao's Huang Chi Ching Shih 邵雍皇极经世 *Cosmological Chronology*

Kuo Yü 国语, *Conversations of States*, by Tso Ch'iu-ming 左丘明

Lao Tzu 老子 or Tao Te Ching 道德经, by Lao Tzu 老子

Li Chi 礼记, *Record of Rites*, edited by Han Dynasty Confucianists

Liu Tsu T'an Ching 六祖坛经 Liu Tsu Fa Pao T'an Ching 六祖法宝坛经, *Platform Scripture by the Sixth Patriarch*, sayings of Hui-neng, 慧能, Edited by Fa-hai 法海 (cited as *Platform Scripture*)

Lu Hsiang Shan Ch'uan Chi 陆象山全集, *Complete Works of Lu Hsiang Shan*

Lun Yü 论语, *Analects*. Sayings of Confucius and some of his disciples

Mencius 孟子, *Meng Tzu*, by Mencius and some of his disciples

Meng Tzu Tzu I Su Cheng 孟子字义疏证, *General Survey of the Meaning of Mencius*, by Tai Chen 戴震

Mo Tzu 墨子, by Mo Tzu and the later Moists

Pao P'u Tzu 抱朴子, *Embracing Simplicity*, by Ko Hung 葛洪

San Kuo Chih 三国志, *History of the Three Kingdoms*, by Ch'en Shou 陈寿

Shen Hui Yü Lu (Tun Huang text) 神会语录敦煌本, *Record of Conversations of Shen-hui* 神会

Shu Ching 书经 or Shang Shu 尚书, *Book of History*

Shuo Wen Chieh Tzu 说文解字, *Explanation of Script and Elucidation of Characters*, by Hsü Shen 许慎 (cited as *Explanation*)

Sung Yüan Hsüeh An 宋元学案, *Writings of Sung and Yuan Philosophers*, ed. by Huang Tsung-hsi 黄宗羲, suppl. by Ch'uan Tsu-wang 全祖望

Tai An Po Shou I Ching 大安般守意经, *Great Anapana Concentrating Thought Sutra*, tr. by An Shih-kao 安世高

T'ai Hsüan 太玄, *Great Mystery*, by Yang Hsiung 扬雄

Ta Hsüeh 大学, *Great Learning*, attributed to Ts'an Tzu 曾子; originally a chapter of the *Record of Rites*, edited into the *Four Books* by Chu Hsi 朱熹

Ts'an T'ung Ch'i 参同契, *Unity of the Trio*, by Wei Po-yang 魏伯阳, （Commentary by Chu Yun-yang）朱云阳

Wang Yang-ming Ch'uan Shu 王阳明全书, *Complete Works of Wang Yang-ming* 王阳明

Wu Chen P'ien 悟真篇, *Book of Awakening Truth*, by Chang Tzu-yang 张紫阳（Commentary by Chu Yün-yang）

Wu Men Kuan 无门关, *The Pass Without a Gate*, by Wu Men Hui K'ai 无门慧开

Wu Teng Hui Yuan 五灯会元, *Five Lamps Meet To-gether on the Source*, ed. by P'u-chi 普济

CHINESE REFERENCES（consulted）

Chung Kuo Che Hsüeh Tz'u Tien 中国哲学辞典 *Dictionary of Chinese Philosophy*, by Wei Cheng-t'ung 韦政通, Taipei: Tai Lin Publishing Co., 1977

Chung Kuo Che HsüehTz'u Tien Tai Ch'uan 中国哲学辞典大全, *Complete Dictionary of Chinese Philosophy*, Chief ed. Wei Cheng-t'ung, Taipei: Shui Niu Publishing Co., 1983

Chung Wen Tai Tz'u Tien 中文大辞典, *Encyclopedic Dictionary of the Chinese Language*, Taipei: China Academy, 1962

Fo HsüehTai Ts'u Tien 佛学大辞典, *Big Dictionary of Buddhism*, ed. by Ting Fu-pao 丁福保, Taipei: Taiwan Sutra Publishing Co., 1974

Harvard-Yenching Institute Sinological Index Series, 哈佛燕京学社引得, Peiping（Peking）: Yenching University, 1940

Hsin Pien ChuTzu Chi Ch'eng 新编诸子集成, *New Complete Works of Philosophers*, Taipei: The World Book Co., 1974

Shih Shan Ching Chu Shu 十三经注疏, *Explanation and Commentary on the Thirteen Confucian Classics*, Taipei: Wen Hua Book Co., 1970

ENGLISH REFERENCES（consulted）

Chan, Wing-tsit, *A Source Book in Chinese Philosophy*（Princeton: Princeton University Press, 1963）

Dubs, Homer H., *The Works of Hsüntze*（London: Arthur Probsthain, 1928）

Feng, Gia-fu and Jane English, *Chuang Tsu, Inner Chapters*（New York: Random House, Vintage Books, 1974）

Fung, Yu-la, *A History of Chinese Philosophy*, tr. Derk Bodde（Princeton, Princeton University Press, 1952-1953）

Legge, James（tr.）, *The Chinese Classics*, Vols. 1-8（Oxford: Clarendon Press, 1895）

Liao, W. K.（tr.）, *Complete Works of Han Fei-tzu*（London: Arthur Probsthain, 1939）

Lin, J. Paul, *A Translation of Lao Tzu's Tao Te Ching and Wang

Pi's Commentary (Michigan: Center for Chinese Studies, U. of Michigan, 1977)

Lin, Yutang, *Chuangtse* (Taipei: World Book Co., 1957)

———, *The Wisdom of Laotse* (New York: Modern Library, 1948)

Pound, Ezra, *Confucius* (New York: New Directions, 1928)

Rump, Ariane and Wing-tsit Chan (tr.), *Commentary on the Lao Tzu by Wang Pi* (Hawaii: University Press of Hawaii, 1979)

Soothill, William Edward and Lewis Hodous, *A Dictionary of Chinese Buddhist Terms* (Taipei: Buddhist Culture Service, 1934)

Sung, Z.D., *The Text of the Yi-King* (New York: Paragon Books, 1969)

Waley, Arthur, *The Analects of Confucius* (New York: Random House, 1938)

Watson, Burton (tr.), *The Complete Works of Chuang Tzu* (New York: Columbia University Press, 1968)

Wilhelm, Richard (tr.), *The I Ching or Book of Changes*, rendered into English by Cary F. Baynes (New York: Pan-theon, 1950)

Wong, Mou-lan (tr.), *Sutra Spoken by the Sixth Patriarch on the High Seat of " The Treasure of the Law"* (Hong Kong: Buddhist Book Distributor Press, 1929, 1952)

Wu, C.H., *Lao Tzu* (New York: St. John's University Press, 1961)

———, *The Golden Age of Zen* (Taipei: United Publishing Center, 1975)

· 读懂中华文化　构建中国心灵 ·

──────── 道善元国学馆新经典丛书 ────────

更多名家音视频课程，敬请关注我们的公众号

在这里，彻底学懂中国传统文化